HERODOTUS

HERODOTUS

BY

TERROT REAVELEY GLOVER

Select Bibliographies Reprint Series

 BOOKS FOR LIBRARIES PRESS
FREEPORT, NEW YORK

First Published 1924
Reprinted 1969

STANDARD BOOK NUMBER:
8369-5090-9

LIBRARY OF CONGRESS CATALOG CARD NUMBER:
70-99661

PRINTED IN THE UNITED STATES OF AMERICA

ALICE

PREFACE

While revising the proofs of this volume, I have often thought of the difference between a course of lectures and a book; and the severe words have returned to my mind, in which Thucydides, not without a glance at my author, distinguished between the show-piece designed for fugitive pleasure and the possession for ever. Listening and reading are different operations; the lecturer has one task, the writer another; and the endeavour to combine them at least helps a man to understand in a new way the art of Herodotus who triumphed over the difficulty. That the Sather Lectures shall be a book is one of the laws laid down for them.

My readers must at once be told that Herodotus makes better reading than any of us who have written upon him. After all, it is the business of the commentator to explore the charm of his author and to set others reading him. If some who heard these lectures in California, and perhaps others who may look at the book, are a little doubtful of their Greek, I would recommend Mr. A. D. Godley's translation in the Loeb Classical Library. The Greek text there faces the English, and I have used both; and I wish to thank the translator for the help that his work has given me. I hope I have not too often borrowed his renderings nor always quite spoiled them by variants of my own contrivance.

For me, this volume will always have the association of a distant ocean, and an unusual climate;* of hills with dark foliage, now half-hidden by the sea-fog, now lit up by the sun—hills, to which, in the familiar language of Scotland and of childhood, I lifted my eyes with happiness and relief, when I grew tired of my proofs. The book will recall pleasant days spent in a community of ten thousand students, with men who added to the ties of kindred studies those of a signal kindness. It will recall the great catastrophe of a burning town and new evidence that goodwill is the foundation of society.

* "The poet," if I may abridge Strabo (C. 150) by way of postscript, "informed through his inquiries of so many expeditions to the uttermost parts and learning by hearsay about the wealth and the other virtues of the country, in fancy placed there the abode of the blest; as Proteus says 'But the deathless gods will escort thee to the ends of the earth, where life is easiest for men. No snow is there, nor yet great storm, nor ever any rain; but always Oceanus sendeth forth the breezes of clear-blowing Zephyrus.' For both the pure air and the gentle breath of Zephyr properly belong to this country, seeing the land is not only in the west but also warm; and the phrase 'at the ends of the earth' well fits it."

CONTENTS

You come and tell us of so many things—
    Satraps and oracles, Nile and Italy,
    And fairy-tales as splendid as there be,
The Phoenix with his father on his wings,
Great marvels of Greek art, strange fates of kings,
    Soils, climates, customs, and the Southern Sea,
    And how Greek citizens battled to be free,
And all the breadth of soul that Freedom brings.
You loved your story, and the things it shows,
    Dear critic, who part doubt and part believe,
Lean, like the Greek you are, to what man knows,
    Yet hold that in long time and other lands
God may do stranger things than Greeks conceive—
    You that have met such wonders on all hands.

Maymyo, Burma,
    Spring, 1916

CHAPTER I

THE PLACE AND THE MAN

I

In one of his later books Mark Twain put a preface, and in the preface he quoted Herodotus; at least he says so. "Along through the book," he wrote, "I have distributed a few anachronisms and unborn historical incidents and such things, so as to help the tale over the difficult places. This idea is not original with me; I got it out of Herodotus. Herodotus says, 'Very few things happen at the right time, and the rest do not happen at all: the conscientious historian will correct these defects.'" I do not myself recall this passage of Herodotus; I believe it to be wanting in the best European texts, and I doubt if any manuscript earlier than 1890 attributes it to the historian. But the view which the humourist elected to propound was not altogether new, a trouble that lies in wait for the most modern. Juvenal had long before coupled the sailing of a Persian fleet through the promontory of Athos with "all the rest that lying Greece ventures in history."[1] He did not foresee that modern travellers would discover the traces of Xerxes' canal across the neck of the promontory;[2] he had not himself visited Athos and he assumed, like other critics, that his own age had little to learn.

[1] Juvenal x, 173-186, on the story of the Expedition of Xerxes.
[2] See the interesting note of How and Wells on Herodotus vii, 24.

The more genial Plutarch lost his temper with Herodotus, and, in the spirit of Juvenal and Mark Twain, declared with cruel misquotation, that the historian "had danced away the truth," οὐ φροντὶς Ἡροδότῳ.[3] The fact was that Herodotus in the fifth century B.C. had not the motives which moved Plutarch in the first century A.D. to emphasize alone what was glorious in Boeotian history. Professor Sayce in our day, on the basis of discoveries made in Egypt, dismisses Herodotus first as inaccurate, and then as a liar, who "resorts to a kind of verbal legerdemain" to convey the impression that he had visited Upper as well as Lower Egypt, when he had done no such thing.[4] So Mark Twain's humour had some support in ancient prejudice and modern archaeology.

But one does not read far in the works of other modern scholars before one discovers that another view altogether is held of Herodotus, and that other canons of criticism are employed. It was unlikely that a canal was dug through the neck of Athos; it was awkward that Herodotus had unpleasant things to record about Thebes; a man may be inaccurate in a great many particulars, and yet no liar. Mr. G. B. Grundy has given to the military side of Herodotus' history a closer study than any other English or American scholar, and he speaks in quite another tone from Professor Sayce. He finds Herodotus "eminently unmilitary himself" and "peculiarly liable to misunderstand the information at his disposal with regard to military matters," but "his painful conscientiousness seems to be genuine, not

---

[3] Plutarch, *De malignitate Herodoti* 33, p. 867 B.
[4] Sayce, edition of Herodotus, i-iii, p. xxvii.

fictitious,"[5] and "he brought to bear upon his material a certain amount of critical acumen which the extreme simplicity of his language has a tendency to conceal."[6] Further discussion of this question of veracity we may for the moment postpone, but so much may be said at once: Any one who will read Herodotus till he knows him with real intimacy will find it hard to hear with patience the suggestion that he is other than the most candid and truthful of men.

The Greek world read Herodotus. Thucydides might correct detail here and there in his predecessor; Ctesias might string together improbabilities on the alleged authority of royal Persian parchments; Strabo the Geographer might reject his statements as to the outlying regions of the world (and not always be right in so doing); Lucian the satirist might scoff at him; the Greek world read Herodotus; from his own day to ours men have read him. In general, if an author wishes to be read, it is as well for him to be readable, and even Plutarch admits that Herodotus was readable; his charm was a snare.[7] But contemporaries and later generations do not always find the same man readable; tastes change, and styles change, and many an age has found it hard to understand how its grandparents could endure the authors they positively enjoyed. And still Herodotus is read, as Homer is read and Shakespeare; they all keep something that fascinates every age. For every one of the three has the great gift of knowing what to say and what not to say, "of knowing what to leave in the inkpot," as somebody

[5] Grundy, *Great Persian War*, p. 373.
[6] Grundy, *Great Persian War*, p. 266.
[7] Plutarch, *De malignitate Herodoti*, 43, p. 874 B.

put it. Each one of them, again, lived in a peculiarly
interesting period, and brought his great gift to bear
on expressing the mind of that period. (Not one of
them used this rather unpleasant and perhaps
Teutonic phrase to describe his work; we agreed that
they were writers of charm.) The periods of Homer,
Herodotus, and Shakespeare were occupied with
problems that have a permanent interest for mankind; they were crucial periods in the history of our
race, ⟨to which it is always illuminating to return.
And lastly, if I am not beginning to go round in a
circle, these periods survive in the pages and in the
thoughts of men peculiarly interested in Man, and
specially gifted to interpret Man—lovers of men, all
three of them.

   "Think as one may of such things," writes a great
and suggestive German historian,[8]

   Greek History remains still the most important page
in the history of mankind. All the battles, which we are
still fighting for truth, for freedom, for equality, were
fought long ago by the Greeks. The whole development,
in the midst of which we stand and work—it lies here
complete and achieved before our eyes; we see Greek
culture rise, and bloom, and bear fruit, to be quenched at
last in the night of spiritual and political despotism; and
the causes of it all lie open for him who has the wit to
read the book of History. The Greeks did not fight in
vain. Our whole modern civilization rests on the foundation of the Hellenic, it is to the Greeks we owe the blessings
that make life worth living at all—our thought, our art,
the ideals of spiritual and political freedom.

Every word of this is true.

   It is because Herodotus lived through the most
formative and illuminating period of Greek history;
because, though neither philosopher, poet nor

[8] Julius Beloch, *Griechische Geschichte*, I, p. 33.

sculptor, he yet was able, in the true old Greek way, to "see the cities of many men and learn their mind," because he loved men and because Love is after all the simplest and most revealing thing in man; because he kept the gifts of a child and added to them the gifts of a man; because, in virtue of all this, he wrote a book, which may have errors and blunders abundant as his critics say, or more abundant, but yet is full of the life and mind of the most richly dowered race that God has yet given us; because of all these things, and for other reasons, such as old acquaintance and love of my author, I ask you to study Herodotus again with me.

II

We must begin with his homeland and his city, for to Greeks then as now the homeland and home town came first, and remained first. His fellow-citizens the Greek might hate, as Constantinists and Venizelists have hated one another of late; but the Greek exile, though the ancient Persian court or the modern New York with all their variety of wealth and splendour might tempt him, preferred, like Odysseus in the poem, his own land, island or canton.

> A land high-tabled in the main
> Westward; the others take the morning sun;
> Rough but a good nurse, and divine in grain
> Her heroes. Never can I gaze upon
> Land to my mind so lovely as that one,
> Land not to be forgotten.[9]

[9] *Odyssey*, ix, 25 (Worsley).

Herodotus was long ago called "the most Homeric of men,"[10] a description to which we must often recur. Certainly his description of Ionia recalls Odysseus, but with a difference which we shall feel the more as we study him. "These Ionians," he says,[11]—and we shall remember that the Dorians who settled in Halicarnassus were their next-door neighbours— "these Ionians had set their cities in places more favoured by skies and seasons than any country known to us. For neither to the north of them, nor to the south, nor to the east, nor to the west, does the land produce the same effect as Ionia, for in one region it is afflicted by the cold and wet, in another by the heat and drought." Europe is wet and cold, Africa and India are hot and dry, Ionia is right. Elsewhere Herodotus says it again. He speaks of long-lived Ethiopians, of Indians whose land abounds in gold, of Arabians blessed with frankincense, of lands where the creatures are larger and stronger and all things more wonderful—"it would seem," he concludes, "that the fairest blessings have been granted to the ends of the earth, just as Hellas has the seasons tempered by far to the kindliest."[12] Odysseus did not quite discuss the effect of climate on character, nor perhaps does Herodotus, but he leads the way for Aristotle, who found the inhabitants of the cold Europe full of spirit but lacking intelligence and skill, the Orientals intelligent and inventive but so spiritless as to be always slaves, but the Greek both high-spirited and intelligent.[13]

[10] Longinus, 13, 3.
[11] Herodotus, i, 142.
[12] Herodotus, iii, 106.
[13] Aristotle, *Politics*, vii, 7, 1327b.

Halicarnassus was, strictly speaking, in Caria, a little to the south of the Ionians, in a lowland belt, that "opens to a wide sea frontage, and with better government would become one of the best agricultural areas in Asia Minor."[14] So says the modern geographer who elsewhere[15] speaks of "the rich littoral districts of Asia Minor," "lands rich and enervated, at the foot of easy roads, leading down from another and a more virile world." The Carians, however, seem to have been virile enough throughout their history, and, as it is interwoven with that of Halicarnassus and other Greek towns of the coast, a digression to the Carians will not be irrelevant. After all, the art of relevant digression is one we have to study in Herodotus. Here then is what Herodotus says of the Carians:[16]

a people who had come to the mainland from the islands. In the old time they were subjects of Minos and were called Leleges, and held the islands. They paid no tribute so far back as I can reach by hearsay, but they manned him ships, when Minos required. Seeing that Minos had subdued much land to himself and was fortunate in war, the Carian nation was of all nations most famous at that time, and very much the most famous. Three inventions they made, which the Greeks used; it was the Carians who first taught the wearing of crests on helmets and devices on shields, and who first made for their shields handles; for till then all who were wont to use shields carried them without handles but with leathern straps to steer them, which they slung about their necks and their left shoulders. But after a long time Dorians and Ionians drove the Carians out of the islands, and so they came to the mainland. This is what the Cretans tell about the Carians; but the Carians themselves do not consent to it, but hold that they themselves are mainlanders, children of the soil, and always had the name they have now.

[14] D. G. Hogarth, *The Nearer East*, p. 34.
[15] D. G. Hogarth, *Ionia and the East*, p. 48.
[16] Herodotus, i, 171.

Herodotus will allow this of the men of Caurus, who however claim to have come from Crete, though their speech and the Carian have come to be similar.[17] Thucydides[18] tells another story; Minos conquered and colonized the Cyclades, and drove the Carians out of them; the Athenians, in "purifying" Delos during the Peloponnesian War, found Carian dead in more than half the graves they opened; the arms buried in the graves and the general mode of burial alike proved it, the same mode being still used by Carians of his day. Modern archaeologists have also opened the graves on the islands and decided that the arms found do not square with what Herodotus says of Carian weapons, and they give their verdict for the Carian tradition of a mainland origin.[19]

With the Carians are grouped the Leleges. Who the Leleges were, serfs latterly of the Carians, perhaps another or an older people, we need not here discuss. Strabo points out that Homer distinguished between Leleges and Carians, and he tells us that all through Caria and in Miletus "graves and fortresses of the Leleges and traces of their dwellings are shown."[20] What Strabo says of northern Asia Minor, is probably true of southern; it is hard to tell the exact distribution of the races, or mark out their frontiers; there were constant invasions by barbarians and wanderers, who could not always hold the land they took and spent their time casting out and cast out.[21] Whatever the Leleges were or had been, the

[17] Herodotus, i, 172.
[18] Thucydides, i, 4, 8.
[19] How and Wells on Herodotus, i, 171.
[20] Strabo, p. 611.
[21] Strabo, p. 564; he adds (p. 665) that the poets mix the peoples still more terribly than the raiders.

Carians, as Herodotus shows in every reference, were a recognizable people, and so they remained down to the days of Alexander, a people of spirit and character, with fighting qualities that won for them from the Persians the nickname of "game-cocks."[22]

Greek history opens with the planting of colonies on the coast of Asia Minor. The Greek, as we know him in history, was what Carlyle calls "a son of Order," and he tidied up the story of this migration as well as he could, and gave it a proper and uniform beginning with decent and intelligible causes: the Dorians migrated and displaced the Achaeans, the Achaeans displaced the Ionians,[23] and by way of Athens, with Athenian leadership, natural to their kinship, and in twelve groups,[24] the Ionians moved over to Asia Minor. Some of these statements, the first at all events and the last, most people would accept; but the whole is probably more symmetrical in the telling than in the process. Herodotus knew very well that it was not all so orderly; Minyans of Orchomenos, Cadmeians, Dryopians, Phocians, Molossians, Pelasgian Arcadians, Dorians of Epidauros, and Abantes of Euboea, and many more took part in the movement; and for kings some chose Lycian descendants of Glaucus, and some descendants of Codrus. That the stocks were mixed, we can believe; for the rest, writes Mr. Hogarth,[25] "what exactly we are to understand by that Migration, when it began and when it ended, it is difficult to say. Certainly it did not pass in any one great horde. . . . The

[22] Plutarch, *Artaxerxes*, 10.
[23] Herodotus, i, 145.
[24] Herodotus, i, 145.
[25] D. G. Hogarth, *Ionia and the East*, p. 103.

landings in Asia probably went on for several generations." If some of it took place in "Mycenaean"
times,[26] it was all, apparently, after Homer's day,
for Homer knows only a Carian Miletus.[27]

> Nastes the Carians of outlandish tongue
> Commanded, who, the infinite leaves among,
> Dwell near Miletus in the mount of Pine,
> Where flowings of Maeander, not unsung,
> Wind through the vale, and o'er the mountain line
> Lifts up her towering heads great Mycale divine.[28]

Afterwards Miletus was Ionian, or was reckoned
as Ionian, for it had curious customs, which Herodotus explains.

> As for those who came from the very town hall of Athens
> and deem themselves the bestborn of the Ionians, these
> did not bring wives with them to their settlements, but
> married women, whose parents they killed. Because of
> this killing these women made a custom and bound them-
> selves by oath (and enjoined the same on their daughters)
> that none would sit at meat with her husband nor call
> him by his name, because the men had married them after
> killing their fathers and husbands and sons. This happened
> at Miletus. (i, 146).

Modern students of Anthropology have another
explanation of these customs, suggested by parallels
widely diffused throughout mankind, far beyond cities
captured by force and cunning from the Carians;
Lohengrin and Tom Tit Tot had a similar reticence
about their names, though they seem not to have
had Carian mothers. But Herodotus' story at least
explains how Miletus became Ionian. That human
"game-cocks," armed with shields of most service-
able design and scimitars like reaping hooks,[29] did

---

[26] E. Meyer, *Forschungen*, i, p. 150.

[27] See Theodor Wiegand, *Das Delphinion in Milet*, p. 407, for archaic
period.

[28] *Iliad* ii, 867 (Worsley); "near" might better have been "in."

[29] Herodotus, v, 112; vii, 93.

not yield town and women-folk and life itself without furious fighting, is obvious enough, and it illumines the age, all other record of which is lost to us. The shore of Asia Minor is sprinkled with Greek cities when history opens for us, cities won by bloodshed long ago, cities of mixed race, colonies with the energy of their planters crossed with strong qualities derived from mothers sprung of a tribe of warriors. Not idly, nor with the scorn of later days, was it said

Of old, Milesians were men of might.[30]

It was demonstrated for the first time in history (for the Trojan war was a problem) that Greeks could beat the world in hand to hand fighting, the lesson that Marathon and Xenophon's retreat made as gloriously clear in later days.

Halicarnassus was a Dorian colony, from Troezen in the Peloponnese. Queen Artemisia, as all know, even though she had a son, already a young man, took part herself in the great expedition of Xerxes.[31] She was the daughter of Lygdamis,— and by descent she was of Halicarnassus on the side of her father but of Crete by her mother. She was ruler of the men of Halicarnassus and Cos and Nisyros and Calydna. "Of these states I declare the people to be all of the Dorian race, those of Halicarnassus being Troezenians, and the rest Epidaurians."[31] Strabo says much the same and tells us that the ancient name of the place was Zephyria,[32]—much, one supposes, as Ammianus Marcellinus, in the fourth century, speaks of a British town "Augusta, which the ancients called

[30] Aristophanes, *Plutus*, 1002.
[31] Herodotus, vii, 99.
[32] Strabo, p. 656.

Lundinium,"[33] and some moderns, too, who know no better. Halicarnassus was, as Strabo says, the capital of the dynasts of Caria, not only of the great Artemisia and her family but of a later house (related or not, who shall say?), famous also in its queens, for their Mausoleum and their friendship with Alexander the Great. When once the Persian garrison was driven out,[34] Queen Ada "adopted" the son of Olympias.

Herodotus, as we have noted, was eminently Greek, but it is also true that he had a friendly feeling for the Carians. He has always leisure for people he likes, and he notes that the Lydian king, Croesus, had a Carian mother (i, 92) and afterwards conquered her country (i, 28); he tells how long ago Carian "men of brass" had raided Egypt along with Ionians, and entered the service of King Psammetichos (ii, 152), and how they and the Ionians settled in the land, and the Carians adopted a phase of Egyptian religion, and, while they join in sacred lament with the Egyptians, go further and cut their brows with knives, which shows they are foreigners, a significant remark (ii, 61); how Harpagos subdued Caria for Cyrus and had more trouble at Pedasos than in all the land beside (i, 175); how most of the Carians joined the Ionians in the Ionian Revolt (v, 103); and how after the revolt failed, they were subdued by force or surrendered (vi, 25); after which we find Artemisia established as queen and in high favour with Xerxes.

[33] Ammianus Marcellinus, xxviii, 3, 1. Elsewhere he uses the old name himself without the new.

[34] Arrian, *Anabasis*, i, 20, 2-23, 8.

It is plain that, in these Asiatic cities, Greek and Carian intermarried (the very names in the families of Artemisia and of Herodotus himself will reveal so much), as Greek and Libyan intermarried at Cyrene (iv, 186), where the racial difference must have been considerably greater, for the modern conjecture is that at least one element in Caria was Indo-European.[35] Herodotus whose interests are very varied, tells us that the garb of Greek women, known to the world as Ionian, the dress that needed no pins, was really in origin Carian (v, 88); and from the story of Miletus we can guess how the confusion (if such it was) came about, while modern scholars tell us that probably the very name Ionian was first used in these mixed towns, and the Ionic dialect, too.[36] But we are straying back into antiquity.

Inscriptions suggest that there was little in language to separate Halicarnassus from the Ionian cities of Asia and the grea intellectual awakening that began among them. One has only to recall such names as Archilochus[37] and Alcaeus, as Thales, Heraclitus, and Xenophanes, to realize how very great a part those cities had in all that we most gratefully call Greek,—in poetry, art, and philosophy. Here almost from the first, certainly from our first historical acquaintance with them, are at work those instincts which S. H. Butcher picked out as peculiarly Greek,—the Greek political instinct in broad contrast with Asiatic despotism, the laymindedness of the Greek that never succumbed, as all Egypt did, to a priesthood, the passion for beauty and for

[35] D. G. Hogarth, *Ionia and the East*, p. 44, quoting Sir W. M. Ramsay.
[36] E. Meyer, *Forschungen*, I, pp. 132-135.
[37] See J. A. K. Thomson, *Greeks and Barbarians*, Chap. I, and especially pp. 26 ff.

reason, and the insatiable thirst for knowledge, the boylike curiosity, that built the habit of observation and laid the foundations of science. The linguistic barrier was slight, yet, till the day of Herodotus and of Hippocrates, the physician of Cos, the awakening is Ionian. Perhaps the correct language of the lapidary obscures small differences, as our own "Doric" is less often found on stone than in song. Perhaps other reasons operated. But the question arises whether Halicarnassus did not in fact lie as it were in a backwater, away from the stream of great movements, a rather conservative place like Cilician Tarsus in the Roman Empire.[38] Was the Carian influence stronger than the Greek? Were the family traditions of Herodotus of another colour altogether than those of Heraclitus? Or is genius, as so often, leading us to overstress the individual? Or is it quite the other way—was "the Greek spirit" not the common heritage of every Greek? These questions we must at least bear in mind.

III

"The city teaches the man," said Simonides, and the story of almost every Greek of significance confirms him; πόλις ἄνδρα διδάσκει. The city stands on a headland, with Cos full in sight, hardly two hours' sail away; and Cos interested the subjects of Artemisia, and the tale of the captive Coan lady was preserved by her fellow-subject (ix, 76). Behind are the mountains and the mainland, in front is the sea,

[38] Dio Chrysostom, Oration xxxiii (*First Tarsian*), 48.

and as the one or the other may predominate, Halicarnassus is in bondage or enjoys freedom. Its politics are written in the landscape and are intelligible at once. If Carians, or Lydians from behind them, or Persians from the back of beyond, come down upon the headland, nothing but the sea and naval support from Europe will save the city. The hills are Asia, the sea is Europe. The heart of the city was the agora, the market place, where all life centred for the Greek, boy and man. Long after his boyhood Herodotus records what he was told the great Cyrus said to the Spartan herald about the Greeks and their agora: "I never yet feared men of the sort who have a place set apart in the midst of their city, where they gather together and perjure themselves and deceive one another. These Spartans, if I keep my health, will have not the sufferings of the Ionians to chatter about (ἔλλεσχα), but some of their own" (i, 153). "The talk of the market" (περιλεσχήνευτος ii, 135) is his term for what is notorious; and, where we say "ten o'clock," he says "when the market was filling."[39] In and about the market, we can believe, the boy went with bright eyes, watching and noting. "He loves," says one of the finest of English scholars,

to watch and depict human nature. He loves the personal element in history . . . . In his pages, statesmen, grooms, doctors, nurses, peasants, gods, thieves, jostle one another. Now a King speaks, now a philosopher, now a café loafer. We see Syloson in the great square of Memphis, strutting in his scarlet cloak, we hear the self-complacency of the fisherman who was asked to dinner with the tyrant of Samos, and the retort of the mother of Ariston to the man who said that a mule-driver was the father of her children.[40]

[39] Herodotus, ii, 173; vii, 223; iv, 181.
[40] R. W. Livingstone, *The Greek Genius*, p. 151.

If that is the man, the boy before him lived amid all the talk of the market place, now political and international, the last word from up country and the very latest from overseas, rumour and lie and gospel; personal talk, old tales of Rhodopis so pretty that she built a pyramid, and modern talk not very different; above all, trade talk,—where the painter got his Sinopic ruddle, wools of Miletus, corn and hides and hemp of Scythia, flax of Colchis, and alum for the dyer from Egypt.[41] There were all sorts of tradesmen and craftsmen to watch and to talk with when they were at leisure, and it takes little imagination to guess that the bright boy found people very apt to be at leisure for him, and very ready to be his friends, as he did in later years. Like the Greek in Plato's tale, he was "always a boy." The old trades, that we find in Homer, smith and potter and carpenter, leather-dresser, boat-builder and goldsmith,—they still flourished, as was bound to be; and other trades there were of less note today, prophet, interpreter of dreams, singer and reciter of Homer. The physician too was there, midway probably between the Homeric leech and the modern Hippocrates, with his science, across the strait at Cos.

Seafaring men must have been about every Greek haven and perhaps less pressed for time than in greater ports like the Peiraieus, and what tales they could tell! Think of the echoes of old stories of sailors and explorers and traders that we catch in Herodotus—of the "men of bronze" who fought in Egypt and made a friend of the king and opened the country (ii, 152, 154); of Phanes the Halicarnassian, "a man of sufficient judgment and valiant

[41] Cf. Herodotus, v, 49; iv, 17, 53; iv, 74; ii, 105; ii, 180.

in war," who fell out with King Amasis, deserted
and was captured, made his guards drunk and got
safely away to the Persian, and never guessed that
his Greek and Carian fellow-soldiers could make war
on his little boys (iii, 4, 11); of the Phocaeans who
explored the west (i, 163); and of Kolaios, a tale no
doubt learnt later at Samos. Did he not enjoy
hearing how Kolaios was blown out of his reckoning
and at last found himself on a clearer day no man
could say where, till two great rocks loomed up
larger and larger to the north and the south with
open sea between, and the Samian knew them to be
the Pillars of Herakles, which no Greek had seen
before; how he seized and used his luck, traded his
pottery for fabulous wealth, and how, noting every
landmark and keeping a sharp lookout against
Carthaginians and Etruscans, he crept back by the
shore (was it the African or the European? there was
danger at either end of Sicily) and carried the way
in his head and went again, and other Greeks followed him? Was there no pleasure for Herodotus,
young or old, in such a tale, which he tells more
briefly than I have? Or in the tale of Skylax of
Caryanda, no distant neighbour in a Carian town,
whom King Darius sent to sail down the river Indus
from the city Caspatyrus to the sea, who found the
river so full of crocodiles that only one river in the
world has more (a fact that Alexander the Great
forgot, to the confusion of the royal geography[42]),

[42] Arrian, *Anabasis*, vi, 1, Alexander conceived that the Indus might
be the upper waters of the Nile, the crocodiles suggesting it; it might run
through desert regions and so lose its name, appear again in Egypt, and
re-named and more famous flow into the Mediterranean. But he sailed
dòwn the Indus himself and learnt the truth.

and who reached the southern sea, turned westwards, and in the thirtieth month was back in Egypt? (iv, 44). Nearer still to his own day came the brave Carian who fought in Cyprus and saved his commander by a sweep of the scimitar, cutting the legs off the Persian general's horse (v, 112); and Queen Artemisia; and Xeinagoras, the Halicarnassian who saved the brother of Xerxes and became ruler of all Cilicia by the gift of the Great King (ix, 107). The moving tale of adventure, the narrative with plenty of life and character in it, the apologue of homely wisdom, and the simpler story of shrewdness, the witty answer, the thing "well said," appeal to Herodotus as we know him in his book. It is obvious that they would not be there, if they had not appealed to him in life. From childhood he must have loved to listen to stories and to tell them; he must have enjoyed talking. He wrote his book, he tells us, that old stories might not be lost (i, 1). The landward tales that he gathered in youth and manhood must wait for another chapter.

IV

It was the tale that interested Herodotus; the chronology did not so much appeal to him, a sad confession to make about a historian whose life overlapped that of Thucydides. Lest the same charge be brought against us in our study of him, let the one comparatively secure date of his life be given now. There was once a student at Athens, who kept a notebook for years, and at last published it with the poetic title of *Attic Nights* perhaps about 160 A.D. Here is one of the Aulus Gellius' notes or extracts unabridged:[43]

Hellanicus, Herodotus, Thucydides, writers of history, flourished with great glory about the same time and were in age not far apart. For Hellanicus appears to have been sixty-five years old at the beginning of the Peloponnesian War, Herodotus fifty-three, and Thucydides forty. This is written in the eleventh book of Pamphila.

Another writer, Apollodorus, who dates men by their *acme*, puts down the prime of Herodotus about 444 B.C. These two statements bring his birth to the year 484, or very near it. Against this may be cited the statement of Eusebius that in 468 B.C. "Herodotus, the historian, began to be known;" but there is little suggestion of personal memory of the Persian Wars to be found in Herodotus' book, and we may conclude (if conclusions are of moment) that he was born within a few years of 484 B.C. He would seem to have died three or four years after the beginning of the Peloponnesian War, for he mentions no event that can certainly be dated after 430 B.C.[44]

When we ask for detail of his family and of his earlier and later life, antiquity, as usually with the great classical writers who did not write their own lives, has little to give us, and that little survives in lexicons of late date. Stephanus of Byzantium wrote after 400 A.D. and under the name Thurii preserves an elegiac quatrain about Herodotus, which in prose (for it is not the work of a great poet) comes to this: "This dust conceals Herodotus son of Lyxes dead, prince (*prytanis*) of ancient Ionic history, sprung from a father-land of Dorians; for, to avoid their

---

[43] Aulus Gellius, *Noctes Atticae*, xv, 23.
[44] How and Wells, *Commentary on Herodotus*, Vol. I, p. 9.

unbearable censure, he had Thurion for fatherland."
It is impossible to guess the date of such a stanza;
lexicons are made of lexicons. The tenth century
A.D. is named as the date of the Lexicon of Suidas,
which likewise rests on predecessors, lexicographers,
historians and scholiasts and others; and it contains
two entries, which concern us closely.[45] They are
both in prose, and not very skilful prose.

Panyasis, son of Polyarchus, a Halicarnassian, a seer
of signs and epic poet, who revived poetry when quenched.
But Duris [a Samian historian] recorded him as son of
Diocles and a Samian, and similarly Herodotus as a
Thurian. Panyasis was said to have been cousin german
(*exadelphos*) of Herodotus the historian. For Panyasis
is son of Polyarchus, and Herodotus of Lyxes brother of
Polyarchus. Some have said not Lyxes, but Rhoio the
mother of Herodotus was sister of Panyasis. Panyasis was
(γέγονε) in the 78th Olympiad [i.e. 464 B.C.] but according
to some a little older; he lived in fact in the Persian War
period. He was killed by Lygdamis the third tyrant of
Halicarnassus. Among poets he is ranked after Homer,
and according to some after Hesiod also and Antimachus.
He wrote a Herakleid in fourteen books, in 9000 lines,
Ionica in pentameter (it is the story of Codrus and Neleus
and the Ionian colonies) in 6000 lines.

Herodotus, son of Lyxes and Dryo, a Halicarnassian,
of the better class, and had a brother Theodorus. He removed to Samos because of Lygdamis, the tyrant of Halicarnassus third after Artemisia. For Pisindelis was son of
Artemisia and Lygdamis of Pisindelis. In Samos then he
was practised in the Ionic dialect and wrote a history in
nine books, starting from Cyrus the Persian and Candaules
King of the Lydians. After coming back to Halicarnassus
and driving out the tyrant, when later he saw himself
envied (or the object of ill will) by the citizens, he went as
a volunteer to Thurion, then being colonized by the
Athenians, and there he died and is buried in the agora.
But some say he died at Pella. His books are inscribed
Muses.

[45] Sir John Sandys, *History of Scholarship*, Vol. I, p. 371, Stephanus;
p. 399, Suidas.

A sentence from a third entry may be added, which appears to corroborate the suggestion that Pella gives of a residence in Macedonia, a suggestion not incredible in view of his many references to Alexander. "And Hellanicus with Herodotus resided with Amyntas."

Some of this is contradictory at first sight, and some of it is wrong. Archaeologists have shown from inscriptions of Halicarnassus that Herodotus did not need to leave home to master the Ionic dialect; he learned it, they say, from his mother. It was moreover the literary dialect of the day which Hippocrates also wrote, himself, as we have seen, a Dorian from Cos. No one believes that the history was written in Samos and before the expulsion of Lygdamis; the established dates relative to the tyrant upset that statement. But there is a general disposition to accept what we are told by Suidas about the family. There is no obvious reason for supposing it invention, nor any very clear motive to be assigned to the inventor. In the historian's character and his interests there is a good deal in the way of kindred taste and outlook to confirm the kinship with Panyasis, and these are not the considerations that weigh with the common hands that compile lexicons. Halicarnassus reclaimed him after he became famous, and it is likely enough that the family names and story were preserved there. The alternative names of the mother—and it was an easy accident for a copyist to mix them—are both Doric, and Panyasis may very well be Carian. Let us at least provisionally accept Suidas' story.

Here then is a family, in which old poetry and the old style of poetry, old legends of Ionia, old

stories of gods and ever new manifestations of the
gods, dominate the intellectual interests, where a
passion for freedom prevails in two generations and
brings to one man death, to another exile and glory
and ill will. No one can say that all this is alien to
the historian. The gods, their myths and legends,
their oracles and theophanies, piety and morals, are
written all over his work. It is worth noting that
both sons of Lyxes have names of piety—"given by
Hera" and "gift of god" are not without significance
in an age when so many men have names with
meanings that do not suggest piety. The giving of
"theophoric" names was in later centuries an accom-
paniment of the revival of religion. "Herodotus,"
writes Dr. Macan,[46] "was trained so to speak in the
school of his uncle Panyasis, one of the last of the
epic poets. His history of the great invasion is but
the application of the principles of Panyasis to a new
subject, the freshest that could have engaged his
attention." Fragments of Panyasis still survive; the
longest are preserved by Athenaeus and therefore, as
one would expect, bear on the convivial, one being
a praise of wine, and the other two leaning a little to
moderation in its use, though not going so far as
prohibition.[47] Others quote smaller pieces, and
Dionysius of Halicarnassus praises his fellow-citizen
as at least in some features the equal or superior
of Hesiod and Antimachus. It is sometimes a little
difficult to be at once patriotic and critical in dealing
with local authors.

On epic poetry, whoever was his uncle, the boy
was nurtured. Rhapsodes were still reciting Homer

[46] Introduction to Herodotus, pp. vii, viii, ix, Vol. I, p. xlviii. Cf.
Amédée Hauvette, *Hérodote*, p. 25.

[47] See Kinkel, *Epicorum Graecorum Fragmenta*, I.

in public a good half-century or more later, as Plato
tells us in the *Ion* and Xenophon in his *Symposion*;
and in Plato's phrase,[48] we can believe that "a certain reverence and friendship" for Homer stayed
with Herodotus from boyhood. We have seen (and
shall see again) how close an intellectual affinity is
recognized between Homer and Herodotus both by
the ancients and by scholars today. He discusses
Homer as a literary artist (ii, 116) and as one of the
great teachers of religion to the Greeks (ii, 53).
He alludes to one of the Cyclic poems, the *Epigonoi*,
"if in real truth Homer wrote that poem" (iv, 32),
and he decides that Homer did not write the *Cypria*
(ii, 117).[49] Sooner or later, he knew a great deal of
Greek poetry; he refers to the successors of Homer
(ii, 117; iv, 32), to Hesiod (ii, 53; iv, 32), Archilochus
(i, 12), Alcaeus (*v*, 95) and Sappho (ii, 135), Solon
(*v*, 113), Arion of Methymna (i, 23, 24, the famous
dolphin story), Simonides of Ceos (*v*, 102; vii, 228)
and Lasos of Hermione (vii, 6), and Anacreon (iii,
121). He also read something of contemporary
poets, which not every man of letters will do.[50] He
quotes Pindar (iii, 38) and refers to Aeschylus (ii,
156), and, as we may see, there were still closer
relations between him and Sophocles. Some Greek
poetry he clearly despised, but lets "the Greeks who
deal in it" go unnamed (ii, 82).

Of his family and his childhood he does not speak,
but certain passages show an interest and pleasure in
children. The cowherd's wife, who saw how big and

[48] Plato *Republic* X, p. 595 B.
[49] On this see the interesting discussion of John A. Scott, *The Unity
of Homer*, pp. 23, 24.
[50] Some students of Latin literature are a little naïve in noticing this
reluctance in Cicero.

fair the baby Cyrus was, fell weeping, and begged
her husband not to expose the child to death (i, 111,
112); the shepherd of Psammetichos with his homely
attentions to the little Egyptian babies, who were
to reveal the primitive language and by calling
for *bekos* proved it to be Phrygian (ii, 1); and the
twisted Labda's baby which "by divine providence
smiled at the man" who was to destroy it and who
preferred to pass the smiling child on to the next
and so round (v, 92, C); these tales illustrate the
simple humanity of the man, and perhaps tell something of his early days, as Xenophon's picture of the
young Cyrus, the most genuine boy in Greek literature, reveals that historian's character.

Herodotus must have had the usual upbringing of
people of quality of his day. He was "of the better
sort," Suidas says; and it is noted that he laughs at
Hecataeus having the vanity to recite his pedigree
of sixteen generations, ending in a god, to the
Egyptian priests; "I told them no pedigree of mine,"
he says (ii, 143). Not he! Simple people do not make
themselves always so ridiculous as the clever. However, he duly learnt to read and write and, more or
less, to spell.[51] There is only one way to all that,
and a fragment of terra cotta has been found at
Athens, with the innocent inscription, which needs
no comment:

ar bar gar dar
er ber ger der.[52]

[51] There are those who find him a little uncertain as to Oriental names.
[52] Paul Girard, *L'Education Athénienne*, p. 131; cf. Kenneth Freeman,
Schools of Hellas, p. 89. Also A. A. Bryant, "Boyhood and Youth" in
Harvard Studies in Classical Philology, XVIII, 1907.

Herodotus looks back as an antiquary to the alphabet and discusses its origin, in the light of the Cadmeian characters which he saw carved in a Theban temple and of the old name that the Ionians gave to them, "phoenicians" (v, 58-61), a fact confirmed by an inscription of Teos (of about 470 B.C.).[53] The Cadmeian letters may have been of later date than he supposed, but Phoenician their origin was. He speaks of Egyptians writing from right to left (ii, 36) but does not seem to have known of Greeks writing *boustrophedon*, first one way and then back. He tells us how Dorians call *san* the letter the Ionians name *sigma* (i, 139). Elsewhere he digresses to the origin of common games; and, forgetful of Patroclus and Nausicaa, or using another chronology, he says that the Lydians in the reign of Atys invented dice and knucklebones and ball games; draughts are not claimed by them (i, 94). Thus, perhaps from the beginning, he was interested not only in things but in their origins and their place in human story. Nothing human is alien to him. The frequent washings and so forth of the Egyptian priests he explains as precautions against lice (ii, 37); perhaps not all Greeks were so careful. John Wesley had in the eighteenth century to say something about such parasites to his converts, and everybody remembers what Burns saw.

There were gaps in his education. His spelling has been compared to the Elizabethan for its spacious freedom. His arithmetic obviously broke down now and then. There is very little reference to music in his pages; he merely says that the Argives were best at it (iii, 131). The music of savages is, of course, quite another thing; it has an anthropological, a

[53] Hicks and Hill, *Greek Historical Inscriptions*, no. 23.

human interest. He does not talk philosophy, but it was clearly an influence in the training of his mind, as we shall see. There is little to show if he ever rode or boxed. Sooner or later he became greatly interested in works of art, though perhaps he was more stirred by the achievements of engineering than by the triumphs of architecture (iii, 60); he liked to see a big building, it was so obviously the victory of human mind over matter.

But, whatever the gaps in his training, it was genuinely Greek. "I visited Thebes, too, and Heliopolis for this very purpose, because I wished to know," he says (ii, 1). Solon, he tells us, travelled "to see" ($\tau\hat{\eta}s$ $\theta\epsilon\omega\rho\ell\eta s$ $\epsilon\ell\nu\epsilon\kappa\epsilon\nu$, i, 30). "Wonder" is one of his characteristic words, and "worth seeing" is another. He "wanted to know" as a boy in the market at home, as a man in Egypt,—"as far as I could learn by inquiry" (ii, 34), "wishing to get some clear knowledge about it whence it was possible so to do" (ii, 44). Modern education too often kills this instinct with which all of us are born who are not mentally deformed. But Greek education left alive in the man the boy's eager and ardent mind, at any rate in the centuries under our review; and, as we shall see in the chapters that follow, the range over which he inquired was a very wide one. "Fortunate Egyptian priests!" exclaims Mr. Livingstone,[54] "who expounded to him the ways of their country, and watched him absorb it all from the three hundred and thirty Sovereigns of Egypt down to the bird that picks the crocodile's teeth!" But, as with all Greeks, the ways and manners of men interested him most.

[54] R. W. Livingstone, *Greek Genius*, p. 150.

He liked pedigrees, even if he would not tell his own; and he gives us a good many, traditional among the Greeks, Spartan and others. One tremendous family tree, which he does not give us, he clearly carried in his head, and it was a feat to do it. Anyone who will work out the details of the royal house of Persia given in his pages will soon realize how much Herodotus was interested in such things, perhaps absorbing them, as some men and more women do, without knowing it. He will pause to tell us something of a man of fine physique,—"of all these men, so many myriads in number, no one for beauty and stature was more worthy than Xerxes to possess this power" (vii, 187). Callicrates was the most beautiful not only of the Spartans but of all the Hellenes of his time; and, doomed to die a lingering death, "it did not grieve him," he said, "to die for Hellas, but that no deed had been done by him worthy of the spirit within him" (ix, 72). Tigranes, next after Xerxes no doubt, excelled the other Persians in beauty and stature (ix, 96). Yet moral quality interests him more, as the saying of Callicrates shows and a hundred other episodes.

V

So far nothing has been said of the Persian Empire, the one constant background of everything in Asia Minor, as the accursed Turk has been since. That subject will occupy us in later chapters. But one thing must be said now. If the date of Herodotus' birth was 484 B.C., then the earliest public event

which he would remember might well be the great
expedition of Xerxes or its more amazing defeat.
What does it mean to grow up in an age of victory
and hope? in an age when the human mind is achiev-
ing all it "desires to know," moulds stone to the
human form, and yokes sea and sky to the human
purpose, charms magic out of words, unlocks the
secrets of the universe—and beats back the despot
from the gates of freedom? "Bliss was it in that
dawn to be alive, but to be young!" And Herodotus
was young, and he drank of that sense of power of
which Athens and all Greece drank, and yet with the
moderation that the old training gave and the old
uncle sang. He has a "naïve yet noble sense of
humanity," but a Greek clearness that saves him
from intoxication, a sense of limit and of law (vii,
104), which is as Greek as the sense of power. He
looks before and after, he will "see the end" (i, 32),
he will be at a universal point of view; travel and
inquiry are stimulated by this sober exultation in the
possibility of knowledge. Grandeur comes very near
our dust, and Herodotus, like any other Greek of that
age, but more soberly, believes he may say "I can;"
he too has the Greek sense of power, but he is not
drunk with it. There were influences to sober any
one at Halicarnassus; Greece might be free, Athens
might have driven back the Persian invader, but
Lygdamis was tyrant of Halicarnassus, and before
he was driven out Herodotus had had new experience of the limitations of man's life.

The story has been told already, all we know of it,
in the awkward entries of Suidas, but two pieces of
epigraphic evidence remain to be noticed.[55]   Sir

[55] See Hicks and Hill, *Greek Historical Inscriptions*, no. 27.

Charles Newton found at Halicarnassus a marble stele, now in the British Museum, which tells of a sworn agreement between Lygdamis, once more in the city after quitting it during some revolution, and his citizens; the outgoing magistrates are not to hand over any lands or houses to their successors; in other words, the owners, returned from exile, are to regain them, subject to proof in due time. A Panyassis is mentioned in the inscription. A later monument[56] reveals that in 454 B.C. Halicarnassus paid *phoros* (tribute) to the Confederacy of Delos; so we may conclude that, by that year at latest, Lygdamis was gone. Herodotus is as silent about his own share in all this as about his pedigree; he has not even so much as the quiet words of Thucydides, "it befel me to be in exile."[57]

But a good deal confirms Suidas. Herodotus' feelings about tyranny will occupy us later on, and his glad proud words that tell how good a thing Freedom is. Tyrants themselves he could not quite dislike, any more than other people; they were sometimes so extremely interesting, and he was obviously proud of the grandmother of Lygdamis. The whole episode fits the man and his mind—hope, and faith in Freedom, knowledge of what it is to be an exile, the triumph of victory, the sad departure from among men whom he had helped to free and who did not feel for him as he had hoped they would. It also confirms the story that he is so full of information about Samos and so interested in the island and its arts and history.

[56] Hicks and Hill, *op. cit.*, no. 33.
[57] Thucydides, v, 26, 5.

The Samians, he says, had made the three greatest works to be seen in any Greek land, the tunnel of Eupalinus that brought the water through the hill, the great mole that enclosed the harbour, and the temple, "the largest of all the temples I know," the architect of which was Rhoecus, a Samian. The temple contained much of beauty well worth seeing (iii, 123). The tunnel is not mentioned elsewhere in literature, and it was quite unknown till it was discovered and the silt cleared out in the nineteenth century. "It is for this cause that I have written at length rather more than ordinary about Samos" (iii, 60); and, no doubt, also because, in their various ways and their various days, Polycrates with his fleet and his ring (iii, 39 ff., 120 ff.), and his brothers (iii, 139 ff.), and Pythagoras, "not the weakest teacher of the Greeks" (iv, 95), and even Theomestor the benefactor of Xerxes at Salamis (viii, 85; ix, 90) were more than ordinarily interesting people; and because the Samians ransomed after Salamis the Athenians whom Xerxes had made prisoners (ix, 99); and because in short the Samians were the only Ionians who combined sense and courage, though, to be sure, the Chians also were brave (vi, 14).

But Samos was an interlude only in his career, well filled as the bare reference above to the stories of the Samians will show and much else—an interlude of expanding acquaintance with old legends and living men. Perhaps, and it is likely, his acquaintance with Athens and Athenians began here, and he realized in a new way the alternative to Persian suzerainty and the tyranny and murders of Lygdamis. We have no direct evidence, but let us put together what indications we have. We have then, first a city under a tyrant with Persia behind him, and later on a city in the Athenian Confederacy free of tyrants; and we have a great book that is one of the chief sources of Athenian fame, written (we are told) largely from an Athenian point of view by a man loyal to Athens and bold to speak her merit in her dark days; and the man came from the city that drove out the tyrant and joined the Confederacy. Later on, as we saw, tradition says that he was unpopular at home. Was it for his eager loyalty to the saviours of Hellas, the source of other men's discomfort in other cities, liberated and ungrateful? There are theories less well founded. It is likely enough that, in his return and in the expulsion of Lygdamis, the Athenian fleet had a part.

To Athens Herodotus turned, it would appear, when Halicarnassus grew uncomfortable. So far as we know, he never saw his native city again; Athens was his centre for the rest of his life—Athens, and for a while her hapless Italian colony, Thurii—and then, most probably (though it is only an inference and is disputed), Athens again. His travels only a bold man would try to date; they fell between the exile of Lygdamis and the historian's death, so much is obvious, unless the Samian period was a long one and varied with journeys. But between 484 and 454 boyhood and youth filled many of the years; and questions have been raised as to how far and how freely a Halicarnassian exile with strong Athenian sympathies could travel in the Persian Empire. One surmises that in a somewhat loose-hung empire, as Persia's always was, in days before paper and printing and passports were so rife as today, a Greek of sense, who knew something of Asia Minor at first hand, might travel with less hindrance than we should suppose. True, the Persians did identify Greek spies now and then.[58] The later period between 454 (or whatever earlier year saw Lygdamis go) and 431 (when the Peloponnesian War began) gives more time, and his visit to Egypt certainly falls into these years, as it was a good while after the battle of Papremis in 460 B.C.[59] All his eastward travels may have been after 448 B.C , the year of the pacification with Persia. However, his travels belong to the next chapter, Athens to this.

How deeply interested he was in Athens, and how familiar with Athenian life, may be read in many places in his book. Eduard Meyer[60] remarks his criticisms of other Greek states, his explicit emphasis on the thoroughgoing Persian policy of Thebes, and on the jealousy that Corinth had for Athens, the rivalry of Adeimantos and Themistocles,—the light irony (or something like it) with which he treats Sparta so intent on festival as to miss the moment of action,— the excuses made for the Medism of Thessaly and of Argos (vii, 148-152), with the latter of which Athens was beginning a *rapprochement*,—his defence of the Alcmaeonid house against contemporary slanders as to their dealings with Cylon and with Persia (vi, 121), —his grudging recognition of the great deeds of Themistocles, and his admiration of Cimon and Pericles, each of whom is brought into the history with an entry well prepared. It is conjectured that a phrase in one place (vii, 162) is borrowed from the funeral speech of Pericles in 439 B.C., in which he described

[58] Herodotus, vii, 146.

[59] Cf. Herodotus, ii, 30, 99; E. Meyer, *Forschungen*, i, 155.

[60] Meyer, *Geschichte des Altertums*, iii, § 142.

the death of young men in the Samian War as taking
the spring from the year.[61] It is guessed that his visit
to the Black Sea was with the expedition of Pericles in
444 B.C.[62] It is a generally accepted view that he
was on friendly terms with Sophocles, the friend of
Pericles, and a congenial nature:

$$\text{ὁ δ' εὔκολος μὲν ἐνθάδ' εὔκολος δ' ἐκεῖ.}[63]$$

The line would serve equally well for the historian
and the poet, both easy tempered here and easy
tempered yonder, wherever yonder might be.

$$\text{Οὔ τοι συνέχθειν ἀλλὰ συμφιλεῖν ἔφυν,}$$

wrote Sophocles,[64] and Herodotus was of the same
mind, "born to join in loving, not in hating." A line
or two survives of a little poem which Sophocles, aged
fifty-five, wrote for him.[65] The story of Miltiades
shows information clearly coloured by the views of
an anti-Periclean group, the friends of Cimon,
Miltiades' son, no doubt. Of all Athenians Themistocles suffers most eclipse in the pages of
Herodotus; his crooked ways,[66] his deals in money,
his footing in both camps, his extortion, revolted
the simple-minded and candid nature from across the
Aegaean. Herodotus undoubtedly met people, who,
like his informants on Cyrus (i, 95), "desired not to
make a fine tale of" Themistocles. He makes no
allusion to the walls of Themistocles, and though the
story of the Great War itself brought out the incom-

[61] E. Meyer, *Forschungen*, ii, 211-233; and J. B. Bury, *Ancient Greek Historians*, p. 63.

[62] Bury, *op. cit.*, p. 41.

[63] Aristophanes, *Frogs*, 82.

[64] Sophocles, *Antigone*, 523.

[65] Plutarch, *An Seni Respublica*, 3.

[66] Cf. viii, 4, 5; 22; 57; 110; 111; 112.

parable services of Themistocles, it was left for
Thucydides, an Athenian and once a politician
himself, to emphasize the real greatness of the man.
Aristides, on the other hand, says Herodotus (vii,
79), "I hold, according to what I hear of his character, to have been the best and most upright of all
Athenians." The most intelligent foreigner does not
always judge a nation's politicians quite as their
adherents will; and Herodotus to the end was sometimes curiously naïve in his ideas of politics.

But whatever he made of party politics and of
politicians, he was clear as to the supreme achievement of Athens. One cannot precisely date each part
of his book, though it is with some scholars a favourite
pastime to try to do so, but it is conjectured that the
passage now to be quoted may have been added to
the book at a late stage when the Greek world was
deluged with an anti-Athenian propaganda and
Athens' services were being obscured. "Here I am
compelled by necessity," he says (vii, 139),

to declare an opinion, which in the eyes of most men will
seem odious, but yet, as it seems to me to be clearly the
truth, I will not refrain. If the Athenians, in dread of the
danger advancing upon them, had left their land, or if they
had stayed and surrendered to Xerxes, no one would have
attempted to withstand Xerxes on the sea. If then nobody
on the sea had withstood Xerxes, something of this sort
would have befallen on land; even if many tunics of walls
had been thrown across the isthmus by the Peloponnesians,
the Spartans would have been abandoned by their allies,
not willingly but of necessity, as city after city was taken
by the barbarian navy, and they would have been left
utterly alone; and left alone they would, after doing great
deeds, have died nobly. Either that would have been their
lot, or before that, when they saw the rest of the Greeks
Medizing, they would have come to terms with Xerxes.
And thus, either way, Hellas would have been brought

under the Persians. Of what use walls thrown across the isthmus could have been, when the King held the sea, I cannot learn. But now, if a man were to call the Athenians the saviours of Hellas, he would not miss the truth; for to whichever side these turned, the balance would incline. They chose that Hellas should survive and be free, and they it was who roused all of Hellas that was left, all that had not Medized, and with the help of the gods drove the King back. Nor did terrible oracles coming from Delphi dismay them and lead them to abandon Hellas, but they stood their ground and endured to receive the invader of their land.

That is a noble passage, and it is true. This Halicarnassian had not travelled the world in vain; he could form a shrewd and sound judgment on *Weltpolitik*. Themistocles "even where he had no experience, was quite competent to form a sufficient judgment," according to Thucydides (i, 138). Herodotus, after the event and with real knowledge of the world in its width and its variety, had an easier task; and yet, after the event and with wide opportunities, how many men still fail to grasp that the world is not the Peloponnese and still miss the significance of the sea? Our old historian's greatness shines in this passage, not least for his resolute candour in putting forward an unpopular truth.

Of Thurii little need be said. Started with a Panhellenic idea, which we can understand appealing to Herodotus,[67] the colony was one of Pericles' failures. The colonists fell to quarrelling, and it was no place for a friend of all the world. Did Herodotus return to Greece, scholars ask,—to Athens? and they waver in their answers. Eduard Meyer does not make up his mind, but thinks from his allusions to the Peloponnesian War that he did return. M. Hauvette

[67] Cf. what the oracle and Herodotus say of Cyrene, iv, 159.

holds that he did not, and Suidas shows that some ancients agreed with him; the Thurians would be glad in after days to boast of his tomb among them; but so did the Macedonians. Mr. How and Mr. Wells emphasize small facts and events of the War, more likely to reach a man in Athens than in Thurii. East or west, in Athens or in Thurii,— somewhere at all events,—he wrote his *History*, and men have gone on reading it ever since. With all his love of digression, and his avowed quest of digression, he did not digress to his own story, but much of it is in his book; and his character is there, transparent and lovable.

CHAPTER II

THE STORY AND THE BOOK

I

It is not often we are in a position to know how the impulse came to a great artist to produce what has proved to be his masterpiece. Probably, as a rule it comes after long preparation, which has been less conscious than instinctive. The subject drew him; he thought much upon it; then one day he saw it in a new way, and wondered, and then perhaps suddenly realized how intensely it suited him, how much of his work was done already; he would finish it. But in working it out, he found he had only begun his work, and it must all be done again; new views broke in upon him, he saw fresh implications, deeper significance; and his task grew under his hand. And then he had to re-learn how to handle it, to experiment with method and approach, to discover or to develope the one style in which he could make all tell—the "inevitable" style. One imagines that somehow so Herodotus came to write his masterpiece. We have seen already how much there was in his situation, his environment and life at Halicarnassus to lead him on to his great theme and to enable him to see it in its true setting of the world. He "wished to know," (ii, 3); he "wondered"; and he became a historian.

A parallel may illustrate his case. "The surprising nature of the events which I have undertaken to relate," says a later Greek historian,[1]

is in itself sufficient to challenge and stimulate the attention of every one, old or young, to the study of my work. Can any one be so trifling or idle as not to care to know by what means and under what kind of polity, almost the whole inhabited world was conquered and brought under the dominion of the single city of Rome, and that within a period of not quite fifty-three years. . . . . It will be a useful and worthy task to discover why it is that the Romans conquer and carry off the palm from their enemies in all the operations of war, that we may not put it all down to Fortune and congratulate them on their good luck, as vulgar minds would, but may know the true causes.

So writes Polybius of a story as wonderful if not so romantic as the Persian War. He too has wondered and wished to know, but he wrote at a later day, and with an older mind than the ever young Herodotus. It is one of the greatest losses in History that it was so, and that the great gifts and powerful mind of Polybius lacked the supreme gift of charm. Still the parallel will serve.

Landward or seaward, whichever way he looked, there lay the region of wonder for Herodotus. The seamen about the harbour, the traders in the agora, all spoke of strange lands over the hills and far away, of strange men and animals, and other manners and customs, of great deeds and splendid adventures. Story-telling ran in the family blood, and Herodotus was a *logopoios* from the cradle; he told the tales again to his brother Theodorus; to his mother and father, to his schoolfellows, and went again to .the

[1] Polybius, i, 1; and xviii, 28; translation of Shuckburgh, with one or two verbal changes.

haven and the market for more stories. He was one of the world's great listeners, and the best of them turn story-tellers; the bright eyes flashed as the point came, and the story-teller at Halicarnassus talked more and more to the boy. "You Greeks are always young; you are always boys at heart," said the Egyptian priest to Solon in Plato's tale; and it was true. It was autobiography in Plato; and it is confirmed by the great story-tellers, Homer, Herodotus, Walter Scott, Dumas, the tellers of tales "without psychology," as the old Englishwoman said of Shakespeare, great, big, genial natures too full of zest and vitality to analyse, but with the boy's quick instinct for life.

Over the hills and far away! What would Alexander have attempted but for that fever at Babylon? To add Europe to Asia? the British Isles to Europe? "I cannot really conjecture," writes Arrian,[2] "and I do not care to guess. One thing I think I can be sure of; it would have been nothing small or mean, nor would Alexander have rested quiet, but would have pressed on, onward into the unknown." "There were many great things," says Herodotus (i, 204) in much the same vein of Cyrus, "that uplifted him and drove him forward; first of all, it was born in him."

It was born in that Greek race to want to know, to wonder, and to range the world. There lay Cos full in view, two hours' sail away, and all the Cyclades were out beyond it, each with a tale to tell, and the mainland of Greece. Farther off lay the lands of wonder, Scythia where feathers fell from the sky, and away beyond it were eaters of men (iv, 106) and

[2] *Anabasis*, vii, 1, 4.

men with goat's feet and men who slept for six
months (iv, 25)—tales which travel might lead a
man to doubt, "credible to another, to me not;" and
southward lay Egypt, true enough, where the one
river overflowed instead of drying up, and the lizards
grew to the size of nightmares; and eastward "all the
fairest things are in the ends of the earth" (iii, 106).
"If there were such darling things as old Chaucer
sings," wrote Charles Lamb to a great Cambridge
explorer,[3] "I would up behind you on the Horse of
Brass, and frisk off for Prester John's country. But
these are all tales." "I wanted to know," and when
Lygdamis was gone and the Halicarnassians showed
no wish to keep their patriot at home, he sailed away
to learn. And probably, quite apart from the wonders
of the world, the greatest of all stories was calling
him. Some have fancied that considerable parts of
his book were originally meant to be a part of a
geography, and were afterwards incorporated in his
history.[4] So critics will conjecture, forgetting
Homer's ways and the aptness of Geography to
Tragedy which Aeschylus saw, forgetting Herodotus
himself, one thinks, who was an artist all through,
and left it to Diodorus and Suidas to "incorporate,"
and, whatever digressions his story sought (iv, 30),
saw to it that nothing was in it but what belonged to
it (cf. iv, 154; v, 72). No! Sooner or later, he realized
that all the calls were one call—the call of the greatest story in the world. Homer had heard the same
call, though it was a different story.

[3] Lamb, Letter to T. Manning, 19 February, 1803.
[4] Bury, *Ancient Greek Historians*, p. 40.

II

"What Herodotus of Halicarnassus [some manu-scripts read "of Thurii"] has learnt by inquiry is here set forth," so his *History* begins, "in order that so the memory of the past may not be blotted out from among men by time, and that great and marvellous deeds done by Greeks and barbarians may not lack fame, least of all the cause for which they warred with one another." After a page or two of tales told by Persians, he says, and by Phoenicians to explain the ancient feud of East and West, "for my own part," he continues

I will not say that it befel so or otherwise; but him whom I know myself to have begun wrong deeds against the Greeks, him I will name and then go on with my story speaking of cities of men [a Homeric phrase from the very beginning of the Odyssey] small and great alike. For many cities which of old were great have become small, and those that were great in my time were in other days small. I know that human prosperity never continues steadfast, so I will make mention alike of both.

Then he starts with Croesus, initiator of evil deeds against the Greeks, and his very good friend long before he says his last word to Cambyses.

He wants to know how the war arose and how they fought it through. He was not a practical soldier, he had had no personal experience of war, Mr. Grundy tells us,[5] and was eminently unmilitary. The struggle with Lygdamis was fought out in the streets of what we should call a little country town, a smaller affair than the revolutions of Paris; and to

[5] Grundy, *Great Persian War*, pp. 266, 291, 373.

hold a barricade or storm a little palace is a different
thing from managing an army and a navy acting
together. The hugeness of the task that Xerxes
imposed upon his admirals and generals in the main
escaped Herodotus; he misreads his sources, he does
not take in naval language, and in manoeuvres
ashore he misses the object of tactics, he fails to see
the real strategy, and once he drops two whole days
out of his story of a big movement.[6] Yet he took
pains to talk with men who had fought the actions;
Mr. Grundy holds that he drew his stories of Artemisium and Plataea from men who had been present,
but who did not know the plans of the commanders.[7]
He travelled over the ground of the great march and
of the famous actions, and Mr. Grundy once and
again remarks his great accuracy in description; at
Thermopylae, at Plataea,—"there can be no real
question that he visited both places, and, not merely
that, but that his examination of them was extremely
careful." It is true that he slews the pass of Thermopylae round through a quarter of the compass,
speaking of the east end of it as the south end, but
at all events it was the Greek end and he did not
confuse it with the Persian. He missed the point of
the combined work of fleet and army on both sides
in the movement from the north to the south end
of the Euripus, as probably many of the hoplites
themselves did, and many perhaps of the sailors.
But important as actions are, the history of a war
is more than the story of its battles, even when they
are as important and tremendous as Thermopylae,
Salamis, and Plataea.

[6] Grundy, *Great Persian War*, p. 319.

[7] Grundy, *Great Persian War*, pp. 319, 333, 340, 472.

"My story was looking for additions," he says; and his real interest comes out in them. Aeschylus does not precisely explain his purpose in writing his *Persians*; he lets the play tell the spectator or reader, who may miss it or hit it. Herodotus does not unfold his design and discuss his own outlooks with the length of a Polybius,—to whom be no disrespect! for his mind has a real affinity with Polybius, though he is a greater artist and conceals his art better. Can any one be so trifling or so idle as not to care to know how Greece and Persia came to fight, the politics, the natures, and the minds that brought about the conflict or were involved in it? He does not theorize offhand in our modern way and call it all inevitable; the Athenians perhaps need not have been "humbugged" by Aristagoras into sending those twenty ships which "were a beginning of evils for Greeks and for barbarians" (v, 97). Nor will he call it all fortune; the hand of God was in it, as we shall see later on. Was it all avoidable? Was it all inevitable? It will, at all events, be a useful task to discover who and what manner of people the combatants were, and how they looked at life; and life, as one looks into it, proves very complex, very manifold, and if you want to understand it, you must know it very well and know it all round; and the story grows in depth and breadth. He goes to see the countries as well as the spots concerned, and there are no marked lines to be drawn on the Mediterranean, and even mountain ranges are not very definite or difficult lines on the land, however abrupt they may look on a map. One land involves another land; one people more means other tribes on its frontiers; his intellectual curiosity is as compelling and as universal as Alexander's; and it is all relevant to his story. "He did not look on history as formed in a vacuum."[8]

Nor did he look upon it, in our modern way, as chiefly composed of abstract nouns: of tendencies, and popular opinions, and economic pressures, and the circumstances of the time. Lygdamis was not driven out by circumstances, though circumstances did help Athens to get rid of Hippias (v, 65); no, in both cases some man had to get comrades and do it, an "Archibald Bell-the-Cat." It was Themistocles who precipitated the fight at Salamis; all the circumstances were against it, and if it had been left to tendency or, in English, drift, that battle would not have been fought. In heroes of one kind and another, in men, Herodotus is as much interested as Carlyle; and, heroes or villains, he loves to watch men. What sort of men, then, did Greece and Persia produce? And the answer is, all sorts of men; Persia, grandees who could jump overboard and drown to save their King (viii, 118), and Greece, commanders who could vote to a man, every one of them, that Themistocles was second best among them (viii, 123). These types the races produced and all the variety that makes a world.

Students of Thucydides have remarked how he will deliberately sum up a situation in a speech, gathering up the ideas that were generally in the air and the things that would be said,—"putting into the mouth of each speaker the sentiments proper to the occasion, expressed as I thought he would be likely to express them, while I endeavoured, as nearly as I

[8] Grundy, *Great Persian War*, p. 220.

could, to give the general purport of what was
actually said."[9] What Thucydides did upon reflection, we may possibly say that Herodotus did by
instinct. Where in Thucydides' pages (i, 72) some
Athenians, who were present for other business, came
forward on invitation and spoke, in the story of
Herodotus we are more behind the scenes and in the
counsels of the men who put the things through; and
of course there was no reporter present, no maker of
précis; but Herodotus, a born story-teller, like Elia
uses the first person, and dialogue with him is neither
deception nor art but nature. Ancient and modern
alike have found the speeches he gives easier to read
than those of Thucydides. In a modern historian his
method, the method of either of them, unless the
modern turned Thucydides' speeches steadily into
a series of vague third persons, would be intolerable.
The daily press stands between us and the real agents
in any political or international transaction. "Current opinion in France is that the Germans' attitude, etc." is the language of today, and in huge
nations the real force, operate only in this muffled
way. In a small Greek town it was different; καί ποτέ
τις εἰπῇσι says Homer, there was talk indeed and
anonymous rumour enough in the agora, but when
the decisive thing was done, it was the speech or act
of some very definite person whom everybody knew.
In a despotism like Persia, the circle in which policies
were decided was a small one, too; and shrewd
observers, and there were plenty among the Persians,
could know, or pretty certainly guess, where the
responsibility lay for one act and another of the Great
King.

[9] Thucydides, i, 22 (Jowett.)

Men and women are always talking, intriguing, reflecting, in the books of Herodotus, and to mingle with them as they talk is one way of understanding History. To understand Canada and Arabia there are two ways open to the modern: one is to amass histories and other books, and Board of Trade returns, statistics of lunacy, illiteracy, wheat production, railroads; another is to ride on the trains or the camels, as may be, and live as Doughty did in Arabia or Martin Allerdale Grainger in lumber camps,[10] and assimilate the people unconsciously. It is well to know how many miles of railroad a country has, it is well for democrats to reflect that 94 per cent of the population of India is illiterate, and the percentage far higher among Hindus than among Christians; but to know how the mind of Greek or Persian, of Scot or Irishman, will instinctively react to circumstances, is a higher and more valuable knowledge. But will not a novel, or a series of novels, tell you this as well? It might, if written by a man of genius. In the case before us, happily, the man of genius wanted to know, not what might happen, but what did happen, and was anxious that great deeds that stirred wonder should never be blotted out by time. He immersed himself in the actual as far as he could get it. Men did not always tell him the truth; men are horribly careless, as Thucydides grumbled,[11] they do not discriminate, they are too ready to accept old traditions or inaccurate statements of the present and to pass them on, to form wrong opinions as to the greatness of the war that

[10] Grainger's *Woodsmen of the West* is as real a picture as I know or can imagine of the life he describes.

[11] Thucydides, i, 20, 22.

absorbs them, to lack historical perspective, to see one side of a question, one facet of an event and forget all else. Herodotus is not so incisive in his criticism of his informants and predecessors, but in his long travels, or perhaps earlier, he grew aware of the human weaknesses that Thucydides pillories. "The task was a laborious one" says Thucydides. "I wanted to know, so I went to Tyre" says Herodotus.

Herodotus travelled further afield than Thucydides—far further. His subject was a larger one, and involved the whole world. A man who will try to get the whole world on to his canvas will make mistakes of his own and fail at times to see where he is deceived. But, broadly, mistakes in detail do not matter much. Herodotus might have been more accurate about the votes of the Spartan kings, but there are two much more fundamental questions to ask about his picture of Sparta. Are those sketches of her kings, of Cleomenes, of Demaratus, of Leonidas true, are they individual, are they alive? Only one answer to that question is likely. They are intensely alive; they are individual; they have every appearance of being as true as a foreigner not contemporary with them could hope to get them. And the second question is this: Is he drawing the real Sparta? Certain things are plain here; he is not idealizing Sparta as Plutarch did; he is not attacking Sparta as Isocrates did; the Sparta which he draws is substantially the Sparta drawn by Thucydides and by Xenophon, and his picture is confirmed by Isocrates and by Plutarch, the critic and the panegyrist. In short, he got the kings alive on to his pages and he gives you the Sparta that was really there,—fighting

her way to Tegea, conquering the Thyreatis, jealous
of Argos, well-disciplined, invincible, mother of men,
and just a little slow.

Let us take two more illustrations. A great deal
of criticism, ancient and modern, has been directed
to Herodotus' accounts of Persia and Egypt; we
shall have to return to these, but for the moment,
let us note that Adolf Erman the Egyptologist calls
Herodotus "an indefatigable and careful observer,"
who "observed exactly those things which are of
special interest to us."[12] Spiegel[13] says at once that
his account of Persia as it stands no one will take for
historical, but it cannot be denied that it has historical traits; taken as a whole it is of high value, for
of all the legendary accounts that the ancients have
preserved from the time of the Persian Empire, none
is so thoroughly Iranian as his. It will be remembered
that for centuries the story of the Achaemenids
virtually rested on the statements of Herodotus
alone, and that in 1837 his narrative received
startling confirmation from Darius' hand upon the
Rock of Behistun deciphered by Henry Rawlinson.
With the judgment of a later Rawlinson we may
leave this phase of our subject. "On the whole,"
writes H. G. Rawlinson,[14] "the account given by
Herodotus of the Indian satrapy is careful and
accurate. It is no doubt drawn from the lost narrative of Skylax; or from firsthand evidence—probably
from accounts given by Persian officials who had
served in India."

[12] Erman, *Egyptian Religion* (English translation), p. 175.
[13] Spiegel, *Eranische Altertümer*, ii, 169.
[14] H. G. Rawlinson, *India and the Western World*, p. 24.

Burke could not, he said, draw an indictment against a nation, and national portraits are as hard to draw. Mrs. Trollope and Charles Dickens and Münsterberg have not altogether satisfied Americans, nor perhaps even Lord Bryce and Goldwin Smith. It is not criticism to ask the miraculous of a human writer, to expect the impossible. If it can be shown that he used to the full, that he transcended, the means and opportunities that lay to his hand, that by some inspired combination of hard work and intuition he can re-create the foreign or the ancient scene and give it you with the people talking, planning, thinking, and emphatically alive all the time; if, in addition, his honesty is such as to enable you to check his statements and sometimes from his data to seize a truer interpretation of his reported facts than he has given;[15] if throughout he is human and makes humanity mean more and more to you as you live with him; then he has surely some strong claim to be called a historian.

III

How he was able to achieve so great a triumph is our next inquiry. It has been of late a favourite exercise with scholars of a certain type to try to discover how great books came to be organic wholes. We are told on ancient authority that Virgil drafted his *Aeneid* and then wrote here and there as fancy led him, trusting at last to give two or three years' revision to the whole and so to remove inconsistencies and temporary passages that served as scaf-

[15] Cf. G. B. Grundy, *Great Persian War*, p. 267, and elsewhere.

folding; then can we trace his movements in his
half-revised poem? Or can we decide what Thucydides in each case means by "this war,"—the whole of
the Peloponnesian War or the so-called "Archi-
damian War," its first ten years; did he write "this
war" and then that war in Sicily, and then join them
somehow with book v and prolong them with book
viii? If he did, he had the whole under his hand all
along, says Eduard Meyer, and is surely right
in saying so. A strong attempt has been made to
prove that Herodotus began with the expedition
of Xerxes and wrote what are now his seventh, eighth
and ninth books, and then expanded gradually his
design to include the world and last of all Egypt.
A contrast is drawn between the piety of the ninth
book and the tone of religious speculation in the
second, which seems to some critics to imply psy-
chologically that the second book is later. Psychology might surely be used equally well to imply
the opposite. If one man inquires more freely in
religion as he grows older, another is more impressed
with the hand of God in human affairs. To this we
shall have to return, but we may remark that the
second book shows greater caution in its references to
the gods than is sometimes noticed. There are
other suggestions as to evidence upon the order
of writing, but perhaps the inquiry is not one to give
very certain results nor one that is supremely
interesting. That his conception of his theme grew
as he handled it, that what he eventually left us is a
book of far larger design and vastly richer content
than what he perhaps planned at first, we can
readily believe; "my tale sought additions from the
start" (iv, 30). The real wonder is that any man was

able to gather so much, and to give so much, without losing his thread; and the wonder grows as we consider the means at his disposal.

Later Greek historians drew largely upon the books of their predecessors, and it is clear enough that Herodotus used written sources. The list of Persian satrapies, for instance, in his third book must evidently have come from some document; that is generally agreed, and perhaps the Royal Road did too. We know, for he tells us, that there were great collections of oracles (vii, 6); perhaps they were copied out together; and it seems highly likely that Herodotus had access to something of the sort, quite probably at Delphi. Lists of priests and of archons were publicly kept, we know, and events were dated by them; and there may have been books of genealogies, though this is perhaps doubtful. There were also geographers, or at least there was Hecataeus, for Herodotus quotes him now and then by name and is supposed to refer to him when he uses the anonymous plural "the Ionians." He also mentions Skylax, as we saw; and other names of men who wrote books at or about his date are known. Charon of Lampsacus wrote a history of Persia down to 492 B.C., which may have been published after 465-4 B.C. Dionysius of Miletus wrote another down to Marathon and the death of Darius. Dionysius of Halicarnassus, centuries later, indicates that their style was somewhat bare if clear and concise. Professor Bury traces their work to the impulse of Hecataeus.[16] There was also a Greek history of Lydia by a Lydian Xanthus. "In any case," says Professor Sayce,[17]

---

[16] Bury, *Ancient Greek Historians*, p. 23.
[17] Sayce, *Herodotus* I–III, Intr., p. xx.

there must have been Greek translations of Persian and Phoenician books as well as of official documents from which Herodotus derived his statements; and the fact that they were translations may explain why he always speaks of his Oriental authorities in the plural. . . . His chief aim was to use their [his predecessors'] materials without letting the fact be known. We must not forget that although there were no publishers or printing-presses in the age of Herodotus, public libraries were not altogether unknown; as the library of Pisistratus at Athens and that of Polycrates at Samos. Pericles at Athens was surrounded by literary men, and books were at any rate cheaper than travelling. He pilfered freely and without acknowledgement; he assumed a knowledge he did not possess; he professed to derive information from personal experience and eye witnesses which really came from the very sources he seeks to disparage and supersede.

It would be difficult to parallel such a tissue of absurdities and false assumptions, all so unworthy of a scholar. For the library of Pisistratus at Athens, the rather confused story of some connexion of the tyrant with the standard text of Homer, and Herodotus' account of Hippias' collection of oracles, are the only warrants. Greek poets came to that court and to Polycrates, but that does not warrant the assertion of public libraries. Pericles was indeed surrounded by men of letters, but that proves nothing as to Charon and Xanthus and the rest. It is a pure assumption to say that books were cheaper than travel; yes, if they are in the shop down the street in quantity, but it might today be cheaper to go to Mexico than to buy Lord Kingsborough's volumes. To say there must have been translations is to beg the question. Greeks did not care for such works; they neglected Latin literature very largely n later days, and Manetho and Berossus were apparently dull, flimsy, and inaccurate, and wrote long after

Herodotus. Can any one name a Persian or Phoenician author, unless it be Zeno or some Stoic disciple?
The one point on which any evidence at all can be
brought is the relation of Herodotus to Hecataeus.

As to Hecataeus the evidence is of two sorts.
Herodotus knew the work of Hecataeus and alluded
to him, so much is certain. That he used him, but
rejected his theories, may be inferred from Herodotus'
pages, but it is an inference. That Herodotus took
verbally from Hecataeus his descriptions of the crocodile hunt and the hippopotamus, without acknowledgment but with all the errors,[18] is a statement that
rests on the assumption that those who first made it
knew for a fact that it was the genuine Hecataeus
which they held in their hands. It is quoted by Eusebius[19] from Porphyry. The authority of Porphyry is
not high, and it is conjectured that he used a book
bearing the name of Hecataeus, which other ancient
authorities knew and doubted. "So," writes Athenaeus,[20] "so says Hecataeus of Miletus in his Description of Asia, if the book is the genuine work
of the historian; for Callimachus entitles it that
of the Islander; whoever made the book then, this
is what he says." The Islander seems not very
easy to identify. Arrian, the historian of Alexander, remarks that "both Herodotus and Hecataeus
the *logopoios* (or whoever wrote the book about
Egypt whether it was some one else or Hecataeus)
both of them call Egypt the gift of the river."[21]

[18] Sayce, *Herodotus*, I–III, p. xxv.

[19] *Praeparatio Evangelii*, X, 3, p. 166B. Müller, *Fragmenta Historicorum Graecorum*, Hecataeus, fr. 292.

[20] Athenaeus, II, p. 70A.

[21] Arrian, *Anabasis*, v, 6, 5.

Eratosthenes, the rival of Callimachus and his successor in the great library of Alexandria, took the
book to be genuine.[22] But it is interesting to note
that for the great libraries of Ptolemy and of the
Attalids (as well as for prophetic purposes) lost books
were found. Galen, the great physician, says: "In
the time of the Attalids and Ptolemies when they
were rivals for the possession of books, the forging
of titles and matter began among people who for
money offered the kings the writings of famous men."
Elsewhere he repeats his statement, "when men who
brought them writings of some ancient writer began
to get money, then indeed they brought them in great
numbers with false inscriptions."[23] It may be, as
Müller suggests, that part of the volume was genuine
and the rest of it fake; and that Porphyry made
or borrowed his statement on the strength of a book
on Egypt, partly composed of Herodotus' own
material. Milton was once convicted of plagiarism
in a similar way, on the evidence of passages taken
from a Latin translation of *Paradise Lost* and attributed (with some slight adjustment) to earlier poets.
Aristotle at any rate quoted the passages supposed
to be stolen without allusion to the theft.[24] At all
events in the 380 fragments attributed to Hecataeus
there is not the least allusion to the Persian wars
properly so called, or the Ionian revolt.[25] Many of
them are mere names of places quoted from him by
lexicographers. Professor Bury counts him one of the
founders of geographical science and associated with

[22] Strabo, i, C. 7.
[23] See Müller, *Fragmenta Historicorum Graecorum, praef.* p. 13; and
Sir John Sandys, *History of Scholarship*, Vol. I, p. 112.
[24] See How and Wells, Vol. I, p. 25.
[25] Hauvette, *Hérodote*, p. 161.

the birth of history and, in a sense, of rationalism—
a bold assertion in view of the scanty evidence.
One cannot but recall the question of Aphrodite in
the Greek epigram,

> Pray, how did Praxiteles see what he shows?[26]

But, in all this as in many other things, the line
of sense is taken by Eduard Meyer.[27] Herodotus, he
says, knew and used his predecessors; not to have
done so would have been a reproach, and indeed
unthinkable. If Xanthus' *Lydiaca* or Hellanicus'
earlier works were already published (which can
neither be proved nor refuted), why should Herodotus trouble about works of detail when for years
past he had collected material himself and had
achieved a complete picture of history? How anybody can speak of his plagiarizing from Hecataeus,
Dr. Meyer does not understand. One is tempted to
add that the habit, at one time, spread among
scholars, like an infectious disease, of attributing
everything possible, whoever the writer, to a neglected and lost predecessor to whom should be the
praise; and the evidence of the casual reader in
antiquity was often accepted, without inquiry as to
his capacity or right to form an opinion.

Herodotus probably had occasional opportunities
to consult collections of legends and myths, of
traditions about migration and colonization, the
settlement and foundation of cities, of pedigrees and
oracles (as we saw), perhaps even of *bons mots*.[28]

[26] *Anth. Planudea*, 162; J. W. Mackail, *Select Epigrams*, § 4,40; Lord
Neaves, *Greek Anthology*, pp. 141, 142.

[27] E. Meyer, *Forschungen*, i, 183.

[28] Macan, *Herodotus*, vii-ix, Vol. I, p. lxxiii.

When Dr. Macan adds army and navy lists, one may
hesitate without disrespect, and concede Simonides'
epigrams and the *Persians* of Aeschylus with some
readiness, and, with a little uncertainty, memoirs.
Nehemiah and Ion of Chios were writing memoirs in
his day, but memoirs of the previous generation have
to be proved, and the attempt to saddle Dicaios with
memoirs is not generally counted successful. Thus,
broadly speaking, all the literature (the poets excepted) which he may have seen—for in that age
still more than in our own post-war days no one can
well dogmatize about the speedy circulation or
availableness of any book, a fact sometimes forgotten—all the accessible literature was probably
on the whole rather dull; and Herodotus is not often
called dull by good judges. So we may take it that,
whatever he found in books, he brought something
of his own, as Shakespeare is allowed to have added
something to the Hamlet of Saxo Grammaticus.
One question may be asked here but hardly answered:
What system or method had he for making all he
read (and all he heard, we shall add) available?
Did he take interminable notes, in an age before
paper? Then, how did he carry them about with
him? What library can he have taken from Naucratis
to Tyre, from the Black Sea to Italy? Weight and
bulk have to be considered as factors in the question
of his literary indebtedness. Little doubt he read
everything he could; we have already seen something
of his acquaintance with Greek literature. The problem of the notebooks remains if we limit him to
oral sources. In any case his memory must have
been a remarkable one, full of minute detail, and
amazingly orderly.

But before we go further, we have to recall the monuments of which he speaks,[29]—the fetters which the Spartans took to Tegea and wore there, which "in my time" were hung around the temple of Athene Alea in Tegea (i, 66); the pillars of Darius, with Assyrian and Greek inscriptions, which the Byzantines used to build the altar of Artemis Orthosia (iv, 87); the picture hung in the Heraeum at Samos which Mandrocles, the architect, had made for himself of the bridge of boats he built for Darius (iv, 88); the offerings innumerable at Delphi, its works of art, and other gifts "worth seeing." "I myself saw" pillars set up by Sesostris in Syria;

also there are in Ionia two figures of this man carven in rock, one on the road from Ephesus to Phocaea, and the other on that from Sardis to Smyrna. In both places there is a man of a height of five ells and a half cut in relief, with a spear in his right hand and a bow in his left, and the rest of his equipment answering thereto; for it is both Egyptian and Ethiopian; and right across the breast from one shoulder to the other there is carven a writing in the Egyptian sacred character, saying: I myself won this land with the might of my shoulders. There is nothing here to show who he is and whence he comes, but it is shown elsewhere (ii, 106).

Professor Garstang[30] accepts the Hittite origin of the monuments on the pass of Kara Bel, and it is generally conceded today; the conical cap and the high boots turning up at the toe and other features connect them with similar figures at Boghaz-Keui. Herodotus puts spear and bow in the wrong hands, and could not, Dr. Garstang holds, himself have seen the monuments: "there is just enough general

[29] A list is given by Macan, *Herodotus* iv-vi, Vol. I, pp. lviii, lix.

[30] Garstang, *Land of the Hittites*, pp. 170-173; cf. How and Wells on ii, 106.

accuracy in his account to identify the monuments, and enough discrepancy to make it apparent that he had not visited them himself." It will be noted that he does not claim to have seen them. His theory of an Egyptian origin is proof of limits to his knowledge of seventh and eighth century Asia, limits which our own knowledge only very recently surmounted.

But probably the great mass of his information was gathered from living men. Three he names —three only—Archias, the Spartan of Pitane, who told him of the siege of Samos (iii, 55); Tymnes, the deputy for Ariapeithes, who gave him information as to the pedigree of Anacharsis (iv, 76); and Thersander of Orchomenos, who told the tale of the banquet which Attaginos gave to Mardonius and the Persians, and how the Persian who shared his couch told him in Greek his ill forebodings for the battle of Plataea and the doom from God that no man could avert (ix, 16). The last is the best, and illustrative of much, of the mind of Herodotus, and of the difficulty of language overcome as a rule by the foreigner and not by the Greek. Herodotus, it has been said, was "at his weakest as linguist."[31] He discovered, he says with pride, what the Persians had not noticed—that their names ("which are of a piece with their persons and their magnificence") all end in the letter S (i, 139). They did in Greek, but the King whom Greeks and others tried to write down as Xerxes and Ahasuerus, was in Persia called Khshayârshâ—sibilant enough but fatal for Herodotus' rule. He also connected Artaxerxes with Xerxes, which the Persians did not, for they called it Artakh-shathra. Wherever Herodotus went, the foreigner

[31] How and Wells on i, 139.

had to talk Greek, and he seems to have been very glad to do it, with such a listener.

A good deal of interesting research has been done as to the Persian friends of Herodotus.[32] He was evidently highly satisfied as to the value of his Persian information (i, 95), which was very various and not always, as he says, consistent, but which was far too much to be due to a single source. Three distinct groups have been noted. When Herodotus tells of the capture of Babylon by the aid of Zopyrus "son of that Megabyzus who was one of the seven destroyers of the Magian" (iii, 153), who mutilated himself and was received as a deserter by the Babylonians (iii, 154-156), he ends his story with a little more about the family: "son of this Zopyrus was Megabyzus who commanded in Egypt against the Athenians and their allies;[33] and son of this Megabyzus was Zopyrus who deserted to Athens from the Persians" (iii, 160). The family was one of high distinction and of independent habits. Megabyzus the second himself revolted from Artaxerxes, was reconciled, banished and restored, and he appears in spite of the great blow he dealt to Athens in Egypt to have been head of the Hellenizing party in Persia. Hence the flight of Zopyrus the second was not a freak, but an act not out of tune with his family's spirit. The date of the desertion may have been in 440 B.C. when the war party in Persia was in the ascendant,[33a] and it is easy to think that Zopyrus and the historian met. At all events Herodotus is able

[32] See J. Wells in *Journal of Hellenic Studies*, XXVII, 1907.

[33] Cf. Thucydides, i, 109, 110; he ruined the Athenian cause there, 455 B.C.

[33a] Thucydides, i, 115.

to tell us that Megabyzus the first, when the Magian was slain, stood for oligarchy (iii, 81). He knows the history of the house for four generations, and it may be to them that he owes his knowledge of what the Persians say "who do not desire to make a fine tale of Cyrus" (i, 95); Cyrus, whom alone, in Darius' opinion, Zopyrus did not surpass for his service to the Persians (iii, 160).

There was another Persian house which Herodotus evidently knew, a house as significant or more so in Greek history. He tells us a rather surprising number of things about Artabazus, son of Pharnaces, and his part in Xerxes' expedition—his capture of Olynthos (viii, 126), his shrewd advice to the king to bribe the Greek leaders (ix, 41f.), his dislike of Mardonius being left to command in Greece and his forecast of Plataea (ix, 66), and his adroit escape from Thessaly after the disaster (ix, 89). From Thucydides we learn of the later history of this man, who was given the satrapy of Daskyleion to promote the intrigues of King Pausanias (Thucydides i, 129). He was succeeded in turn by his son Pharnabazus I and his grandson Pharnaces II (satrap 430-414); and Xenophon draws a pleasant picture of the fifth generation, Pharnabazus II (satrap 413-389), a lover of hunting and gardens, a great gentleman, certainly a man, perhaps something of a great man.[34]

The third Persian noble family was originally Greek. In or about 491 B.C. King Demaratus was exiled from Sparta.[35] Ninety years later Xenophon alludes to his descendant, with the old Herakleid

[34] See Babelon, *Les Perses*, p. xxxv, for the coinage of this house. Xenophon, *Hellenica* iii, and iv, especially iv, 1, 29-38.
[35] Herodotus, vi, 61-70.

name of Procles, and a brother Eurysthenes, more than once intervening in the fortunes of the Ten Thousand.[36] King Darius gave Demaratus land and cities, and Xenophon found the family established near the Dardanelles and in possession of Pergamon, Teuthrania, and Halisarna. It is natural to suppose that they had been there throughout, and the abundance of reference in the pages of Herodotus to Demaratus suggests that Herodotus knew them, and knew them well. The full tale of the exile and his generous reception, of his acute suggestion to Xerxes at the critical time of his succession (vii, 3), of his frequent talks with the Great King whom he very frankly informed as to Spartan character (vii, 101), correctly predicting in the face of Xerxes' incredulity that the Spartans would fight at Thermopylae (vii, 209), of his advice to Xerxes as to how the Greek fleet might be broken up at once and safely—advice not taken (vii, 235), and the king's defence of him against Persian criticism (vii, 237); where else could all this have been so familiar and so interesting as in his own family? Who but his own kin could have known, or cared to invent, the story of Demaratus' part in the palace intrigues on Darius' death?

Now let us try to translate all this into life—three noble houses and a guest from Halicarnassus—and the words of Callimachus the poet come back, when he speaks of his friend from that old city: "I remembered how often we two saw the sun set as we talked, O Halicarnassian guest; and yet thy nightingale-notes live, nor shall death that plunders all lay hand on

[36] Xenophon, *Anab.* ii, 1, 3; vii, 8, 17; *Hell.*, iii, 1, 6; See Babelon, *Les Perses*, p. lxix f., for the coins of Procles as dynast of Teuthrania.

them."[37] Herodotus was not, like Heraclitus, a poet,
of course; but who can doubt of the rest? The bright-
eyed traveller, with a boy's zest and a man's quick
mind, full of travel, full of tales, and always at
leisure to hear old legends and old family traditions,
anything and everything that bore on his great
themes, the old War and the eternal nature of man—
who would not be glad to know him and talk with
him, and tell so eager a listener the best there was to
tell? How else did he ever amass the boundless store
from which he chooses what to give us? Think of
the memory, the interest, the perennial freshness
of the mind that gathered not alone the traditions of
three noble houses but of all Persia and all the world,
and remembered and fitted new detail into its right
place as he got it. Take the story of the physician
Democedes; where did he get it? All in a piece in the
west, seventy years after Democedes' day, or some
of it in Italy, some in Samos, and some in Persia?
Who in Croton would know, as he knew, the influence
of Queen Atossa? For queens live and die, and
distant democracies will know little of them, and
little of eastern palace etiquette.[38] Who told him of
the Persian registers (vii, 100; viii, 90), who gave up
leisure to inform him of Persian life and thought,
politics, history and religion, the spread of Persia
eastward to the Panjāb, north into Scythia, to the
Aegaean, to Egypt and Cyrene? Not three noble
houses alone; his informants and friends must have
been legion, all over the world; and what one said in
Heliopolis tallied or clashed with what he had heard
in Babylon or Byzantion, and he noticed it, as minds

[37] *Anth. Palatina*, vii, 80.
[38] See How and Wells on iii, 129-138.

of that sort do, without recourse to notes. A little discreet use of the imagination, with a map marked to show the points Herodotus reached, will do much toward a real sense of his achievement and of the powers it implies.

To some such friendly discussion with a Persian, Professor Bury refers those early chapters of the first book of Herodotus, which strike a modern reader so oddly. What have Europa and Helen to do with the Persian war? "As for Europe," he says elsewhere (iv, 45),

it is not clear who gave the name, unless we are to say that the land took its name from the Tyrian Europa and before that was nameless as the other lands. But she is plainly of Asian origin and never came to this land which the Greeks now call Europe, but only from Phoenice to Crete and from Crete to Lycia. Now that so much is said, let it suffice; we will use the ordinary names.

Similarly, as we have already seen, after recording this exchange of alleged precedents, he turns off from what Persian and Phoenician talk to tell what he knows.

IV

Now to sum up what we have reached. We saw him started on his travels and his inquiries by the call of the greatest story in the world, and we have seen how the whole world is gradually taken up into its greatest story, how race after race is involved, and how, like others who inquire and research, he finds his outlook grow and his views change. Whatever his earlier feelings as to Persian power, in the days when he hated Lygdamis and his rule—and it must be noted again that he does not tell his own story and that his reticence extends to his contemporaries[39] and to things familiar to them—he saw more to admire in the Persians as he knew them better and he found them more and more interesting. "No writer," says Mr. Sikes,[40] "is more free from prejudice." He wrote avowedly that the great and marvellous deeds of barbarians—not "Greek victories and barbarian defeats," as Lucian re-modelled it—might never be lost. He obviously felt the fascination of Egypt; but where did he not find interest and friendship? What does it mean, this charm that one finds in race after race? An ancient writer, if we except Polybius and his kind, does not analyse his own work for the reader, but we may recognize throughout Herodotus his response to the challenge of the foreigner, an appeal that many good patriots never feel. Plutarch called him in angry criticism "a lover of barbarians" φιλοβάρβαρος. The world is not all Greek; a great deal of the best of it is not Greek at all, nor even Anglo-Saxon, and Herodotus' work is largely a study of the history of civilization, the contact and collision of the progressive types that go to develope the mind of the world. Long before Freeman he realizes the unity of history. At a later point we shall return to his study of the foreigner and his customs good and bad,—generally interesting, rarely called bad,[41]—his political and religious ideas, his myths and legends.

[39] cf. John Burnet, *Early Greek Philosophy*, p. 95; cf. Herodotus, ii, 123; i, 51; iv, 48. Cimon and Pericles are natural exceptions.

[40] E. E. Sikes, *Anthropology of the Greeks*, pp. 73, 74.

[41] Sikes, *Anthropology of the Greeks*, p. 74; Herodotus i, 194, 199.

Side by side there rises the greater challenge the full effect of which we reach only in the Stoics, the challenge of nature. Men were already noting and speculating upon soils and climates and their effect on animal and human life. River and sea and desert, natural phaenomena and their causes, were growing in interest. It was perhaps a side-product of the sophistic movement. Herodotus was, as we have seen, a keen student of topography. Sometimes it bore immediately and visibly upon ordinary history, like the ebb at Potidaea (viii, 129) and the currents of the Propontis (vii, 136), or gave a local bias to industry and trade, like the swift stream of the Euphrates (i, 193, 194). But often great problems in physical geography are raised by him, as in the case of the Nile and its summer overflow. It made Egypt; that was evident about the busy river; but why should it reverse the ordinary habits of rivers and be fuller in the time of heat? What problems of wind or snow, or what not, did it involve? An unpractical problem, but to a Greek mind fascinating. We shall have later on to linger over the outer edges of the world.

But in this world most of us will agree with what Herodotus does not say but surely thinks: that Greeks are really in their variety, their restlessness, and their impossibility, the most interesting of all peoples. We shall find that of all their wonderful discoveries the most wonderful—and that puts it far beyond anything that barbarians have achieved—is the discovery of Freedom and its positive value in making men real and adding dignity and stability to political life. We must return to this, and watch with him the rise of the Greeks, and their discovery and development of Freedom; and so we shall reach

the central theme of the whole book, the conflict
in which this supreme achievement of Hellas was put
to the test. Would it, could it, survive the attack of
the best organized monarchy that the world had ever
seen, would it prove equal to the strain upon it, or
would it break down into anarchy and be lost?
Was Law in Liberty to prove master?

These are great themes, and the parallel of
Polybius has suggested to us that a great theme of
unequalled interest may, like the heroes before
Agamemnon, lack the inspired touch that shall bring
it into every man's business and bosom. There is
perhaps in every day's issue of *The Times* as much
variety of old and new, near and distant, as in
Herodotus; certainly no encyclopaedia but has it.
Herodotus brought something more to his work than
the widest range of knowledge then available of all
the world, more than accuracy and the alert inquiring
intellect. He was one of the great artists of Greece,
so great that his instinctive art conceals itself till you
look for it, and perhaps even then. One may read
him over and over again, and note with surprise how
much one has missed. He is an incomparable "source,"
as historians say. But his art is more wonderful even
than his range of knowledge, and his mind and
personality than his art. He is the Greek world in
person, he is ancient humanity, yes! and he is
Herodotus of Halicarnassus.

His avowed object in writing we have already discussed and the great purpose of his work. From time
to time he speaks of his method and his plans, generally when he is conscious of some possible challenge
or criticism. He will omit the native chieftains who
commanded their tribes in Xerxes' levy; he is not

obliged to give them, he says, his story does not
require it; they were not persons who deserve mention and there were so many of them in each nation
(vii, 96). That his story was on the lookout for additions, we have seen (iv, 30); and he adds accordingly
a curious fact about mules in Elis, and elsewhere he
says his account of Rhegians and Tarentines is an
inset (παρενθήκη, vii, 171). He will give two or three
variants of a story. He contrasts the Corinthian
and the Athenian statements as to the services of
Corinth at Salamis; and the former is supported by
the general voice of Greece, says the historian, who is
supposed to dislike Corinth and to glorify Athens
(viii, 94). He knows more than one variant of
Cyrus' early adventures and confines himself to one
(i, 95), or he gives a story both ways and his readers
may decide which to believe (v, 45). He will not tell
them what they know already; Greeks are familiar
with the general look of the camel, so he only adds
one detail "not generally known," but admitted, it is
said, by modern naturalists (iii, 103). Again and
again he is careful to state that he does not exactly
know, he could not exactly learn;[42] he thinks, or he is
of opinion;[43] he cannot convince himself, but at any
rate this is what he has heard[44]—and sometimes this
is what people say and others may believe it, he
cannot himself;[45] or he offers no opinion, his business
is simply to record what he is told[46]—though he will
add "yet all things are possible" (iv, 195), the sensible comment of the much-travelled man who has

[42] Herodotus, vi, 14; vii, 54; viii, 87, 133; ix, 84.
[43] Herodotus, vii, 185, 186, 187; ix, 32.
[44] Herodotus, iv, 77; vii, 35, 55; ix, 95.
[45] Herodotus, v, 86; cf. iv, 42; iii, 116; iv, 25; viii, 119, 120.
[46] Herodotus, vii, 152; ii, 123.

seen a good many things that clever people who stay at home would recognize at once as impossible. "How, I cannot for my part conceive," he says again, "but everything is possible in long ages" (v, 9). Once he says definitely that he will not mention something which he knows, being well aware that people who have not themselves visited Babylonia will not believe it (i, 195). Such passages are surely overlooked by some critics of his credulity,—generally people who have not travelled and do not realize that it is often folly *not* to believe what you are told in a strange land. On the other hand, when he says categorically, as he now and then does, that he *knows*, he should surely have the credit that his general caution seems to warrant (cf. i, 140).

Otherwise, he does not discuss method or art. But it is abundantly evident that he based himself on long thought and practice; he had told tales for years before he wrote his book, and he has the tale-teller's art. He watches his listeners and (in the Greek sense) he *economizes*, he manages his tale, he cuts things out, he makes circuits, he amplifies, he digresses; and by each movement the tale is richer in colour and life, more full of feeling and intensity, or in some subtle way the humour is heightened. But he has his eyes on his audience throughout and he never loses them. Yet it may be better to say no more at this point, but to let the Greeks who came after him give us their impressions and criticisms.

V

Thucydides said he was inaccurate. He never mentions Herodotus by name, but he makes it quite plain to whom he refers. "There are many other matters," he says,[47]

not obscured by time but contemporary, about which the other Hellenes are equally mistaken. For example, they imagine that the kings of Sparta in their council have not one but two votes each and that in the army of the Spartans there is a division called the Pitanate; whereas they never had anything of the sort. So little trouble do men take in the search after truth; so readily do they accept whatever comes first to hand.

He knows that Greek readers will remember that Herodotus made both of these unlucky statements,[48] and others as bad. When Thucydides speaks (i, 126) of Cylon's conspiracy and its failure, he says the nine Archons were in charge, and he adds severely: "for in those days public affairs were chiefly administered by the nine Archons." The guilty Herodotus had said "the prytaneis of the naukraries" were responsible (v, 71). A little before 431 B.C., he says (ii, 8) "the island of Delos had been shaken by an earthquake for the first time within the memory of Hellenes." Herodotus had said that the Delians had reported to him that the one earthquake in their history was when Datis sailed on from them to Euboea in 490 B.C.; there had never been another before nor since that one "down to my own time" (vi, 97). Herodotus had talked of Mnesiphilus suggesting ideas to The-

[47] Thucydides, i, 20.
[48] Herodotus, vi, 57; ix, 53.

mistocles (viii, 58); but Themistocles was equal to
divining the right plan by sheer force of nature, without assistance, says Thucydides (i, 138, 3). There
are some other corrections of the same austere kind.[49]
But his most caustic criticism is in his most famous
phrase. "Very likely the strictly historical (literally:
the non-mythical) character of my narrative may be
disappointing to the ear. My history is a possession
for ever, not a prize composition which is heard and
forgotten." (i, 22.) "The ear"—"heard and forgotten"—and the suggestion of a show performance;
is there truth then in the story that Herodotus read
his history or part of it aloud in Athens, and that
Anytos, whose name at least recalls the accuser of
Socrates, moved for an award of ten talents to him?
Plutarch quotes the story as from Diyllos, a fourth
century Athenian historian.[50] Thucydides' language
would lose its sting if there had been no recitation,
and he disliked carelessness, as he says. A date about
446-445 B.C. is given by Jerome for the recitation and
scholars consider it possible enough. Thucydides was
of age to follow[51] the whole course of the Peloponnesian war which began in 431, and he died about
399 B.C. It would not have been a specially long life,
if he was twenty or so when the recitation took place,
if it did take place; and yet there are legends that he
wept for emulation.[52]

[49] Thucydides, ii, 97; ii, 2-6; i, 89 and perhaps i, 14.

[50] Plutarch, *De malignitate Herodoti*, c. 26. Professor Bury (*Anc. Gk. Historians*, p. 65) sees "nothing incredible" in the story of public recita-
tions. E. Meyer, *Forschungen*, i, p. 200, suggests that the ten talents
were for diplomatic services eastward, but this does not find favour.

[51] Thucydides, v, 26.

[52] Marcellinus, *Life of Thucydides*, p. 54.

The *History* of Herodotus lasted better than Thucydides predicted. Isocrates in his *Panegyric* (which he was writing for a good while and published in 380 B.C.) wished to emphasize a sort of natural hatred between Athens and Persia, and amongst other signs of it he noted that "even where stories are concerned we linger with most pleasure over the Trojan and Persian wars, in which we can learn of their disasters. . . . I think that even Homer's poetry has greater glory, because he praised right well those who fought the barbarians."[53] We may accept the fact both as to Homer and Herodotus, and perhaps guess other reasons. Later on, Strabo speaks contemptuously of Herodotus' geography as less reliable than Homer's;[54] some of it, as we shall see, was very wrong, but at least once the older writer was correct against Strabo.

But the most famous of ancient attacks on Herodotus was made by Plutarch who wrote a tract on his *Malignity*. Herodotus, we are told, uses hard names when he might use kinder; he loves to introduce ill reports against peoples in wanton zest of abuse, and conversely to omit what is good about them; he prefers the worse account where there are several, and the worst explanation where the real reason is obscure; he damns with faint praise; he takes away the character of Io; he is a lover of barbarians and suggests that Greeks learnt their religion from them; he first makes Croesus a fool and then a sage; he accuses Cleisthenes of bribing the Delphian priestess; he calls the burning of Sardis the beginning of trouble, when it was a stroke for

[53] Isocrates, *Panegyricus*, §§ 158, 159.
[54] Strabo, C., i, 508.

freedom; he muddles the full moon at Marathon and throws the day and the story into confusion; his style is "all twists, and nothing sound, but all about;"[55] he bitterly slanders Thebes; Aristophanes the Boeotian says it was because he asked and failed to get money from the Thebans; in short, like his own Hippocleides he dances away the truth, and "Herodotus don't care"; "he can write and his story is pleasant, there is grace and cleverness and bloom upon his tales, . . . he charms and seduces everybody." The general verdict seems to be that Plutarch this time has written himself down an ass (unless the tract be spurious, which plea is rejected,[56]) and that the whole thing is "a monument of critical incompetence," based on an absurd patriotism—and a false conception of history.

Halicarnassus produced after some four centuries a second historian, who, besides writing on early Italy at some length, wrote a number of essays (or letters) on Style. Dionysius deals with his townsman and commends him as against Thucydides. Herodotus chose a more attractive subject, victory rather than defeat; he showed more judgment in knowing where to begin and where to leave off, and what to put in and what to omit; he chose to vary his story in the Homeric way, copying Homer, and indeed, "if we take his book we like it to the last syllable and always wish for more," while Thucydides rarely attempts variety; and Dionysius finds Thucydides' chronology boring. Then Herodotus has the kindlier disposition, while Thucydides had a grudge against

---

[55] Euripides, *Andromache*, 448.

[56] Georg Busolt, *Griech. Geschichte*, Vol. II, p. 616n, on the genuineness. See also Hauvette, *Hérodote*, pp. 98 ff.; E. Meyer, *Forschungen*, ii, p. 211.

his country. Both are great writers, Herodotus the superior in character drawing and natural writing, Thucydides in pathos and a clever style; the beauty of Herodotus is bright and happy, that of Thucydides terrible.[57]

"He chose to vary his story in the Homeric way." So also hints Longinus, a far surer and stronger critic—"Herodotus most Homeric" is his phrase.[58] It is not the common eulogy of a historian, but let us look at it, first recalling Matthew Arnold's four notes of Homer's style: he is simple in thought, simple in language, rapid, and noble. If these terms be given the meaning that Arnold intended, they are not far from a true description of the style and mind of Herodotus. He is so simple in narrative, so easy and plain, that many readers wholly miss the clarity, with which he takes an idea, and with which he judges it. Arnold found in Homer some traits, not all, of Voltaire. Herodotus had seen more of the world than Voltaire and was less dogmatic; he was kindlier-natured; but was he really less clear? Do not the kindlier nature, the larger sympathies, the "human catholic" quality, which we all feel in him, the leisure for all mankind, the quick keen interest, suggest that the parallel with Homer is not idle? He has not Homer's zest for battle, he had seen little of fighting, except in the town streets of his home; and he did not wish to be classed with poets. Homer or some older poet invented, he supposes, the name Oceanus and brought it into his poetry, but he carried his tale into the unknown, where proof or disproof is

[57] Summary of part of the *Letter to Pompeius*. His *de Compositione* may be consulted for occasional additions of detail.
[58] Longinus, 13, 3.

impossible (ii, 23). He dismisses Greeks who have
dealt in poetry and made play with forecasts (ii, 83);
Aristeas of Proconnesus, "making poetry and possessed by Phoebus (Φοιβόλαμπτος)" does not convince him as to the One-Eyed (iv, 13-16); and elsewhere he gives us a caution about "trusting the Epic
poets" (ii, 120). But candour is not un-Homeric.

He writes a "book of good faith," and he can be
read and known in every page of it; and that is
Homeric. He takes a large canvas and he fills it,
and every paragraph contributes to the general
theme, as it does in the *Odyssey*. He is said to
digress; but in Homer and in Herodotus every digression is centripetal;[59] and there are historians and
poets of whom that cannot be said. He loves
variety and he loves a good story—and he tells a
good story—as Homer does; and these are not
superficial resemblances, for they rest on something
fundamental, love of man and love of this world
and its wonder. Both find a fascination in seafaring,
—not
                              the foam
        Of perilous seas, in faery lands forlorn—

No! but the real sea and the lands beyond; both are
honestly charmed with Geography[60]—word of prose
for thing of poetry! They both knew the joy of the
explorer better than we do, in spite of La Salle and
Livingstone, heroes more fit for Homer and Herodotus than for our day. Herodotus has the Homeric
impulse to make men realize the wonder of the world
he lives in, and achieves it;—to make men see the
characters that he watches, and they speak their own

---

[59] Cf. J. L. Myres in *Anthropology and the Classics*, p. 156.
[60] Cf. A. D. Godley, *Herodotus* (Loeb series), Vol. II, p. xiii.

words and go their own way in his pages as in
Homer's; and you listen to them and watch them,
and you like them as you read; you are won for a
larger humanity, whether it is Homer who wins you
or Herodotus. He loves, as Homer loves, a pageant,
the marshalling of men, in all that variety of gear
that expresses the variety of life and land and climate. Like Homer he rejoices in the skill of the
craftsman who weaves the rich web, who works dead
metal into life, who catches colour and keeps it. He
loves the scene, the movement, be it scandalous as
the Spartan king sitting on the glove of money
(vi, 72), or noble as the other Spartan king in the
pass, preparing to die. He is not afraid of wickedness;
he saw plenty of it; and, though he never leaves you
in doubt as to his mind on it, he cannot hate the
sinner any more than Homer could. Are there two
writers in Greek literature who stand nearer together
than these two, in knowledge of men, or in that love
of men which makes it their master-aim to interpret
men, or in the power they have to make one proud
of one's race and glad to be a man? Longinus was
assuredly right in calling Herodotus "most Homeric."

CHAPTER III

THE OLD GREEK LIFE

I

We have seen that in telling the story of the Persian War Herodotus rested to some extent on the authority of monuments and of books, with some doubt on our part as to how many books were available to him, but that his chief source of knowledge was the living voice of man. But one of the great features of his work was his realization that history is not made in a vacuum, that it is the life of men, of men with grandfathers and traditions, and that "the Greek race is of one blood and one speech; it has temples of the gods in common, common sacrifices and ways of like kind" (viii, 144). To show something of these common ideas and ways of like kind was part of the task of the historian of the Persian War. Expansiveness is the mark of true History; the reader must know the peoples, if their War is to interest him; and to know one generation you must know several. Herodotus then looks back—his tale sought additions—and the old days of Greece were relevant to the heroic Persian epoch.

But here the authorities were fewer and more uncertain; and to understand how Herodotus thought of them and how he used them, it will help us to see how Thucydides treated them. Their methods are different. The striking chapters which serve as introduction to Thucydides' history are of quite another texture and spirit from the stories of old Greece which Herodotus weaves into his narrative. "If one may trust the epic poets" says Herodotus (ii, 120), and both the historians did trust them in the main, at least so far as they could identify them with Homer (Hdt. iv, 32). Thucydides expresses no doubt as to the fact of the Trojan War, and he rationalizes the legend. The heroes did not go to Troy because, when suitors of Helen, they had bound themselves by oath to her father, but because Agamemnon was the most powerful king of his time; he had succeeded to the throne and the power of rulers whom we today consider hardly even so much as doubtfully historical, and he became the greatest naval potentate of his time; the princes followed him, not from goodwill but from fear. He is described as "the king of many islands and of all Argos;" and without a navy, a ruler of the mainland could not have ruled "many" islands, for the islands off his coast would not be "many."[1] Herodotus warned his reader that towns rose and fell in greatness and in power, and Thucydides argues against supposing Mycenae to have been small from the case of Sparta in his own times; "it has no splendid temples or other edifices; it rather resembles a straggling village like the ancient towns of Hellas, and would therefore make a poor show;" "distant ages would be very unwilling to believe that the power of the Lacedaemonians was at all equal to their fame."[2] Thucydides accepts the tradition of Greek wanderings, and with it an established chronology. In the sixtieth year after the fall of Troy

[1] Thucydides, i, 9.   [2] Thucydides, i, 10.

the Boeotians settled in the land once called Cadmeis
and now Boeotia; and twenty years later the Dorians
led by the Herakleids conquered the Peloponnese;
the Athenians colonized Ionia, the Peloponnesians
(he means Corinth chiefly) the greater part of Italy
and Sicily and various places in Greece,—all after the
Trojan War.[3]

Thucydides is thus dependent on the same authorities as Herodotus—epic poetry and what today we
vaguely call folk-memory. Thucydides conceived
that Homer as a poet might be expected to exaggerate
(i, 10), and we have noted already the caution of
Herodotus. Archaeology in the modern sense had not
begun. The treasuries of Mycenae were happily
unexplored and so was Crete; and whatever "antiquities" had been found, the comparative study of
human civilization had not advanced so far as to
allow a reliable and scientific appraisal of their
historical worth and meaning. Thucydides had
indeed seized the comparative method, and used the
present-day customs of barbarians to illustrate the
ancient usages and manners of Greeks—the preva-
lence of piracy, the habitual carrying of arms in
everyday life, and so forth.[4]

Folk-memory is a very modern term, and it seems
to imply a new attitude to tradition. Once tradition
was thoroughly accepted, though, as a concession to
rationalism, if legend said King Cecrops had a
serpent's tail, that tail was removed; for a man of
course would not have a tail, it was a poetic addition.
Then came doubt, and in the nineteenth century
most ancient traditions were doubted; it was seen
that Cecrops and his tail were really indivisible, they

[3] Thucydides, i, 12.   [4] Thucydides, i, 4.

went together or they remained together. A change is perhaps coming over criticism and a higher value is being attached to the stories of the peoples. Legend said, for instance, that Bunyan wrote his *Pilgrim's Progress* in the jail in the bridge at Bedford; antiquaries proved that he could not have, as his long imprisonments were on a warrant or warrants that would send him elsewhere. But Dr. John Brown, his brilliant biographer, stuck to the jail in the bridge; he refused to believe that popular tradition had blundered as to the jails, and he used an argument from dates of publication to support his view. He was justified by the sudden emergence into the sales room of another warrant altogether, an incontestable document of the year he had surmised, which would have, and, quite obviously, had, sent Bunyan to the bridge. Folk-memory will keep facts that impress the contemporary imagination; it will certainly let slip other facts perhaps as vital. But in the case of Greek legend, we are not in a position to decide how much exactly is folk-memory and how much mere legend. Tradition, then, kept detail about Agamemnon and Minos and Periander. Thucydides, using the experience and the ideas of his day, and impressed by sea power and hegemony, gave an interpretation of Agamemnon and Minos that would appeal to thoughtful men; they were rulers of the sea, precursors of the Confederacy of Delos, lords of many islands in earnest. Thucydides rationalized his material; and modern criticism does not here sustain him.

Herodotus moved on another plane; he had his own point of view. He preserved stories of Spartan

wars with Tegea, and of Periander's family, and
incidentally of Periander's colonies, stories that
might much more conceivably be matter of folk-
memory. If we are told that into all his stories,
whether of the Persian War or of Periander, there
steals an anachronistic element, a flavour of his
own day, History seems rarely to escape it, and
indeed History is seldom alive without it. There
are degrees in anachronism; it may be patent or it
may be subtle. It may be the application of the true
historian's faith that all history is one history and
that human motives remain much the same through
the ages—*votum timor ira voluptas gaudia.* Periander's family story as given by Herodotus may be
more reliable than Minos' and Agamemnon's lordship of the sea; and his daughter's use of proverbs in
dealing with her brother may be sound, even if
Herodotus supplies the particular proverbs. Most
people, when trying to heal family feuds have recourse to sense; and proverbs are the language of
sense on such occasions. To use the first person in
such a narrative is not to falsify history, at least not
to falsify history so thoroughly as the creation of a
blue water school before the beginning of years. For
here Herodotus is more sceptical than Thucydides;
he is not sure if Minos was a man at all.[5]

Such elements of History as Archaeology can
prove to us to have lain behind Homer, neither
Thucydides nor Herodotus could be expected by
rational criticism to know. The amateur antiquary,
who proved the Carian occupation of the islands
from the graves he opened, was not necessarily a fool
any more than his modern successor who theorizes as

[5] See the remarkable chapter, Herodotus, iii, 122.

to mound builders; perhaps he was less of a fool; both are laying the foundations of history, both are preparing the way for better things, pioneers in directing attention to the real records, even if they do not read them wholly aright. The collector of folklore is not giving us history in one sense of the word; in another he surely is. No story is told quite the same by two generations, whether it is folklore or whether it is meant for history; but the story is again and again our only chance of recapturing history. The arrowheads from Cape Cod that I possess and the flint axe from Bottisham, near Cambridge, give us history, though they do it without chronology. The stories of Jack Cade and Wat Tyler, even if some years ago they got mixed with Mr. Lloyd George, give us history, and Foxe's *Book of Martyrs* sums up a century as soundly and truly as James Gairdner's work at the Record Office did. Is this to sacrifice too much? Can we call it history, if we sacrifice chronology once for all, if we are for ever deducting something more or something less for anachronism, if we allow some important facts to have been lost and others misconceived?

Aliter non fit, Avite, liber![6]

We must take history as it is written, and not forget that we are perhaps less likely to be led astray when we are aware of our danger.

Modern readers and critics give us at least enough warning of the besetting sins of Herodotus. But here we may modestly recall what Samuel Butler said of commentaries on great poems—they are useful if you wish to learn the mind of the commentator—a warn-

[6] Martial, i, 16.

ing about those who give us warning. We are told
that Herodotus is too theological, he allows to the
gods a hand in human affairs, sometimes in the
control of the elements (viii, 13, 129), sometimes in
the event that follows right act or wrong act (ii, 120),
sometimes in stranger ways (v, 80; i, 67, 68). He
loves marvel—oracle, dream, and portent; and the
"supra-naturalistic" story, as Dr. Macan calls it,[7]
may supplant a more natural one. He loves a moral
even more. He uses myth to widen the historical
horizon but in a petty style, as the Io story shows;
so says Gomperz,[8] but perhaps the Io story shows
something else, if you look at it again. He contra-
dicts himself; he quotes now one version of a story
and elsewhere another—not perhaps inexplicably, if
we recall his mass of material, the physical difficulties
of the notebook and the obvious breadth of years
over which his work was spread; and he borrows and
mixes his chronologies,[9] with some insouciance; and
he is not meticulous about minute detail. He sometimes misses the true cause behind an act or a policy,
as sometimes happens in modern politics among the
actors themselves. Doubts are expressed as to the
fulness and sureness with which he realized character; even Plutarch, who habitually failed to understand such men as Pericles and Themistocles, attacks Herodotus for making Croesus first a fool and
a knave, and later on the mentor of Cyrus.[10] He ex-
aggerates numbers, we are told; though the evidence
for this might equally well warrant no more than the

[7] Macan, *Herodotus*, vii-ix, Vol. I, p. lxxxvii.

[8] Gomperz, *Greek Thinkers*, Vol. I, p. 260.

[9] See How and Wells, *Herodotus*, Vol. I, p. 375; appendix xiv; and on
bk. vi, 125.

[10] Plutarch, *de malignitate Herodoti*, § 18, p. 858, D.

statement that others exaggerated the numbers and he quoted them; and we have seen that arithmetic was not one of his interests. Above all, he loves anecdotes, he prefers the concrete to the abstract, the *bon mot* to the conscious rationale of political events. So says Dr. Macan;[11] but Edward Freeman[12] thought better of anecdotes, for even a false anecdote to pass current at all must have a kind of truth, a certain degree of probability, and it may throw light on the character of the person of whom it is told. Herodotus, as we saw, loved the man more than the abstract idea.

When all is said, and his critics take a lot of time to say it, they make admissions of another kind. It is, in a way, easier to tell what is wrong with a work of art, or with a great historian, than what is right, and it seems to suggest more shrewdness in the critic, though it is really more properly the function of criticism to show what is right, when it is so right as to preserve the work of art for ages, at a constant cost of human labour. A great poem or a history does not survive of itself like a buried statue; it calls for the copyist, the printer, the editor, and it takes toll of brains and energy, gladly given, but why? Allow all that is said in criticism of Herodotus, and how much remains! What would or could Greek history have been without him, his incomparable store of knowledge, and his unflagging instinct for what lives? Modern criticism is justified as far as it goes, but the history of the discrediting of Herodotus' critics is not the least diverting or the least instructive phase of the modern progress of knowledge. The criticisms

[11] Macan, *Herodotus*, vii-ix, Vol. I, p. lxxxv.
[12] Freeman, *Historical Essays*, Series II, p. 168.

that can be sustained touch a very small part of his activity or his value; he conceived of a whole world, all inter-related, all a unity, and he made men see it and be interested in it.

Herodotus in general accepts the current construction of the most ancient Greek history—the migrations, the foreign influences (which Plutarch resented[13]), the colonizations. He was not unconscious of the difference between what we call the mythical and the historical periods—"Polycrates was the first Greek, of whom I have knowledge, to aim at the mastery of the sea, leaving out of account Minos of Cnossus and any others who before him held maritime dominion; of such as may be called men Polycrates was the first so to do" (iii, 122). Whatever the value in each case of the traditions which he quotes, he has a wide acquaintance with ancient tribes and families, their migrations and movements, with Minyae and Gephyraeans and Bacchiads— some legendary, perhaps, and others not clumsily accurate in reporting pedigree and ancient story. Even if there were no Minyae or Gephyraeans or Bacchiads, men and groups of the kind there were; but in any case, whatever we make of Minyae, or of the kinship of the Bacchiads with Herakles, Bacchiads seem as historical as Plantagenets in England or Adamses in New England. Herodotus believes that Phoenicians at one time haunted Greek waters as Homer said; and most of the letters of the alphabet seemed to him to point to their share in the early development of Greek civilization.[14] Legend and

[13] Plutarch, *de malignitate Herodoti*, §§ 12-15, p. 857.
[14] See general discussion in How and Wells, Vol. I, pp. 347-350; on iv, 147.

popular phrase that told of "Lemnian deeds" (vi, 138) remind him of episodes, which explain the bare fact that Thucydides notes of the habit of bearing arms in daily life. The expulsion of the Pelasgians, their raid and the capture of women, the long enduring contempt shown by the women in their new home, and by their half-breed sons with the Attic speech, for the children of the island, and the murders that followed—whatever the value of the detail, it all makes a picture that would impress the imagination and would survive, especially if the rest of the world were consciously farther on upon the road to decent life and ordered ways. Siphnos again was a rich island by reason of gold and silver mines; and the men of Siphnos asked the god at Delphi, if their well-being was like to abide long, and they were bidden beware of a wooden ambush and a red herald. But the Siphnians forgot the old days of Greece, when all ships were painted with vermilion; so when the fleet of Polycrates came, they would not "lend" ten talents and were fined a hundred (iii, 57, 58). This was no ancient deed, it was a Samian deed of the sixth century, a generation before Herodotus was born. So history had some continuity, and an inference from the present to the past might not always be wrong.

II

But the Pelasgians remind us of a great racial problem belonging to the early days and of questions of more import bound up with it. "Among the Greeks Croesus found upon inquiry that the Lacedaemonians were chief among them of Doric stock and

the Athenians of Ionic. These races, Ionian and
and Dorian, were the foremost in ancient time, the
first a Pelasgian and the second an Hellenic people.
The Pelasgian stock has never yet left its habitation,
the Doric is assuredly a much-wandered race;"[15] and
he traces their wanderings from Phthia, where they
dwelt in King Deucalion's day, to the lands below
Ossa and Olympus in King Dorus' time, and so
onward to the Peloponnese. The Pelasgian language
he cannot accurately determine; but he knows of
Pelasgians dwelling at Creston near the Etruscans
(though once in what now is Thessaly), and of others
in two places on the Hellespont "who came to dwell
among the Athenians," and of other townships
"once Pelasgian which changed the name;" and
from these he judges that the Pelasgians had a
barbarian tongue. If then—the hypothetical form
must be noted—"if, then, all the Pelasgic stock so
spoke, then the Attic nation, being Pelasgian, when
it changed to be Hellenic, must have changed its
language too," for it seems clear that the people of
Creston have not changed theirs. "But the Hellenic
stock, as to me seems clear, has ever used the same
language since it was. While separated from the
the Pelasgians it was but few in numbers, but starting
by being originally small it has grown to be a multitude of nations, since the Pelasgians especially and
many other foreign stocks united themselves with
them. Before that, however, as I at least think, the
Pelasgic stock on its side nowhere was greatly
increased." (i, 58.)

[15] Herodotus, i, 56, 57.

Homer mentions Pelasgians in the Catalogue and in the *Odyssey*, and Pelasgian is one of his epithets for Zeus of Dodona, and for that Argos where Myrmidons, Hellenes and Achaeans dwell. Hesiod calls Dodona "seat of Pelasgians." Gradually a mythical Pelasgos comes into the pedigrees to be the ancestor of Pelasgians as Hellen was of Hellenes. The tribe or people is. particularly associated with Attica for some reason. Identification with existing groups, who called themselves or were called Pelasgian, was not difficult; it was obvious. So we reach, as we have seen, a Greek world that was not Greek at all (ii, 56, 171), and learn that Aeolians and Ionians were all of Pelasgic origin (vii, 94-95), Arcadians too (i, 146; ii, 171) and some others. Some of this is, no doubt, tradition and some of it theory. Possibly to the son of a Dorian town, who thought not over-highly of Ionians, there was a certain satisfaction in thinking that the only real Greeks from the beginning were the Dorians. Yet elsewhere, as we have seen, he links the tie of blood among Hellenes of his day with those of language, religion, and culture (viii, 144),—a kinship between Spartans and Athenians asserted in the hour of danger. A purist might excuse the contradiction on the ground that in one place Herodotus gives his own view, in the other the Athenian opinion. But to be precise on such questions is to court disaster. The English race is a composite one, and presumably so was the Hellenic. The origins of such peoples are hardly to be made out from the past; close observation of modern Burma with its many races, continued over a long enough span of centuries to come, might tell us a great deal more.

It is noted that Herodotus was at least shrewder than some philologists of the nineteenth century and noted that a nation may acquire a language by contact.[16] He knows of people who have acquired Carian without being Carian (i, 171), and he tells us that the Aethiopians of Asia and Africa differ in language as well as hair (vii, 70). He appears to believe that the oldest language will probably be spoken by the oldest race, whether we choose ourselves or not to accept the result of King Psammetichus' experiment. (One of the Scottish kings made it again, and the children, one reporter tells us, spoke good Hebrew, though we do not, I think, know the extent of their vocabulary.) In any case Herodotus holds that a good deal of "Greek" religion was of Pelasgian origin, particularly the traditional representation of Hermes. This "came from the Pelasgians, from whom the Athenians were the first to take it, and the rest from them. For the Athenians were then already reckoned as Greeks, when the Pelasgians came to dwell in the land with them and so began to count as Greeks too. The Pelasgians told a sacred tale about this [form of image], which is set forth in the Samothracian mysteries" (ii, 51). An earlier stage seems represented in his next chapter, which is confirmed by modern students of primitive religion—

formerly in all their sacrifices the Pelasgians called on the gods (as I know, for I heard it at Dodona), without giving name or appellation to any one of them; for they had not yet heard them. They called them gods from some idea that they set all things in order and had the distribution of all. Afterwards, when long time had passed, they learnt the names of the rest of the gods, when these came

[16] E. E. Sikes, *Anthropology of the Greeks*, p. 76.

from Egypt; but of Dionysus much later still. After a while they sought an oracle about the names at Dodona; for this place of divination is held to be the most ancient in Hellas, and at that time it was the only one. When then the Pelasgians inquired at Dodona as to whether they should adopt the names that come from the barbarians the oracle bade them use them. From that time they used the names of the gods in their sacrifices; and the Greeks received these from the Pelasgians later on (ii, 52).

The story grows confused, as well it may. The Pelasgians never wandered as the Dorians did, but they came to dwell with the Athenians and so began to count as Greeks. They learnt to speak Greek too, but already they had a Greek etymology for their Greek word for gods (θεοὺς and θέντας); and, as the story stands, they distinguished themselves from barbarians, or Herodotus did it for them. Thus, or in part thus, all Greece came to share gods as well as language; and there are gaps enough in the story.

Physique is not a test that Herodotus applies as a modern would; and even as a modern researcher of training and caution would apply it, it would probably have told little in the matter. Dorians appear to have had black hair, and Achaeans yellow; and presumably the original Mediterranean stock black. But cranial and other measurement could hardly have yielded much result, where stocks so small and presumably so near akin were mixed so thoroughly, and for so long a time, as by the day of Herodotus the Greeks were. But Greek thinkers laid more stress on climatic conditions, and especially on the effect of the sun, and held that "generally human physique and character follow the nature of the country."[17] Theophrastus, in his introduction to his *Characters*,

[17] Hippocrates, quoted by E. E. Sikes, *Anthropology of the Greeks*, p. 78.

says he has often wondered, and perhaps he will never stop wondering, why it is that, while all Greece lies under the same sky and all Greeks have a similar education, the characters of Greek men are so very different. As he says that he is ninety-nine years of age, perhaps he went on wondering to the end, or perhaps,—a hypothesis which the rest of the book supports,—he was not wholly serious. Still the form of his problem harmonizes with the Greek view. We have already heard Aristotle on the effects of the continents and their climates, and we shall have to return to the matter.

Once more, we have to guess at any chronology that may be involved in this theory about the Pelasgians. Where in the process of Hellenization does Homer come, who knew the names of the gods, but had no common name of Greek for the people, though they all seem to have spoken one language? Or was it Homer who taught them the names? (ii, 53). Anthropology and philology are sciences where the road to knowledge is found by endless blunderings. Herodotus had started.

III

He says with apparent conviction that he believes Homer and Hesiod lived four hundred years before himself, and not more than four hundred (ii, 53). Moderns, after bringing Homer so far down history, are perhaps tending to give him an earlier date. At all events, as we well know, there was a dark period between Homer and the rise of Ionian literature.

If we except the story of Lycurgus and the migrations, Herodotus has little to tell us of historical events before 700 B.C., and naturally his information is fuller for the sixth century than for the seventh. It may be urged that his subject did not require him to recount all that had befallen since Deucalion; and that he starts at the natural moment and in a reasonable way, with Greece as it was, when the first real clash of war began between Greeks and barbarians, when Croesus thought it of interest to know which were the leading powers in European Greece and to cultivate the oracle of Delphi. At this point his story really begins; and, though he knows a number of facts about the earlier days, they are not of the essence of his theme, and he does little more than allude to them.

For instance, one of the most significant events of early Greek history appears to have been the war of Chalcis and Eretria for the Lelantine plain of Euboea. Two manufacturing cities, on the Euripus with its beds of murex—if they had recovered from Phoenician over-fishing—with a rich sheep-growing plain between them, the question rose sharply as to which was to control the wool crop; and the Greek world was divided between them. It is not in Herodotus' story, but it comes in as a memory. Aristagoras got the Eretrians to send five triremes to the aid of Miletus, "for the Milesians in former times had borne with the Eretrians the burden of all that war which they had with the Chalcidians, at the time when the Chalcidians on their side were helped by the Samians against the Eretrians and Milesians" (v, 99). The war was epoch-making in early Greece; the whole Greek world, Thucydides says (i, 15), was

most divided and took the greatest part in it. Mercantile centres as they were and dividing the world's
commerce so far, it appears that they fought out
their struggle ashore, and that it was decided by
cavalry. "In old times," says Aristotle,[18] "the cities
whose strength lay in the cavalry were oligarchies,
and they used cavalry in wars against their neighbours; as was the practice of Eretrians and Chalcidians." Corinth also was among the allies of
Chalcis, which was victorious, thanks to the aid of
Thessalian cavalry.[19] It has been concluded by
scholars that the division of the world for colonizing
and trading purposes was connected with this
cleavage of the Euboean cities and their allies.
Miletus and Megara, at all events, had a practical
monopoly of the Black Sea and lined it with colonies;
Corinth and Samos looked westward. Bury and
Eduard Meyer put the war down to the beginning
of the seventh century, while Busolt dates it a
century earlier. The year commonly assigned to the
foundation of Byzantium is 660 B.C., and the rest
of the Black Sea cities follow. The planting of the
west is given a series of earlier dates, rightly or
wrongly; Naxos 735 B.C., Corcyra and Syracuse
734 B.C., Sybaris 721 B.C., and so forth. Doubt has
been cast on these dates, but the definite planting
of a town gives at least to its inhabitants a fixed era
from which to reckon, as reliable perhaps as a famous
earthquake or eclipse,[20] which in this early period
and indeed later gave men a landmark for memory.
At the same time we have to remember that very
often the source from which we derive the date of

[18] Aristotle, *Politics*, IV, 3, 3, p. 1289 b.
[19] Plutarch, *Amatorius*, c 17 (*Moralia*, p. 760 F).
[20] Herodotus, i, 74.

a colony's foundation is quite late, and that our dates may depend on a reckoning of generations perhaps made by Alexandrian scholars, and not on local tradition.[21]

The seventh and sixth centuries B.C. saw a number of developments in the Greek world, to some of which Herodotus merely alludes, while he lingers over others. It was the age when poetry and wisdom and law-making began to fascinate the Greek mind, when trade and exploration and foreign adventure tempted the Greek youth to range the Mediterranean, when a new type of religion was added to Greek ideas of worship, when metallurgy and coinage began to influence economic conditions and through them political speculation. We have already noted Herodotus' references to some of the poets and to the seamen and the adventurers. The tyrannies we may reserve for later treatment, and confine ourselves here to three groups of events, the great raids into Asia Minor, the rise of Sparta, and the founding of Cyrene, all of which Herodotus happily paused to notice.

The monuments of Assyria enable us to date the great age of invasions.[22] Sargon (King 722-705) speaks of Gimirrai and Iskuza, who are in more Greek form Cimmerians and Scythians. Esarhaddon (681-668) and Asshurbanipal (668-626) speak of victories over the Cimmerians. Herodotus tells us that the Cimmerians were driven from their own home in South Russia by the Scythians (i, 15) —the Crimea is considered to preserve their name—

---

[21] Cf. E. Meyer, *Gesch. des Altertums*, II, § 285; Julius Beloch, *Griech. Gesch.*, I, p. 173.

[22] Cf. How and Wells on Herodotus, i, 15.

they broke into Asia Minor, they raided and robbed
the Greeks but failed in general to take their cities
(i, 6), they attacked the Lydians and compelled King
Gyges to ask the aid of the Assyrian,—to "take the
yoke of my Kingdom," as the Assyrian monarch
preferred to put it. A little later, as we learn from
Strabo, the Cimmerian chief, whose name appears to
have been Tugdami though Lygdamis was an irresistible confusion for Greek copyists, let loose his
troops upon the lands, and overran Pontus, Paphla-
gonia and Phrygia, "at which time Midas drank
bull's blood, they say, and went to his doom. Lygdamis however at the head of his own soldiers
marched as far as Lydia and Ionia and captured
Sardis, but lost his life in Cilicia."[23] The capture of
Sardis, except the citadel, Herodotus records (i, 15).
"Often" continues Strabo, "the Cimmerians and the
Treres made raids of this kind, but they say that the
Treres and Cobus were finally driven out by Madys
king of the Scythians." Herodotus called this
Scythian chief Madyes, son of Protothyes, and said
he drove the Cimmerians out of Asia, and in pur-
suing them, reached the land of the Medes and there
worsted Kyaxares the Mede, who was warring
against the Assyrians. After defeating the Medes,
the Scythians swept on toward the Egyptian frontier, but in that part of Syria called Palestine King
Psammetichus met them and with gifts and prayers
prevailed on them to come no farther. The Scythians
ruled Asia for twenty-eight years, and all was
wasted by their violence (*hybris*) and pride; for one
thing they would exact tribute from all, and quite
apart from the tribute they would ride round the

[23] Strabo, i, C. 61.

country and carry off every man's possessions. At last, by lavishly entertaining them and making them drunk, Kyaxares and the Medes were able to destroy them and win back their empire.[24] From the Jewish prophet Jeremiah we gather what impression the Scythians made in that part of Syria called Palestine:[25] "a people cometh from the north country; and a great nation shall be stirred from the uttermost parts of the earth. They lay hold on bow and spear; they are cruel and have no mercy; their voice roareth like the sea[26] and they ride upon horses."

The effects of these raids may be traced in the weakening of both Assyrians and Medes, and perhaps we should associate with them the settlement of the Bithynians in Asia[27] and the rise of the Armenians. The Greeks in their walled towns on the sea escaped the worst effects of the invasions, and the Lydians, who suffered, may have so far strengthened their position in Asia in that they suffered less than the great powers to the east of them. But for Greeks of the sixth and fifth centuries there was little outlook east of Lydia and Phrygia. In the main they missed the early significance of the Hittites, and though Herodotus indeed mentions them under the name of Syrians (i, 72) he believed, as we have seen, their striking monument in Western Asia to be Egyptian, and he was not aware of their connexion with the Royal Road into farther Asia (v 49-52).[28] When once the raids were over, Greek

[24] Herodotus, i, 103-106, abridged.
[25] Jeremiah, vi, 22-23.
[26] Compare the *barritus* of fourth century Germans.
[27] Herodotus, vii, 75.
[28] See Sir William Ramsay, *Historical Geography of Asia Minor*, pp. 27-41. E. Meyer, *Gesch. des Altertums*, III, § 39; H. F. Tozer, *History of Ancient Geography*, pp. 90, 91.

foreign policy in Asia Minor was to be summed up in resistance to Lydia, but to that we return later; in the meantime Herodotus has given us the historical background of Croesus and Cyrus and the Greeks of Asia.

When Croesus set to work to inquire very carefully who were the most powerful of the Hellenes that he might make friends of them (i, 56), while "he strove to win the favour of the Delphian god" (i, 50), he learnt easily of the growing power of Sparta among the Dorians. To that city we now turn, and in Herodotus' pages we can learn something but not all about its rise and growth. Some part of the story has only been revealed by modern archaeology, and some of it goes back into the twilight of myth. To the conquest of Messenia Herodotus alludes twice. The clever Aristagoras contrasts the rich and broad lands of Asia, so easy to win, with the hard struggles of the Spartans to conquer lands nearer home "not very big and not very good, and confines but small, at the risk of battles against Messenians, a fair match for you, and against Arcadians and Argives" (v, 49, 8). Elsewhere Herodotus drops a strange hint that "the Samians aforetime came to their aid with ships against the Messenians" (iii, 47). Tyrtaeus, the Spartan poet of the second Messenian war, he does not mention (he was of course, as he said, not bound to mention everything, any more than those who write of him); and the considerable development of poetry, if not by Spartans, at least round and in Sparta, we learn from elsewhere. Between the eleventh Olympiad (736 B.C.) and the restoration of Messenia in the fourth century, only one Messenian victory at Olympia is recorded;[29] Messenia disappears for nearly four centuries. In 720 B.C., the fifteenth Olympiad, the first Spartan victor is noted at Olympia and a long list of successes reaches down to 576 B.C., after which date they too cease and rather abruptly.[30] Seventh century Sparta is different altogether from the Sparta of later history and of the great legend. It is a progressive state with a fresh keen life, which has introduced a new element in the Greek world, for nowhere else is there so early the full democratic equality of citizens. Poetry flourished, and, as excavation on Spartan sites reveals, art with it,—particularly the delicate carving of ivory,—and athletics. The sixth century shows a people concentrating on conquest of their neighbours, developing into a more and more exclusive caste, forswearing all the arts, and trade and commerce too, and living under a very peculiar and rigid discipline which greatly interested posterity.

It is the sixth century Sparta that Herodotus knows, not the earlier; that was gone and so thoroughly forgotten that Athens, to explain Tyrtaeus, made him a lame Athenian schoolmaster lent to Sparta; the ivories were underground. What men heard who were allowed to linger in Sparta was another story altogether, from which the real seventh century was omitted. Away back in the eighth century Sparta was lawless at home and inglorious in war, the worst governed community of Greece. But one Lycurgus went to Delphi and was greeted as a god by the Pythian priestess, who, "some say, declared to him the whole governance now estab-

[29] E. Norman Gardiner, *Greek Athletic Sports*, p. 54.
[30] *Ibid.*, p. 56.

lished for the Spartiates; but the Lacedaemonians say that it was from Crete that Lycurgus brought these customs." He changed all the ways of the country and established all their military usages, their sworn companies and bands of thirty, and their common meals, and their government by ephors and a council of elders. So they changed their bad laws for good; and for Lycurgus, when he died, they set up a shrine (or temple) and revered him greatly. And, as you would expect in a good land full of men, they at once flourished and prospered, and proposed to conquer Arcadia.[31]

But the subjection of Tegea was all the god would allow them and all they effected, nor could they manage even this till they should find and bring home the bones of Orestes. So said the god at Delphi; but where were the bones? In a place in Arcadia, said the god,

> Where blow winds twain, of strong necessity,
> Where shock meets shock, and woe on woe is laid.

But when they heard this, they seemed no nearer finding what they sought, till Lichas their envoy, using luck and cleverness, lit on it. For Lichas one day entered a smithy at Tegea, and watched the smith at work and marvelled at what he made. "Laconian," said the smith,

you wonder at the working of iron, but had you seen what I have seen, you would indeed have had somewhat to wonder at. For I was making me a well in this yard, and as I dug I came upon a coffin seven cubits long. I could not believe that there had ever been men taller than those of our day, so I opened the coffin, and found in it the dead man as long as the coffin. I measured him and buried him again.

[31] Herodotus, i, 65, 66.

So Lichas watched him and thought, and he noted how, when the smith forced the bellows down, of necessity winds blew, and how anvil and hammer gave shock and received shock; and he reflected that iron had been discovered for man's undoing. Lichas drew an inference, and it was right; and Orestes' bones in time came home, and Tegea felt the power of Sparta, somewhere about 550 B.C. by our reckoning.[32]

Not only northward did the Spartans encroach on their neighbours but eastward too, and they fought the Argives in respect of the country called Thyrea, for till then the land west of Argos and south to Malea belonged to the Argives. It was covenanted, however, that not all the armies of both states should fight, but three hundred picked men on each side, and the rest should withdraw and leave them. So the six hundred fought till two Argives and one Spartan alone lived at nightfall. The Argives counting themselves victors went off to Argos; but Othryades the Spartan spoiled the Argive dead and remained in his place. Next day when the armies returned, both claimed the victory. The Argives had indeed the more men left;—but they had fled the field, the Spartans rejoined. So the armies fell to it and fought, and the Spartans had the victory. Ever after this the Argives, who had of old worn their hair long, shaved their heads, and made a law, strengthened with a curse, that none should grow long hair, nor any Argive woman wear gold, till they win again the Thyreatis. But the Spartans in triumph changed their short hair for long; and, as we learn from Aristophanes, it was their distinguishing feature in his day,

[32] Herodotus, i, 67, 68, abridged.

and the friends of Sparta aped the custom. But Othryades thought it shame to survive his comrades and slew himself on the spot at Thyreai.[33]

"You see, comrade, how he takes your spirit with him through the place, and turns hearing into seeing." So writes Longinus of another passage of our historian, where he addresses the reader in his own person and sets him at the centre of action. He does not use the second person here, but can one read such stories and not see?[34] It is tempting to think of King Cleomenes, but to tell his great deeds and his strange end would carry us outside the period with which we are dealing. Suffice it to say that, whether friend or foe told the king's history to Herodotus, sane or mad (v, 42; vi, 75), sober or drinking like the Scythians (vi, 84), the king never comes on the scene, whether trying to enter the Athenian temple (v, 72) or studying the Ionian map of brass in his own house with the clever traveller from Miletus (v, 49), resisting the Samian bribe (iii, 148), or getting King Demaratus of the other house deposed (iii, 61), but the page fascinates the reader, and he is back in the ancient Sparta, he lives again the life of the Spartans, and has a hand himself in all the complicated policies and adventures of one of the most interesting of men. But then all the men of whom Herodotus tells are interesting. It is not accident; it is purpose, it is art, and above all it is humanity. And "the man can write," as Plutarch said (γραφικὸς ἀνήρ).[35]

[33] Herodotus, i, 82; this victory also is dated about 500 B.C.
[34] Longinus, 26, 2; of Herodotus, ii, 29, Meroe.
[35] Plutarch, De malignitate Herodoti, § 43, p. 874 B.

The story of the planting of Cyrene will serve two purposes for us. It will illustrate once more the art of Herodotus, his range of interests from pedigrees to geography, his love of adventure and legend and men; and its sequel (which we must reserve for a later point), upon the ways and customs of the Libyans, reveals again the fascination which he found in what we call Anthropology but he happily did not. At the same time, whatever caution we are told to exercise, when he takes us so far out of his own century, we shall at all events see something of Greek life in an age that had passed away.

Those Pelasgians, who had carried off the Athenian women and held Lemnos, drove out the descendants of the Argonauts. They sailed away and landed on Spartan soil and lit a fire on Mount Taygetus. The Spartans sent to ask who they were, and they told how they were Minyae, sons of the Argonauts, begotten during their stay in Lemnos, and they had now returned, as was just, to the land of their fathers. The sons of Tyndareus had indeed sailed on the Argo, so the Spartans received them and intermarried with them. But the Minyae claimed too much as time went on, and the Spartans resolved to kill them and to this end cast them into prison, for the Spartans kill men by night and not by day. Their Spartan wives asked leave to speak with them; and, little suspecting what they would do, their fathers gave them leave; and ere long the wives were in the prison and the men again on Taygetus. Now Theras, maternal uncle of the twin kings, and long their guardian, was unwilling to remain a subject where he had been a ruler, and he planned to sail to Thera then called Calliste; and he begged that he

might take the Minyae with him. So he sailed but
not with all of them, for some remained in the
Peloponnese and went westward and founded six
cities in Triphylia. So far Spartans and Theraeans
tell one tale.

     After this, as the men of Thera say, long after it,
the king of the island came to Delphi with a heca-
tomb, and the god bade his people found a city in
Libya. "Nay, O King," said Grinnus, "I am an old
man by now and heavy to stir; but do thou bid one
of these younger men do this," and he pointed to
Battus, son of Polymnestus of the Minyan stock.
But the Theraeans did not know where Libya was;
and they were afraid to send out a colony to an uncertain goal. Then for seven years there was no rain,
and they were bidden again to colonize Libya. They
sent to Crete to see if any knew of Libya, and found
one Corobios who had been driven there by the wind,
all out of his course to an island called Platea.
Corobios was willing to pilot them, and he took
certain Theraeans thither, who left him on the island
once more, with food for so many months, and sailed
again to Thera; and he was found there in want by
Kolaios on his famous voyage. The Theraeans mean-
while drew lots in their homeland to send out one of
every two brothers, under the leadership of Battus
in two fifty-oared ships to Platea. So say the
Theraeans.

     The Cyrenians have a more romantic tale of a
Cretan stepmother devising death for her step-
daughter, and how the girl was sunk in the open sea
by a trader, Themison, trapped into the deed by an
oath; but he was a kindly man, and put ropes about
her when he sank her, and drew her aboard ship

again. At Thera she became the concubine of Polymnestus and bore him a son of weak and stammering speech, who was called Battus, though some say that *battus* is the Libyan word for king. Whatever his own name, he hated his voice and went to Delphi to ask the god's aid in mending it; but the god had greater things for him, a colony and a kingdom in Libya. Once more there was reluctance, but the god would have it so; and Battus went, but to Platea not Libya itself; and for two years things went ill. The god was again consulted; "if thou," he replied, "dost know sheep-rearing Libya better than I, thou who hast not been there better than I who have, greatly do I commend thee for thy wisdom." So they left the island and settled upon the mainland; and thereafter for eight generations the house of Battus ruled Cyrene, as readers of Pindar will remember. Herodotus tells the tale of the house and its ups and downs to the days when the Persians came into their land,—stories of civil strife and the Mantineian peacemaker, of the siege of Barca and its capture by a trick, and of the horrible vengeance that the Greek princess Pheretime took upon the Barcaeans whom the Persians gave into her hands. He implies that by his day the dynasty reigned no more.

No story told by Herodotus is improved when it is shortened by another hand; and posterity was better served, undoubtedly, by those who copied his manuscripts word for word than by those who write comments upon him, a great deal of their own and a little of the original. Yet there come times when that too must be done. Of what men have written and surmised as to this story of Cyrene,

How and Wells write: "All these guesses and combinations are as devoid of real evidence as the story
in Herodotus; they have the additional disadvantage
of being more than 2000 years further from the facts."
We will not try to penetrate here and now to the true
detail of the planting of Cyrene, some three hundred
years before Herodotus' day; but we should at least
reflect that he is giving us the story as it was told
in the sixth century and in the fifth, that he gives
us variants, and that if we are uncertain how the
elements of truth and fable are woven into the fabric,
the fabric as we have it is evidence as to how Greeks
looked at the world in the great formative period that
led up to the Persian wars. To watch the growth of
the general mind of Greece is what Herodotus
assuredly gives us; and no detail in the story is so
valuable as the familiarity and intimacy with that
growing mind, into which every sympathetic reader
of his pages comes, consciously or unconsciously,
but in reality.

IV

How entirely at home Herodotus is in the story
of the great century before him, is shown by a
curious detail in the narrative about Kolaios.
Kolaios and his men came "under divine escort" to
Tartessus; "now this was at that time a virgin port;
wherefore the Samians brought back from it so great
a profit on their wares as no Greeks ever did, of
whom we have any exact knowledge, save only
Sostratos of Aegina, son of Laodamas; for with him
none could vie" (iv, 152). Every reader would wish

to know the story of Sostratos, but no man knows it;
Herodotus did. Why did he not digress more? And
then what was it that Kolaios brought back, that was
so profitable—was it silver, as some guess? Then
look again at the whole narrative of Cyrene, and
better, in Herodotus' own text, and note the unem-
phasized fulness of illumination. Of course men went
to Delphi, and Delphi knew the Mediterranean and
sent them here and there, to relieve their minds by
doing the god's bidding and to find new livelihood in
places they had themselves overlooked. They went
in fifty-oared galleys, painted red, as the tale of
Siphnos told us (iii, 58); and the base of red paint
in those days was *miltos*. This was found in various
parts of the world; the Libyans, "called Maxyes,
wear their hair long on the right side of their heads
and shave the left, and they paint their bodies with
vermilion" (iv, 191). But the Greeks got it from
central Asia Minor and called it "Sinopic," because
they imported it from Sinope, as we call birds turkeys
and trees Lombardy poplars and cheeses Stilton,
which have nothing to do with those places. But in
each case the name has a tale of its own to tell, which
reveals old history. Sinope had been the port of Asia
Minor, in the old Hittite days. And while we talk
of paints, we must notice that Corobios was a
"trader in purple," a murex-fisher probably (iv, 151);
and a glimpse is given us at one of the big industries
that stimulated exploration and made one lake of the
Mediterranean, and at an ancient fashion in clothing,
a taste in colour, that made industries then and gave
their proper hue to imperial and papal dignitaries
for ever. Kolaios' votive offering was "a bronze
vessel, like an Argolic cauldron, with griffins' heads

projecting from the rim all round, and supported by three colossal kneeling figures of bronze, each seven cubits high." Herodotus had surely seen it in the temple of Hera at Samos (iv, 152); and it tells a tale of art and its development in early days and of the interest a later age was taking in it.

The spot where the Greeks settled in Libya had "the heaven above it pierced with holes" (iv, 158); and there again we must be touching old tradition and hearing the actual voice of men. When the oracle admonished all Greeks to go to Cyrene, in the reign of Battus II the Fortunate, and told them that whoso came late and missed the division of the land would be sorry for it, what a picture opens of crowded Greek cities, swarming with hungry men and women, and the real impulse to colonization. What the American Indian suffered in the Middle West in the eighteenth century A.D. the Libyan feared in that age; and the Pontiac of the times was Adikran. This chief sent to Egypt to get King Apries (Hophra) to help him against the Greeks who swarmed into the land and meant to stay; and Apries sent an army, and the Greeks (how terse it is!) "marched out to Irasa, and at the spring Thestes joined battle with the Egyptians and conquered them in battle; for before this the Egyptians had not made trial of the Greeks and despised them and were destroyed." (iv, 159).[36] There emerges the Greek fighting man in armour, the *hoplite*, who for sheer fighting value beat every soldier in the Mediterranean basin and a long way east of it; the armour and the weapons he made were too good, as the Persians, brave men and heroes as they were, found at Plataea (ix, 62); and the spirit,

[36] Beloch, *Griechische Geschichte*, I, p. 198, dates this about 570 B.C.

with which he fought, with which he flung himself armed into the *ôthismos*, "the push" and used his sword, was irresistible, when he chose. Then a digression; it was Aryandes, satrap (*hyparchos*) of Egypt, who came to Pheretime's aid and took Barca; and later on in King Darius' day he came to grief in a curious way, for presuming to imitate the King; "for Darius had coined money of gold refined to an extreme purity; and Aryandes, then ruling Egypt, made a like silver coinage; and now there is no silver money so pure as the Aryandic. But when Darius heard he was doing this, he put him to death, not on this plea but as a rebel" (iv, 166). Darius' darics are still extant, with only three per cent of alloy in them; the last century has seen great finds of them; one hoard of three hundred was turned up in Xerxes' canal by Mount Athos.[37]   And finally the horrid end of Pheretime, the same that afterwards befel Herod, has a meaning, "so wroth, it would seem, are the gods with over-violent human vengeance" (iv, 205). Vengeance without excess might, every Greek thought, be a reasonable enough thing in the eyes of the gods,—as Thucydides and Euripides note, with little enough sympathy for the view.

The books of Herodotus abound with detail of the kind that illuminates the life and mind of his people. When he speaks of Egyptian ways (ii, 35) or of Persian (i, 133), the contrasts that he draws tell posterity a great deal about the domestic habits and table manners of his own people, what men and women do inside the house and what without. The eructation of a modern Turkish guest after a meal is a matter of good breeding; an ancient Persian, we

[37] Percy Gardner, *History of Ancient Coinage*, p. 90.

learn, did not like to vomit in another's presence.
The greeting of a stranger proclaims the foreigner
or the profession, and Herodotus notes how Persians
greet each other as they meet, and how social etiquette is seen in their approach; how Egyptians
refuse certain cordialities of the Greek; and so forth.
He looks backward too, and sometimes (as we have
seen) incidentally tells of old ways, and sometimes
particularly notes changes of dress that times have
brought, Carian dress for Dorian among women
(v, 88) and long hair among the Spartans (i, 82).
He notes the common meals of Sparta (vi, 57) and
the privileges of their kings, with some detail. The
Pelasgian capture of Athenian girls as they fetched
water from the spring of Enneakrounos reminds
him that in old days "neither Athenians nor the
other Hellenes had household slaves" (vi, 137).
The adventures of this man and that, always relevant
to some phase of the story, show a world of unfamiliar trades. The Aeginetans publicly hired Democedes at a talent a year to be their physician; that
was equal to 82 Attic minae; so the Athenians
offered him 100 next year; and the third year saw
him with Polycrates at Samos at two talents; and
then, as we know, he was found far away in Persia
a prisoner "among the slaves of Oroites, somewhere
or other, neglected, fettered and in rags," and
became court physician to Darius (iii, 131, 129). We
come on the track of diviners who travel in the same
way and are hired by communities and can charge
good prices (ix, 33-38), and of poets who haunt the
courts of princes, and public heralds whose office is
hereditary, and seamen and athletes and adventurers
without number; and prophets among them.

Of the oracles perhaps enough has been said for the moment, and of the vague dreads allayed by such expedients as the recovery of Orestes' bones; nor need we linger over the games, dear to the Greek then as in the days of Homer, and as in the days of Chrysostom. Herodotus will often pause to tell us that such a man who comes into his story had won the pentathlon or the pancration, was a Pythian victor, or ran a four-horse chariot.[38] Gods and oracles and temples and religious beliefs fill his pages to such an extent that we note with interest that at least one subject, which largely occupies the modern student, has little place in his book. "At the time of the fall of the Pythagoreans," writes Professor Bury,

the Orphic religion was no longer a danger to Greece. It was otherwise in the lifetime of Pythagoras himself. Then it seemed as if the Orphic doctrines had been revealed as the salvation which men's minds craved; and if those doctrines had taken firm hold of Greece, all the priesthoods of the national temples would have admitted the new religion, become its ministers, and thereby exercised an enormous sacerdotal power.

One divines little of this from Herodotus, who knows indeed a good deal about Pythagoras, and says less than he knows, as we may see. We have to allow for omissions; he says little of the intellectual awakening of Greece in so many words, but it lies in the story never very far away; his own mind shows it. But the possibility of the rise of a Brahmanate or a Roman episcopate is hardly to be guessed from Herodotus' story; and there, I feel, his evidence in what it omits is of high significance.

[38] Here is a handful of references to athletics (including chariot races) from three books: vi, 35, 70, 92, 103, 125; viii, 26, 47; ix, 33, 75, 105.

Out of the whole story of these early days emerges, as we think over what we read, the Hellen himself, restless in mind and body, born to wander far in the realm of the mind as over the physical world, an explorer, and a pioneer by nature, an individualist in grain. The Egyptian would stay in Egypt, unmoved and aloof, refusing the customs of other men (ii, 79;91). The Scythian would kill Anacharsis for meddling with Greek religion and using the customs of the foreigner (iv, 76); and Skyles their half-Greek king fared no better (iv, 78-80). The Persian was very different; he was a man indeed, a creature of spirit and courage (ix, 62), and he kept his eyes open for the customs of other men and adopted them freely (i, 135), or rejected them with reason (i, 133; vii, 9, b). The Greeks were much of the same mind; they, like the Persians, would adopt the dress of another people, not Median (i, 135) but Carian (v, 87), the shield and the helmet of Egypt (iv, 180), the four-horse chariots and the religious howlings of the Libyan (iv, 189), Carian arms and crests and plumes (i, 171), the alphabet of the Phoenician (v, 58), and even the Egyptian census (ii, 177). Adaptable, critical, at home everywhere but with only one home anywhere (i, 165), individualist,—the Greek would have his city free and he would be free himself; he would sail the sea, mould the bronze, make poetry; he would think and he would adventure. Those may believe who will that Xerxes said to Artabanos: "It is better to have good courage about everything and to suffer half the evils that threaten, than to have fear beforehand about everything and not to suffer any evil at all" (vii, 50). That is not the spirit of Oriental monarchy, it is the vital breath of the Greek adventurer shown all over the Mediterranean—Democedes in Susa, Kolaios at Tartessos, all of them. The story of the sixth century as we gather it from Herodotus illustrates the essential Greek character. The fights with the tyrants of which he tells in that age, the splendid fight with Persia, which is his theme, in the fifth century, the reluctance with which league or hegemony is tolerated after the Greek deliverance, the intrigues and miseries of the fourth century as men struggle to be rid of Spartan harmost and Persian agent—all these come out of the Greek mind and are its expression. If the great speech in which Pericles sets forth the mind and life of Athens does not convince us, if we ask the evidence for it, Herodotus will help us. He knew that mind and shared it; his pages are full of it. He can interpret the Greeks because he is Greek—Greek above all things, and Greek beyond all Greeks—thank God!

CHAPTER IV

THE BARBARIAN NEIGHBOURS

I

One of the unhappiest features of the older classical training was its isolation of the Greek. The Greek had undoubtedly lived his life, and developed mind and character, against the background of the older Mediterranean cultures, and in the full stream of Mediterranean influences. In the later days of Greece there were Greeks who surrendered blindly to the traditions of Egypt and the East as interpreted by Manetho and Berossos, men, whose learning seems to have been as dull as it was inaccurate,—or by others more lively and probably still more inaccurate, who lived on the credulity of their disciples. Yet even then Greeks might boast, and not without justice, that they had given the Orient in Hellenism all the culture it ever had. In the earlier times neither the surrender nor the boast was made. Men might indeed distinguish between Greeks and barbarians; but the view that it was the rôle of the Greek to rule and to teach was hardly held before the time of Pericles; before Salamis it would have been nonsense. Neither Herodotus, nor Xenophon, nor Alexander the Great can be called wanting in the true feeling for Greece, or deficient in the Greek spirit. They were eminently Greek; but, unlike some

Greek writers who formed the tradition, they had personal contact with the barbarian, and they honestly liked and admired him. And so had the earlier Greek of the centuries of expansion. War of course there had been between Greek and barbarian, but no more than between Greek and Greek; and in the intervals of war there had been intercourse, and the reaction of ideas. To understand the development of Greece, its historical course must be known; and it is one of the great merits of Herodotus as a historian that he realized something of the great maze of influences in which Greece matured, and that, when he wrote his history, he gave as vivid a picture of the nascent Greece among those influences as could well be asked.

To the scholars of the Renaissance, and of the centuries that followed, the marvel of Greek literature as a thing apart must have been overwhelming. What its re-discovery meant, no one who associates with Greek literature from the dawn of his intelligence onward without a break can guess; but let a scholar take ten years of his life and devote them solely to Latin or to late Greek writers, and see what the great Classical Greek period means to him. *Crede experto!* But we at least have no excuse for a concentration that has no ground in history. How could the Hellen of Ionia but be conscious of the barbarian? The barbarian was not like the Americans that Columbus or even that Cortés discovered, a curiosity, an exception, a thing remote; he was at the door, he was in the family, and life was not to be thought of without intercourse with him. How in sense could it be? Barbarians, civilized like the Lydian, half-civilized like the Carian, strange of

custom altogether like the Lycian, were not remote
at all. Asia Minor had many a tribe, as it still has,
barbarous in every suggestion of the word; and
Thrace perhaps was more solidly barbarous than
Asia Minor. If people would read Xenophon's
Anabasis, they would realize what the Greek's
environment was. For if Xenophon did not roam
so far as Herodotus, he was perhaps in stranger
places, certainly in places where the native barbarian
was more militant. Or look westward and think of
Sikels in Sicilian hills, of Sabellians in Italy, and
others whose names even Thucydides seems to have
confused,[1]—"so careless are men in the search for
Truth!"[2] Think of Massilia in a land of barbarians,
and of all the strange tribes along the northern coast
of Africa.

Herodotus, as we saw, grew up in an outpost of
Greece, and had perhaps Carian blood in his veins.
More probably than not from childhood he had been
familiar with stories of travel in the back country
and over the seas. Plutarch long after accused him
of malignity for turning Isagoras into a Carian and
Aristogeiton into a Phoenician,—a sneer in each case.[3]
To Herodotus it is hard to say whether the accusa-
tion of malignity or the evidence for it would have
been more amazing. Why should not Isagoras have
had Carian blood in his veins? What was the matter
with Carian blood? Miletus, Halicarnassus, the bold
Carians themselves—and Carian blood a taunt? Or
Phoenician descent a sneer—an infamy to be

---

[1] Thucydides, vi, 103; vii, 53; Etruscans, whom Diodorus, viii, 44,
calls Campanians, and rightly, as E. Meyer says, comparing Strabo, C.
242.

[2] Thucydides, i, 20; cf. p. 69.

[3] Plutarch, *De malignitate Herodoti*, § 23, p. 860 E.

descended from Cadmus who brought letters and civilization? What could be said of the mind that could conceive of such a tract as that of Plutarch—idea or execution?

He travelled himself, and, as we have also seen, he thoroughly enjoyed his intercourse with barbarians of every kind. There was a fascination, the keenest of delights, in learning the minds of men and seeing their cities, getting a hold of their ideas and comparing them, and tracing connexions among the thoughts of men the whole world over. How he was affected by their traditions and beliefs as to gods and cults we shall see at a later stage; and in the next chapter his study of the outer edges of the world will occupy us—the geography of them and the natural history of man and animal, for all of these aspects of life interested him, nor these alone. Social usage and manners, the superficial tastes and decencies of life, he notices as well as the greater things, marriage customs, diet, and climate.

He has always an open eye for trade and commerce,—so much so that men have asked whether he had been a trader himself and with his own goods, and perhaps ship, wandered from land to land.[4] The spices of the East and the perils of their gathering—the small winged snakes that infest the trees that bear frankincense (iii, 107), the winged creatures like bats that attack the gatherers of cassia (iii, 110), the great birds that build their nests of cinnamon sticks and the Sindbad-like device by which the cinnamon is got from them (iii, 111)—all these are romantic tales that take a man far out of the ordinary round. But hemp (iv, 74) and horns,

[4] See How and Wells, Vol. I, p. 17.

even if they are very large (vii, 126), seem very com-
monplace commodities, and salt fish as little romantic
as any article of daily food. A river abounding with
sturgeon and self-formed crusts of salt near its
mouth, handy for their salting, suggest that he is
writing for traders and the market (iv, 53). It is like
our modern books on South America. Sweetmeats
(vii, 31) and linen (ii, 105) are not much better;
honey was a common staple of life in antiquity, and
he twice notices how substitutes are made for it,—
artificial honey of flour and tamarisk juice in Lydia
(vii, 31) and also in some way not described among
the Libyans (vii, 194). Boat transport on the Nile
(ii, 96), and on the Euphrates (i, 194) interests him;
and he stops to describe the huge Nile *baris* of many
thousand talents burden, built of acacia wood and
caulked with byblus, taken downstream by the
current, and towed upstream unless the breeze is
brisk, and the boat of frame and skin that floats down
the Euphrates with a live ass aboard to carry the
hides home up the river to be used again. As no
river of Greece is navigable, the reader can understand how these huge streams with their commerce,
and others as large among the Scythians (the
Dnieper, iv, 53), would hold his attention. He
notices strange trading customs of which men speak
(iv, 24; 196), and he uses now and then what appear
to be trade terms (iv, 61; 152).

National tastes differ as to what a gentleman may
or may not do. "No youth of parts," says Plutarch,[5] "because he saw the Zeus of Olympia, would
wish therefore to be a Pheidias." But Solon, Plutarch
reports, engaged in trade in youth,—ἐμπορία, imply-

ing not a store in a street, but travel from place to place. His father had reduced his property by his generosity, and the young Solon felt shame about receiving when the family tradition was to give. Some, says Plutarch,[6] said that Solon travelled more for experience and inquiry—Herodotus' own word ἱστορίη[7]—than to make money; but a good man, who thinks of his city, may very well neither magnify the acquisition of the needless nor despise the use of the necessary. In those times, at any rate, continues Plutarch, as Hesiod puts it, "work was no reproach," nor did a craft make a distinction, but trade had a certain glory of its own in making native what was foreign, winning the friendship of kings and giving citizens experience. Some too became founders of great cities, as Protis, beloved by the Celts about the Rhone, founded Massilia. Thales, too, they say, engaged in trade, and Hippocrates the mathematician; and Plato found means for travel in the disposal of some oil in Egypt. So Herodotus was in good company, if he went abroad to trade as well as to learn.

But before passing on to deal with the barbarian world, I may be allowed for a moment to digress to two points connected with the mercantile side of Herodotus' travels. During the war I was in Burma for a while, and there I read Herodotus through again and found (as one constantly does) new points of interest in his journeying. In Europe one may or may not notice such matters, but for the reader in the East there is something that comes home to him in

[6] Plutarch, *Solon*, 2.
[7] Herodotus, i, 29, 30, says Solon after his legislation went abroad, κατὰ θεωρίης πρόφασιν.

the Greek's allusions to the seas he has himself
crossed. Our Indian Ocean Herodotus knows under
two names—"the land where the Persians dwell
reaches down to the Southern Sea, called the Red"
(iv, 37). The Euphrates, a wide, deep, and swift
river, flows from Armenia and issues into the Red
Sea (i, 180). Our Red Sea of uncomfortable memory
is also known. "In Arabia not far from Egypt there
is a gulf of the sea entering in from the sea called
Red, of which the length and narrowness is such as I
shall show: for length it is a forty days' voyage for a
ship rowed by oars from its inner end out to the open
sea, and for breadth it is half a day's voyage at the
widest. Every day the tide ebbs and flows therein"
(ii, 11). Happily one can get through it in less than
forty days by now. To the Persian gulf he gives no
particular name.

My other point is his constant attention to mines,
to mining methods, and their returns. The gold and
silver mines of Siphnos we have noticed already
(iii, 57). He alludes of course to the Athenian silver
mines at Laureion (vii, 144) and to gold and silver
mines in Pangaion (vii, 112). The gold mines at
Scapte Hyle and on Thasos—"I myself saw these
mines, and by much the most marvellous of them are
those which the Phoenicians discovered . . . there
is a great mountain which has been all turned up in
the search for metal" (vi, 46, 47). He has a friendly
word for Sophanes the Athenian, who, after the
Persian wars, was killed, after proving himself a good
man, by the Edonians at Daton, in a fight for the
gold mines (ix, 75). Near Lake Prasias in Macedonia

[8] See H. F. Tozer, *History of Ancient Geography*, pp. 80-82; How and
Wells on Herodotus, i, 1.

is a mine from which Alexander drew a talent of silver a day (v, 17); and of the mines of Thrace the Persian was quick to see the significance (v, 23). Herodotus knows that to the north of Europe there is far more gold than anywhere else,[9] "but how it is got, I cannot with certainty say; some will have it that Arimaspians, one-eyed men, steal it from the griffins; but neither of this am I convinced that there are men born with one eye only, while in the rest of their nature like other men" (iii, 116). In India, men, it is said, steal gold dust turned up with the earth from their holes by ants as large as foxes (iii, 102)— a tale explained in various ways by moderns, but apparently one of several genuine Indian legends which have reached Herodotus somehow.[10] He knows of gold dredging on an island off the Libyan coast (iv, 195). He alludes to the gold of Croesus (i, 69) and of Pythios (vii, 27, 28) (perhaps a grandson of Croesus); to gold dust from Tmolus, which he calls the most remarkable thing in Lydia (i, 93). Strabo long afterwards described the gold-washing in the Pactolus from which that wealth came (C. 626).

Embodied in the main story of his work, five great sections deal with barbarian peoples, sections not

[9] How and Wells on iv, 71, say 20,000 gold objects have been found in Scythian lands, and were mostly in the Hermitage at Petrograd. Where are they now?

See Diodorus, iii, 12-14, on mining; and Ure, *Origin of Tyranny*, p. 46, a picture from a sixth century Corinthian terra cotta of a miner at work, uncomfortably enough.

[10] See H. G. Rawlinson, *India and Western World*, p. 25, viz., perhaps Hippocleides (vi, 110) from the Jataka (a peacock there), cf. p. 209, the wife of Intaphernes (iii, 18); and the Hyperboreans, transferred from the Himalaya.

irrelevant to his theme, as we have seen, but distinguishable. In the first book we have the Lydians, in the first and again in the third, the Persians. The Egyptians fill the second, and Scythians and Libyans divide the fourth book. It is noticeable that he has little or nothing to say of the native peoples of Sicily or Italy. He speaks of course of the Etruscans. Western Europe, it may be urged, could hardly be included in his subject. The Libyans touched Cyrene, and, under the circumstances, when he had the information and it was so extraordinarily interesting from so many points of view, it would have been hardly human to leave it out. But a sentence or two will show how ignorant he really was of the North West (if we may call it so) of the Mediterranean region, and then we may turn back to Asia Minor.

"The Ister," he says, using the other name for the Danube (ii, 33),

flows from the land of the Celts and the city of Pyrene, cutting Europe across the midst. The Celts are outside the Pillars of Hercules, and are neighbours of the Kynesioi, who are the westernmost of all nations inhabiting Europe. The Ister then flows clean across Europe, and it ends its course in the Euxine Sea at Istria, which is inhabited by Milesian colonists.

We are told that there was an actual town Pyrene at the foot of the Pyrenees, today Port Vendres;[11] so that we need not perhaps, with Professor Sayce, accuse the historian of turning the range into a town, but it will be hard to explain what has become of the Rhone. Elsewhere (iv, 49) he repeats his statement about the Danube.

[11] So say How and Wells on ii, 33.

The Carpis and another river called the Alpis also flow northward from the country north of the Ombrikoi[12] to issue into it (the Ister); for the Ister traverses the whole of Europe, rising among the Celts who, save only the Cynetes, are the most westerly dwellers in Europe; and, flowing thus clean across Europe, it issues forth along the borders of Scythia.

Here Carpathians and Alps seem to disappear as the Rhone has, or at least to lend their names to rivers. No one who has studied even a little the early geography of America will want abruptly to deny that there were rivers Carpis and Alpis. But a Cambridge man need hardly go to America for illustration, when through his town there lingers a slow stream, formerly known as the Rhee, and in part still familiar as the Granta, a stream never called Cam till the sixteenth century, when Grantabridge worn down to Cambridge suggested it.[13] The general slightness of Herodotus' acquaintance with the West may explain his insistence that he knows of no such islands as the Cassiterides, in one of the very few passages of his book that suggest a shade (or more than a shade) of annoyance (iii, 115).

II

"Phrygians" Sir William Ramsay has said, "bulked more impressively in the Greek mind than any other non-Greek monarchy" till the Mermnad dynasty came to the throne of Lydia. But, in the times of which Herodotus writes, the Lydian power

[12] Cf. i, 94, where among the Ombrikoi the Lydians settle and take the name of Etruscan. It is the Umbria of the Romans.

[13] See Atkinson and Clark, *Cambridge Described and Illustrated*, p. 5.

for five reigns carried on intermittent but frequent
wars with the Greeks of the Asian coast, acquired a
suzerainty over them, and then suddenly collapsed
before the Persian. The Phrygian is altogether on
the outer edge of the penumbra of his story; the
Lydian is an essential part of the story itself. Whatever ancient legends men may tell of Phoenician or
Trojan, "I will name him whom I know to have been
the first to do unprovoked wrong to the Greeks"
(i, 5); and he tells us that, as soon as Gyges came to
the throne, he led an army into the lands of Miletus
and Smyrna and took Colophon (i, 15).

Scholars today incline to the bold guess made
forty years ago by Professor Sayce that Lydia had
once been a Hittite satrapy, but this is not in Herodotus' survey. His one allusion to the Hittites, whom
the Greeks call Syrians, describes them as subjects
of the Medes (i, 72). His story begins, as he said,
with Gyges, though he alludes to the long years of
the dynasties of Atys and Herakles. The last of the
Herakleids was supplanted by Gyges about 670 B.C.
Asia Minor has always been a borderland between
Europe and Asia,[14]—the frontier sometimes at the
Hellespont, sometimes at Mount Taurus, and for
long bad years north and west of the Danube. To
this day it contains "the débris of many races."[15]
Into this borderland have pressed migrant tribes
from Europe,—Phrygian, Bithynian, Cimmerian,
Scythian, Galatian,—and from Asia, great empires,
great raiders, and barbarian tribes like the Turks.
In the eighth and seventh centuries, as we saw, the
Cimmerian invaders were breaking up every estab-

[14] See G. B. Grundy, *Great Persian War*, p. 7; from whom a good deal
of what follows is taken. Cf. also D. G. Hogarth, *Ionia and the East*, p. 75.
[15] Sir Edwin Pears, *Turkey and its people*, chap. XI, p. 246.

lished government.[16]   Phrygia went down before
them, and Lydia rose up to battle with them, led
at last by an able and energetic king in Gyges. How
Gyges became king, Herodotus tells us in a famous
tale,[17] which at least so far corroborates history as it
shows in Gyges a man of sense and a man of action;
the rest draws toward the Arabian Nights. When
Assyria failed to help him, Gyges set to work to
help himself and his country, and, though he fell
in his last battle against the raiders (657 B.C.), he had
done a good deal. He had established a dynasty
which made itself felt in Asia Minor for 130 or 140
years, a dynasty stable and rich, with a policy for
East and West which it steadily and successfully
pursued. It saw at last the end of the Cimmerians,
it survived the Scythians, it came to terms with the
Medes. The eclipse, which marked the settlement
with the Medes, and which the Greeks proudly tell
that Thales foretold (i, 74), is fixed for 28 May 585
B.C., and the kingdom lasted forty years more.
Westward Gyges pushed for the Aegaean—a line of
policy which his successors pursued.

So far in their history, unless we take Priam and
Minos as war-lords of great and consolidated empires,
—which, as we have seen, Herodotus hesitated to do
—the Greeks had not been face to face with any single
power of more significance than a big city or a large
horde of raiders. Egypt was far away and not in

[16] Cf. Pears, *Turkey and its people*, p. 253, "In presence of the constant stream of nomad immigrants, deterioration rapidly ensued."

[17] Nicolaus of Damascus (fragment 49) has a different account of how
Gyges became king, one more like normal history, but not necessarily
therefore more historical, though Radet, *La Lydie*, seems to prefer it.
There are also variants in Plato (the ring of Gyges, *Rep*. ii, 359D) and
Plutarch.

Aegaean politics. Now at last there stood Lydia, organized and rich, and in possession of a policy and of a
base of attack. The Lydian king held the interior,
enough of it united to be powerful; and all the roads
led down to isolated Greek sea towns—his "natural
ports," as a modern would say—towns cut off from
one another by the sea and by mountains, by their
history and by the Greek spirit. Nature had divided
them, the Lydian would rule them, and gradually he
did. The Ephesians were the first that Croesus
attacked, after coming to the throne about 560 B.C.,
"and afterwards he made war on the Ionian and
Aeolian cities in turn, each on a separate pretext"
(i, 26), till he "had subdued and made tributary to
himself all the Asiatic Greeks of the mainland"
(i, 27). The Greeks had a story to tell as to how Bias
of Priene, or Pittacus of Mitylene, headed him off
from attacking the islanders. But the king, who made
friends with Delphi, was perhaps equal to being
grateful for advice which he did not need—an art
which may explain a good many episodes at the
Persian court. Landward Croesus "subdued well
nigh all the nations west of the Halys, except only
the Cilicians and the Lycians" (i, 29).

But the consolidated kingdom did more than
subjugate the Greeks. It gave them an idea of
wealth which they had not known since the dark
ages swept away the throne of Agamemnon. Greeks,
with more feeling for comedy than chronology, told
how Alcmaeon, the Athenian, was offered by Croesus
as much gold as he could carry away at one time on
his own person. So Alcmaeon

put on a large tunic, leaving a deep fold in the tunic to hang
down in front, and he drew on his feet the widest boots
which he could find, and so went to the treasury where they

led him. He threw himself on a heap of gold dust; and first he packed in by his shins as much gold as the boots would hold, and then he filled the whole fold of the tunic with gold, and he sprinkled the hair of his head with gold dust, and some more in his mouth. Thus he went forth of the treasury, dragging along his boots with difficulty, and looking like anything rather than a human being; for his mouth was stuffed full and every part of him padded out. Laughter fell upon Croesus when he saw him, and he gave him all that and more still. So that house became rich exceedingly; and this Alcmaeon set up a four-horse-chariot and won the Olympia (vi, 125).

Perhaps Alcmaeon's family had a less amusing but more historical account to give of the source of their wealth, but the story is illuminative. Croesus was rich and he used his riches in making friends for himself in Greece; and a good century later Delphi had a friendly memory of him, and could quote oracles to show how Apollo convinced the king of his superiority as a prophet, and some others to show that oracles may be misinterpreted.

The suggestion has been made that the Alc-maeonid wealth came from trade with Asia Minor, and particularly with Lydia. The stories of Samos and Miletus are full of references to trade,—to Samian pottery, Milesian fabrics, and oil. Even Thales is recorded to have made a corner in oil-presses in anticipation of a better season than his neighbours expected. They had reproached him with his poverty; but, when the olive harvest came on and many wanted the presses all at once, he let them out at any rate he pleased and made a quantity of money. Thus, says Aristotle, he showed the world that philosophers can easily be rich if they like, but that their ambition is of another sort.[18] Herodotus has two very striking things to say of Lydian interest

[18] Aristotle, *Politics*, I, 11, 8-10, p. 1259a.

in trade. The Lydians "were the first men (known to us) who coined and used gold and silver currency, and they were the first retail traders" (i, 94). Historians tell us that retail trade was common enough in Egypt and Babylon at an earlier date; but Herodotus gives us the Greek view of the Lydians, a nation of shopkeepers, who had practices still more shameful. It has been suggested that the rôle of the Lydians, as of the Phoenicians, was to receive influences from other peoples, to assimilate them and to transmit.[19] But, be that as it may, whether they invented coinage or adroitly adopted the idea, with them Herodotus associates it; and there is much to be said for the modern estimate that few single inventions have had so much influence upon the history of the world.[20] It was soon adopted by Persians and by Greeks, and coin quickly changed the economic relations of every Greek city, and of every class in each city. Coin and armour, the twin products of advancing metallurgy, transformed Greek politics and made democracy possible and inevitable.

Wealth and a certain progress in art[21] and music,[22] combined with conquest, made Lydia an influence, which in morals and tone showed the Orient,—an eastern conception of woman and an eastern theory of monarchy. Croesus was not in the same category as the kings of Sparta; whether they had one vote each or two on the Gerusia, the Lydian king was free of such an encumbrance. Greece had to face

[19] Radet, *La Lydie*, pp. 268, 273.

[20] G. B. Grundy, *Great Persian War*, p. 20.

[21] Pliny, *Natural History*, vii, 57, 6 quotes Aristotle for their early achievement in brass founding.

[22] Anacreon fr. 17, the Lydian *magades* with twenty chords and Plato, *Rep.* 398 E.

in Lydia despotism on a great scale, and the Asiatic Greek went down before it. The Lydians are said to have given the Greeks the word *tyrannos*, and, more certainly, another political term. *Medism* tells its own story; when the rumour of the Medes reached the Aegaean, the Greek patriot *Medized*; any power that would break Lydia was contributing to Greek freedom. At first the change from Mede to Persian in the great menace from the far East escaped notice, and the old word remained. The shrewder politicians of the Greek cities had learned their lesson from the truce of 28 May 585 B.C. (the day of the eclipse). In spite of the overtures of Cyrus (i, 141), in the language of modern diplomacy, they put their money on the wrong horse. They believed in the permanence of Lydia and disbelieved in Persia; they stood by Croesus till too late. They lost their market, and were forcibly subdued and put safely under Greek tyrants (i, 161 ff.). At Miletus people were wiser, or were luckier after the event; for Cyrus allowed them the same terms as they had from Lydia.[23] The mistake of the rest was natural, and Mr. Grundy says that "the sudden collapse of Lydia is one of the most remarkable incidents in history."[24] It was one of the least expected, and it ruined the reputation of the Lydians with posterity.

Once again it is well to remember what a world of hard fighting Herodotus reveals in Asia Minor. In spite of the doubts of Herodotus, the Ionians were fighters. The old line of Anacreon,

> Long since in war's alarms
> Milesians shone in arms—[25]

[23] Herodotus, i, 141, 169.
[24] *Great Persian War*, p. 28.
[25] Aristophanes, *Plutus*, 1003; Athenaeus, xii, 26.

was used to imply a change; but the power which had
impressed itself on the Hellespont and the Black Sea,
and lined the shores with "splendid colonies," was no
mean one. It had taken Lydia some generations to be
mistress of the littoral, but she had beaten down all
resistance at last, and had survived Cimmerian and
Scythian attacks. Wise after the event, Greeks told
how a certain Lydian, the sage Sandanis, counselled
Croesus:

> O king, you prepare to march against men who wear
> breeches of leather, and the rest of their gear is leather,
> and they eat not what they would but what they have;
> for their land is rough. And moreover they use not wine
> but are water-drinkers, nor have they figs nor anything
> else that is good. Now, first, if you conquer them, of what
> will you deprive them, who have nothing? and, second,
> if . . . . (i, 71).

Herodotus bears witness to the fighting capacity
of the Lydians: "At that time there was no nation in Asia more valiant or warlike than the Lydians.
It was their custom to fight on horseback, they
carried long spears, and they were skilled in the
management of horses"²⁶ (i, 79).

Croesus crossed the Halys—in the momentous
phrase of the oracle. He drove the Syrians out of
their homes "though they had done him no harm"
(i, 76). He fought a stubborn but indecisive battle
with Cyrus in the country near Pterie. Cyrus did not
attack next day; and Croesus, whose army was much
the smaller, fell back on Sardis to make preparations
for renewing the war five months later. But Cyrus
was not inclined to wait so long, and "himself
brought word of his arrival" to Croesus. A second

²⁶ The same is implied in his story of i, 27. Radet, *La Lydie*, p. 43,
also speaks of the horse on Lydian monuments.

battle was fought on the plain outside Sardis, where
the cavalry of Croesus seemed to promise much.
But Cyrus knew some natural history, or Harpagus
did, coming from the East. They put all the baggage
camels in front of the Persian line; for "horses fear
camels and can endure neither the sight nor the smell
of them," and, as was expected, the Lydian horses
bolted and "all Croesus' hope was lost. Nevertheless, the Lydians were no cowards; when they saw
what was happening, they leaped from their horses
and fought the Persians on foot" (i, 80). Modern
travellers tell of the same nervousness of the horse
about the camel.[27] Polybius has a curious parallel.[28]
At the battle of Raphia in 217 B.C. most of Ptolemy's
elephants, he says, as is the way with Libyan elephants, shirked the fight; for they cannot endure the
smell or the trumpeting of the Indian elephant. He
supposes that they are afraid of the size and strength
of the Indian animal, though one would have guessed
that the African was the heavier. Whatever the
reason, Ptolemy's elephants bolted at once and threw
his guard into disorder.

Cyrus won the battle, and it was not long before
he took Sardis, and its king with it. Herodotus tells
us that Cyrus at first proposed to burn Croesus alive,
that he might know if any deity would save him;
that Croesus recalled Solon's saying that none should
be called happy while he yet lived, and cried aloud the
sage's name; that Cyrus asked what it meant, and
then repented of his purpose, bethinking himself
"that he being but a man was burning another man
alive, once his equal for good fortune; moreover he

[27] Cf. P. M. Sykes, *History of Persia*, Vol. I, p. 146, note; and D. G.
Hogarth, *Wandering Scholar in the Levant*, p. 46.
[28] Polybius, v, 84.

feared retribution and reflected that nothing is stable in human affairs." He ordered the fire to be extinguished, but too late; then the god in answer to prayer drenched the pyre with violent rain. Croesus lives on through many a pleasant page, the companion and adviser of Cyrus. When Bacchylides' *Odes* were recovered from the Egyptian papyrus in 1896, another version of the story appeared. Croesus himself "not minded to await the further woe of grievous slavery, caused a pyre to be built. . . . he mounted thereon with his true wife and his daughters with beauteous locks who wailed inconsolably." He called on the god, resolved to die, but as soon as the pyre was lit,

Zeus brought a dark rain-cloud above it and began to quench the yellow flame. Nothing is past belief that is wrought by the care of the gods. Then Delos-born Apollo carried the old man to the Hyperboreans with his daughters of slender ankle, and there gave him rest, in requital of his piety; because of all mortals he had sent up the largest gifts to divine Pytho.

The historians who appear to confirm the story of Herodotus may merely derive it from him, though Ctesias often preferred to contradict him at all costs. Bacchylides is the older authority, and a red-figured vase, dating from the end of the sixth or the beginning of the fifth century B.C.—made before Herodotus was born—pictures the scene with Croesus pouring a libation and every suggestion of its being a voluntary end.[29] It is suggested that the one tale comes from Delphi, and the other from Delos, though Bacchylides' mentions both. It is urged that a Persian would not pollute fire with a dead body; but Cyrus appears not to have been so thorough a

[29] See Sir Richard Jebb, on Bacchylides, *Ode* iii, p. 195.

Zoroastrian as Darius. It is pointed out that self-immolation by fire was the end of Hercules in the myth, and of the last king of Assyria and of Hamilcar in history; and in the connexion between Lydian kings (of another house) and Hercules under various forms and names a special reason is sought for Croesus' regarding death in the flames as appropriate.[30] In any case Herodotus, with his historical principles, may be credited with not inventing for himself the version he gives; he may well have known the other, and preferred what he has given us, a tale more full of marvel, obviously, and not without a moral (more than one in fact), and, to rise to a higher plane of criticism, a tale more fragrant with wise and genial humanity. What reader but likes Cyrus and Croesus better, as he overhears their talks in the years of their consorting?

The customs of the Lydians, says Herodotus (i, 94), are like those of the Greeks, with one marked and happy exception. A hundred years of intercourse in war and peace and under suzerainty had brought that about. One might call it the earliest beginnings of that more general Hellenization of Asia Minor which went on so effectively under Alexander and his successors. The influence was not all on one side. Possibly the Ionians, and Thales among them,[31] first at Sardis became acquainted with the elements of Babylonian astronomy, which the Greeks were to transcend.[32] Certainly Xenophanes saw Lydian in-

---

[30] Sir James G. Frazer, *Adonis Attis Osiris*, p. 89.

[31] Thales, cf. Herodotus, i, 74.

[32] Burnet, *Greek Philosophy*, I, p. 19, with some caution, and Gomperz, *Greek Thinkers*, I, p. 532, suggest that Thales may have touched Babylonian astronomy in Lydia; Dreyer, *Planetary Systems*, p. 12, prefers Egypt as the source.

fluence on another side of life. "They," he says of his countrymen,

learnt dainty and unprofitable ways from the Lydians, so long as they were free from hateful tyranny, and went to the market place with cloaks all of purple—yes! a thousand, no less, at once—vainglorious and proud of their comely tresses, reeking with fragrance from cunning salves.[33]

Alcman and Sappho have hints in the same direction, and speak of articles of luxury that were of Lydian origin. Plato would banish Lydian music from his ideal state, soft or drinking harmonies, the Ionian and the Lydian, of the type called "relaxed."[34] Stimulus to thought came to Greece more richly from another quarter.

III

"Concerning Egypt," says Herodotus (ii, 35)

I will lengthen my tale, because it has more wonders than all the world beside, and shows works beyond speech to match all the world. For this reason more shall be said about it. The Egyptians have at once a climate peculiar to themselves, and in their river one that is different in nature from all other rivers; and even so have they made themselves customs and laws contrary to those of all other men. Among them the women buy and sell, the men abide at home and weave; and whereas in weaving all others push the woof upwards, the Egyptians push it down. As for burdens, men carry them on their heads, and women on their shoulders. They do their easement within doors and eat abroad in the streets, and they give the reason that things unseemly but necessary should be done in secret, things not unseemly openly. No woman is dedi-

[33] Fragment 3, Diels, *Fragmente der Vorsokratiker*, and Burnet, *Early Greek Philosophers*, p. 130.
[34] Plato, *Rep.* 398 E.

cated to the service of any god or goddess; men are dedicated to all gods and all goddesses. Sons are not compelled
against their will to support their parents, but daughters
must do so of necessity even against their will. Everywhere
else the priests of the gods wear their hair long; in Egypt
they are shaven. Among other men, when the dead are
mourned, it is custom for those most concerned to have
their heads shaven; Egyptians are shaven at other times,
but after a death they let their hair and beard grow.
Other men have their daily living separate from their
animals, the Egyptians live with theirs. Other men live
on wheat and barley; to an Egyptian, who lives on these,
it is the greatest reproach, but they make food from a
coarse grain which some call spelt. They knead dough
with their feet and clay with their hands, and they will
use their hands to pick up dung. The Egyptians, and those
who have learnt it from them, are the only people who
practise circumcision. Every man of them has two garments, every woman one. The rings and sheets of sails
are made fast elsewhere outside the boat, but inside it in
Egypt. The Greeks write characters and reckon with
pebbles, moving the hand toward the right, but Egyptians
from right to left; yet all the same they say their way of
writing is toward the right and the Greek way to the left.
They use two kinds of letters; one is called sacred and the
other common. They are beyond measure religious, far
more than any other nation.

To Professor Sayce's views of Herodotus and his
travels we need not again refer. Mr. Llewelyn Griffith leans as a critic of Herodotus to the sterner side,
but with moderation.[35] He remarks that the art of
travel, as now practised, was then unknown and that
we do not find in Herodotus the definite pictures of
sights and scenes, photographed on the memory,
such as modern travellers give us. (This is not all
loss by the way.) He holds, as others have held, that
Herodotus was "entirely dependent on cicerones"
for what he saw and what he heard; just as a tourist
in a cathedral is apt to see and hear what the verger

[35] In *Authority and Archaeology* (1899), pp. 162-190.

chooses; "the few keen or critical observations" which Herodotus gives us may have been suggested to him by his guides or companions; and, broadly, that his story has a great deal that is wrong in it and leaves out much that we should have valued. He admits the great debt of gratitude which Egyptologists owe him and that he wins their affection, and that he probably had not "more than an ordinary share of absurdity poured into his ears." Indeed, here as elsewhere, what Herodotus reports has often given modern research a useful clue. That a traveller, so fond of human beings and their talk as Herodotus, should have confined himself to guides or to the hereditary interpreters whom he mentions (the Greek-speaking Egyptians, ii, 154), and whose interpretation of an inscription he well remembers (ii, 125), and a very absurd one too, is not very likely. So much Mr. Griffith admits. But he frequented the company of Greeks and Carians, long domiciled in the country, as his language distinctly implies:—"it comes of our intercourse with these settlers in Egypt (long ago in King Psammetichus' time) that we Greeks have accurate knowledge of the history of Egypt from the reign of Psammetichus onward; for they were the first men of alien speech domiciled in the country" (ii, 154). He says quite explicitly that he *saw* things,[36] that he *heard* this or that at such a place;[37] and once he adds "I have nothing to say but what was told me" by the priests of Sais; his own observation showed him that they were "talking nonsense" (ii, 130, 131). This may be called discriminating quotation. He is quite definite in divid-

---

[36] E.g., ii, 5; 12; 97; 99; 127 (he measured a pyramid); 147; 148.
[37] E.g., ii, 10; 99; 147.

ing up his material, "so far it is my own sight and judgment and inquiry that speak; from this point I come to Egyptian stories, which I shall tell as I heard them, adding a little from my own sight" (ii, 99); and by and by he marks a third section: "This is what Egyptians themselves say; I now pass to what is recorded alike by Egyptians and foreigners, adding a little from my own sight" (ii, 147).

Why he should be supposed to owe his "keen or critical observations" to the interpreters or to his friends, domiciled in Egypt, it is hard to conjecture. He had seen more of the world than most men; and that he was fairly capable of making such observations himself, his History surely bears sufficient witness.

We have thus something that is really of far more interest and far higher value than exact information, given objectively, of Egypt about 450 B.C. We have the reaction of Egypt on the general Greek mind, expressed by a man of singular sensitiveness, solid honesty and real sympathy, who was intensely interested in Egypt and rather more apt to overvalue Egyptian ideas than to undervalue them.[38] The country and the climate, the people and the animals, were a constant surprise and challenge, very much as Japan with its customs and Australia with its fauna have challenged the modern traveller. The common instinct is to prefer one's own customs; the English were long in discarding the silk hat in India. "If it were proposed to all nations to choose the best customs

[38] How and Wells on ii, 2, call him "a philo-Egyptian," and in their Introduction ((Vol. I, p. 14) quote Bauer's description of his attitude in the Egyptian book as "Anti-Hellenic"—a judgment which they appear to endorse in a note referring to iv, 36; 95; 96. I would not put it at all so strongly.

from all the customs of men, each group would on inquiry choose its own; so well is each persuaded that its own are by far the best" (iii, 38). Yet Egypt has the priority in everything; Egypt knew the names of the gods first (ii, 50) and first taught immortality (ii, 123); Egypt first had a well determined and really workable calendar (ii, 4); Egyptian physicians were many and were specialists (ii, 84; iii, 1); Egypt was again and again the teacher of Greece, though some Greeks do not know the fact, and others were interested in concealing it (ii, 82, 123). To his interest in the climate, the river, the animals and the religion, we must return at later points.

The immense ancient history of Egypt impressed Herodotus. He did not know the whole of it; archaeologists are continually discovering facts and situations and whole eras that are new to us. But the great span of years that Egyptian story covered, and that Egyptian geology required, were in sharp contrast with the short annals of the Greeks. Homer and Hesiod he considered, as we saw, to have lived only four hundred years before himself (ii, 53); and in the history of those four centuries there were huge gaps.

If the Nile shall choose to turn his stream into the Arabian gulf, what hinders that, as his stream runs, the gulf should not be silted up within twenty thousand years? Nay, I think myself it would be silted up within ten thousand. Is it then to be believed that in the ages before my birth a gulf even much greater than this could not be made into land by a river so great and so busy? (ii, 11).

But the recorded history of Egypt, so he was told by the priests, exceeded ten thousand years.

Hecataeus the historian was once at Thebes, and told his pedigree and connected his lineage with a god in the sixteenth generation. And the priests of Zeus did for him what they did for me, though I told them no pedigree of mine. They brought me into the great inner court of the temple and showed me there wooden figures which they counted up to the number that I mentioned (viz., three hundred and forty-one, ii, 142); for every high priest sets up there in his lifetime an image of himself. Counting and pointing them out, the priests showed me that each inherited from his father, going through them all from the image of him who died last, till they displayed them all. (ii, 143).

And in not one of the three hundred and forty-five generations, not once in the 11,340 years which they covered, had there been a king who was a god in human form, or before or after them, though before them the gods had indeed ruled Egypt; and they did not believe that a man could be begotten by a god. They told him what was as remarkable, however,— that four times in those 11,340 years "the sun rose contrary to his wont; twice he rose where he now sets, and twice he set where he now rises; yet Egypt at these times underwent no change, neither in the produce of the river and the land, nor in the matter of sickness and death." There seems to be a mistake here somewhere; perhaps the priests translated badly or misunderstood their traditions. In any case both they and Herodotus seem to have fallen short of Heraclitus' conception of law—"the sun will not transgress his bounds; otherwise the Erinnyes, aiders of Justice, will find him out"[39]— unless we are to suppose that the sun is uniformly driven by winds from his customary course (ii, 24).

But does the extreme antiquity, the ancient settled order, of Egypt really matter? "Better fifty years of Europe than a cycle of Cathay," says the

[39] Diels, *Vorsokratiker*, Heraclitus fr. 94.

Victorian young man in Tennyson's poem. The
real value of the discovery of the age of Egypt is at
least twofold. It shows the original history of
civilization; where Greek belief or culture overlapped,
it was not here as with the Lydians a case of mutual
influence; the Egyptians "keep the ordinances of
their fathers and add none other to them" (ii, 79);
"the Egyptian ceremonies are manifestly very
ancient and the Greek are of late origin" (ii, 58).
The Greeks have borrowed, that is the true history
of civilization; from which it follows that they may
borrow again. Further, the presence in the world of
a civilization, an order and a tradition so old, meant
something further, hard to put into words. The
Greek was battling with disorder and change in a
world where all was flux. To him, as Mr. J. A. K.
Thomson lately suggested, not disorder, unchartered
freedom, the ancient rule of Rob Roy, was romantic,
as the young men's revolt against the eighteenth
century persuaded Europe in the Romanticist
Revival; but rather the victory of Cosmos over Chaos,
of an ordered society over "anarchy with its democratic voice" (δημόθρους ἀναρχία).[40] Herodotus, as we
have seen and shall see again, loved liberty, but
Egypt may well have suggested to him what Sparta
clearly suggested later on to Plato, that a thought-out
system of society has advantages as against one
swinging loose among Hecataean gods and Pindaric
demigods, high-born athletes and cultured tyrants,
and the casual improvisations of Ionian republics.

[40] Aeschylus, *Agamemmon*, 883. There are features in the new cities
of the prairies which the European, with centuries of order behind him,
finds conventional and trivial, but the resident admires them, as sym-
bols of his victory over wild nature.

Any race may be sure that its own customs are best, and can be sure of it without reflection. But an ancient civilization, different in principle, in conception, from king and priest down to weaver and brickmaker following other ways, and quite good ways, a contrast in every detail of life, and yet a successful expression of the human spirit—my language grows too modern and abstract—such a civilization may say nothing to the unreflective, but to the thoughtful there is no end to its wealth of suggestion. It means the quiet rethinking of all life. Scythian customs differed from Greek, and it hardly mattered, though even Scythians could on occasion make stimulating criticisms of Greek ideas (iv, 79).[41] Scythian life was savage and undeveloped; but Egypt had been a civilized and ordered land ten millenniums before Homer.

"The Egyptians are divided into seven classes, severally entitled priests, warriors, cowherds, swineherds, retail dealers, interpreters and pilots. So many classes there are, each named after its vocation. The warriors are divided" into two groups, whose members "may practise no trade but only war, which is their hereditary calling" (ii, 164, 166). He implies that the other trades are hereditary, for at a later period he returns to it;

in this the Spartans are at one with the Egyptians, for their heralds and flute-players and cooks inherit their trades from their fathers, and flute-player is the son of flute-player, cook of cook, and herald of herald; other men do not lay hands on the office because they have loud and clear voices and so shut them out of it, but they practise their craft by inheritance from their fathers (vi, 60).

[41] See p. 149.

That the Egyptians had this caste system was the general belief of the Greeks, and as foreigners sometimes do, they systematized it more than the Egyptians would seem to have done, at least in earlier periods.

Whether this separation, like other customs, has come to Greece from Egypt, I cannot definitely decide. I see that Thracians, Scythians, Persians, Lydians, and nearly all the barbarians have less esteem for those citizens who learn trades and for their offspring than for others, and count as honourable those who are free from artisan work with the hands, and particularly those who are free to practise war. At all events this has been learnt by all the Greeks and especially the Lacedaemonians. The Corinthians have least contempt for artisans (ii, 167).

Contempt for hand workers is not quite the caste system, it is social, not religious; but Herodotus noted, or heard, with astonishment another thing: "No Egyptian man or woman will kiss a Greek man, or use a knife or a spit or a caldron belonging to a Greek, or taste the flesh of an unblemished ox that has been cut up with a Greek knife" (ii, 41). He is not very clear about the reason he assigns, but so much is evident, that he associates the exclusiveness with religion. The Greeks had been in Egypt for two hundred years and were still unclean, as Europeans and Americans are *Mleccha* in India to this day. This Egyptian attitude and their worship of animals, the embalming of dead cats, and the decoration of living crocodiles (ii, 69), the Greeks found it hard to understand. But the full and interesting accounts which Herodotus gives of their practices in regard to sacred animals, we must pass over. His curious eye "observed exactly those things which are of special interest to us," says a modern Egyptologist.[42]

[42] See Erman, *Handbook of Egyptian Religion*, pp. 175-181.

The adventures of the Greek settlers in Egypt did not escape his sympathetic attention, and what a story they make! From the bronze men who appeared and ravaged the land, the first Carians and Ionians, whom Psammetichus (664-610 B.C.) recognized as fulfilling the prediction and whom he enlisted on the spot with the happiest results in his own permanent ascendancy (ii, 152),—to the Egyptian reaction under Amasis (569-526 B.C.), who was sagacious enough to head a nationalist movement and yet to maintain and reëstablish the foreigner in the land, to appear to restrict the Greeks' privilege of trading as they would and to give them a "concession" at Naucratis (ii, 178) where a Greek city of real importance developed,[43]—we trace the fortunes of the adventurers. There is constant coming and going, and the colony (if we may use the word in a restricted modern sense) had its own traditions, which would have made a companion volume to Mr. Busteed's lively book *Echoes from Old Calcutta*, with Rhodopis perhaps for Madame Talleyrand (ii, 134, 135). Some Greeks said she built herself a pyramid with a base 280 feet square, but Herodotus saw that that was nonsense. She was the subject of many stories; she came into Sappho's poetry as Herodotus says; and Strabo (C. 808) preserves a Cinderella-like story about an eagle swooping off with her slipper and dropping it into the king's lap at Memphis; and she appears to have become confused with a rosy-cheeked sphinx that haunted the pyramids and survives in Arab legend. After this it seems a little dull to say that Sappho's brother, her

---

[43] Breasted, *History of the Ancient Egyptians*, p. 412.

lover, was in the wine trade,[44] of which Herodotus has something interesting to tell us about the jars[45] (iii, 6). The historian says that, if any one wishes to know what the exact wealth of Rhodopis was, he may calculate it from the tenth she dedicated at Delphi. Once more we may remark the skill and charm with which he crowds his pages with information—life, trade, poetry, scandal—and all lightly and incidentally woven into a digression.

We may digress ourselves at this point and recall that Naucratis and other Greek sites in Egypt have been examined, Naucratis itself several times. A graveyard of foreign mercenaries has been found at Nebesheh, where the dead lie with their heads to the east, contrary to the Egyptian practice of laying them to the west. Sherds of pottery and spear-heads date these burials between 650 and 500 B.C.[46] More interesting still, in the excavation of the Greek temple (*temenos*) in 1903 the base of a vase was found with broken letters round it, thus: H . . Δ O T O Y. [47] No Greek had an assured monopoly of a name, where none had more than one, but it is attractive to think that the vase was dedicated by the man we think of, and handled by the fingers that wrote the book.

[44] Strabo says he brought Lesbian wine to Naucratis.

[45] Compare the secondary uses of kerosene tins all over India.

[46] W. M. Flinders Petrie, *Journal of Hellenic Studies*, Vol. X, 1890, p. 273.

[47] D. G. Hogarth and others, *Journal of Hellenic Studies*, Vol. XXV, 1905, p. 116.

IV

Egypt, when Herodotus visited it, had been for some years a peaceful province of the Persian. The battle at Papremis was long ago, and the bones and skulls of the fallen allowed him to make a deduction as to the effect of the sun on the shaven Egyptian head (iii, 12). A Persian authority watched over the old Egyptian dam at Memphis (ii, 99). Of the old royal houses we hear legends and traditions, but nowhere is it implied that Herodotus met Egyptians of family or nobility. His observations are mainly of customs of daily life and dress, of polite manners (ii, 80), food taboos (ii, 18; 37; 47), cleanliness (ii, 37), mummies and the care of the dead, and above all, religion. Politically Egypt was extinct, a province; and apart from such matters as have just been summarized, the most interesting people perhaps in Egypt were Persians. Here as always we take the Greeks for granted.

It is preëminently for his references to the Persians that Plutarch calls Herodotus a lover of barbarians; and admiration is to be read and felt not only in his general account of them but again and again as he tells his story. Like Xenophon and Alexander, he was impressed with the character of the Persian noble, his bearing, his manliness and frankness. Their very names are "like their bodily shape and their nobility" (i, 139)—long names with something about them that suggests magnificence. It is not often that we find a Greek confessing to feeling the lure and music of a foreign name, though

Aeschylus clearly knew it; what they would have said
to Anglo-Saxon monosyllabic names, abridged or
complete, it is better not to guess. The Persian
habits of courtesy and respect impress him (i, 134),—
more even, we might say, than the Egyptian (ii, 80).
Greek manners, we may on the whole conclude, were
bad,[48] quite apart from the Cleons. The emphasis
which Xenophon lays on the manners of the young
Spartan, his modesty, his deference to his elders, his
resemblance to the English public school boy,[49] seems
to suggest that at Athens, as elsewhere, the democratic child was father to the democratic man, and
shared his manners, as Plato hints, with slave and
donkey. In Persia it was different. "After valour
in battle, it is reckoned as manly merit to show the
greatest number of sons; the King sends gifts yearly
to him who can show most. Numbers, they hold, are
strength. They teach their sons from five years old to
twenty, three things only—to ride the horse, to
shoot with the bow and tell the truth" (i, 136). "Of
what they may not do, they may not even speak.
Lying is among them the most shameful thing, and,
next to that, debt—for many reasons and especially,
they say, because the debtor is bound to lie to some
extent" (i, 138). The training made men,—men like
Pharnabazos whom Xenophon obviously liked, men
like the nobles who appealed to Alexander, men like
the Persian friends of Herodotus.

He realized to the full the spirit and courage of
the Persian, who in a linen tunic would face the

---

[48] So the Romans thought too; see Mahaffy, *Silver Age of the Greek
World*, pp. 169-171; *humeris gestum agebant* (Cicero, *pro Rabirio Post.*,
36).

[49] See Xenophon, *Republic of Lacedaemonians*, 3, 4-6.

heavily-mailed Spartan hoplite and fight as bril-
liantly as he did, and at such a disadvantage (ix, 62).
He recognized their chivalry and munificence; even
of Xerxes he has stories to tell that would make any
one like the King. Darius was a greater man than
any of their kings; and when he would have set up
his statue by that of Sesostris in Egypt, the priest of
Hephaestus forbade it; Sesostris had subdued the
Scythians, and many more nations, and Darius had
not subdued the Scythians. "Which speech, they
say, Darius took in good part" (ii, 110). The story
may be an invention of Egyptian vanity, as is suggested; but it is well invented and it struck Herodotus
as right, it squared with his conception of that Great
King's character. Why should he quote that other
tale of Cyrus, which also may be legend, how the
King described the Greek agora, "a place set apart
for people to go and cheat each other on oath"
(i, 153)? He admires the Persian administration of
their vast empire; and his account of it in its detail
is one of the additions that his tale sought out. He
tells their legends and tells them well, as Spiegel
assures us; and he knew their history, far better than
some of his critics allowed, as Darius' own inscription
on the rock of Behistun has proved. Their queens
and princesses come into his pages—queens indeed,
wicked it may be and savage-hearted, but the kind of
women that Greece never knew till the Ptolemies
reigned. Herodotus presumably never saw one of
them, but like Aeschylus he knew how to draw
Atossa.[50] Rawlinson was right when he wrote of the
historian's feelings for the Persians:—"their valour,
their simplicity and hardiness, their love of truth,

[50] Perhaps Medea owes something to Persian queens.

their devoted loyalty to their princes, their wise customs and laws are spoken of with a sincerity and strength of admiration which marks his superiority to the narrow spirit of national prejudice."[51] A man can be known by what he admires, and his picture of the Persian reveals Herodotus.

Herodotus was a good Greek; he believed in Hellenic liberty and it is hard to think of a better book to teach the young to love freedom, heroism, and self-sacrifice. Persia and Greece were in conflict, as other peoples have been in conflict, both sides intelligibly. He does not make the mistake of vilifying the enemy; "vituperation," wrote an English soldier about 1916, "is a civilian's trade." He respects the Persian and likes him; and the verdict of historians is with him.[52] The Zend-Avesta had inculcated truth; Darius emphasizes it in the Behistun inscription, not speaking as an abstract moralist, but more naturally and showing his attitude. It is often doubted whether any people can be trusted long to govern another. The Roman did it well, if with lapses. We shall have to note lapses in the Persian, but if we compare his government with that of the Semite whom he replaced, with that of the Turk who rules his lands today, and there are others with which we might compare it—the Persian's achievement is high. He was no Assyrian, even when he made war, still less as a ruler. Cyrus was a wise and sympathetic conqueror, and Darius an exceptionally able administrator. To the Persian religion we shall return; it

[51] Rawlinson, *Herodotus*, Vol. I, p. 80.
[52] G. B. Grundy, *Great Persian War*, p. 33; Rawlinson, *Ancient Monarchies*, Vol. III, p. 166; Eduard Meyer, *Gesch. des Altertums*, Vol. III, §§ 12, 21.

was fundamentally monotheistic, the doctrine of a prophet, intensely ethical, and based on clear thought. That it was corrupted by contact with the Semitic world is clear from the inscriptions of the kings that followed Darius, though he himself is judged to have been keenly Zoroastrian and a monotheist. It impressed Herodotus, as well it might. Greek religion was traditional, a popular development of animism, with little relation to conduct and perhaps none at all to truth; and Asia (apart from Judaism which was so far hardly known) had nothing to offer even on the Greek level. The Moslem swept Persia into the faith of Muhammad, but even yet at Yazd and Bombay Zoroaster's disciples maintain the faith he taught them, and with all the corruptions of ages of heathen contact it has still great elements.[53] The Magi, with whom it is associated, and the magic in which their name survives, are intruders, as Herodotus perhaps half realizes, neither Persian nor Zoroastrian.

If Lydia impressed the Greek mind, much more did the Persian power—the prowess of Persian arms, the sweep of their rule, and its character, the nature of the people, lovers of horses, of gardens and of truth. Later Greeks knew a contaminated Persia, probably of mixed blood, certainly a society and a faith confused and degraded by the practice of imperial rule, by compromise, and by the seductions of the Nearer East. No men are more apt, said Herodotus, to adopt foreign customs, and they took over too much from the lower races whom they had to rule. But his picture of the original Persian, the man of one God, who wore leather breeches, drank

---

[53] See the sympathetic and scholarly treatment of J. H. Moulton in his *Treasure of the Magi*.

water, rode horses, and told the truth, is an impressive one, and a true one. Of all peoples of the East, Persia has longest continued to contribute to European literature and thought. The people of Hafiz, Sadi, and Omar, the people of Zoroaster and of the Moslem mystics, has been a great people; and Herodotus, who knew none of these claims to greatness, knew that he was face to face with men, when he met and made friends of the Persians.

The foreigner, if more especially the Egyptian and the Persian, yet also the Indian, the Scythian, and the Libyan, gave the historian much—stimulus to thought, width in sympathy. He moved here and there in the world, and saw strange men with strange ways, different from those familiar to Greece but not wrong. Cambyses, he says, "commanded [in Egypt] the doing of a thing contrary to the custom of both peoples" (iii, 16); "I hold it in every way proved that Cambyses was very mad, else he would never have set himself to mock religion and custom" (iii, 38). He concludes that it is rightly said in Pindar's poem that Custom is King of all.[54] The conclusion sounds very conservative, but it does not represent his whole mind. Tolerant as he is and not easily shocked, he meets customs that disgust him. Again and again he recognizes the acceptance of foreign ways by one people and another, of Median dress, of Carian weapons, of the religious ideas of Egypt. He notes foreign criticism of Greece, whether Persian or Scythian. The comment of Mardonius on the extreme folly of Greek warfare he sets out plainly:

they make war, as I hear, with utter want of counsel, in wrong-headedness and want of sense. For when they have

[54] Pindar, *fragment* 169; Plato, *Gorgias*, 484 B.

proclaimed war on one another, they find out first the fairest and most level ground, descend into it and fight, so that the victors come off with great harm. Of the defeated I say nothing at all; they are blotted out. Being men of one tongue, they ought to use heralds and messengers and settle their differences and do anything rather than fight; or if they must at all costs go to war, then they should find out where they are hardest to handle and try that way (vii, 9 b).

The criticism was right, but Greeks could never see their patches of good and level land harried; they had so little of it and lived on it. So they fought on in just this way till Rome stopped all their wars. The Scythians were properly conservative, and thought ill of Dionysus and his frenzied rites; "they make it a reproach against the Greeks, saying it is not reasonable to set up a god who leads men on to madness" (iv, 79). Perhaps the most striking criticism of Herodotus is one he does not make, except by silent contrast when he sets forth the purity and quiet and sense of Persian monotheism.

Greece has learnt from the barbarian and can yet learn, so he holds; but after all, and here once more history sustains him, "from the most ancient times the Hellenic has ever been distinguished from the barbarian stock by its greater cleverness, its freedom from trivial foolishness" (i, 60). There speaks the Greek—and the historian.

CHAPTER V
THE OUTER EDGES OF THE WORLD
I

"Doriscos is a sea-beach and a great plain in Thrace, and through it flows a great river, the Hebrus;" and there, on his way to Greece, Xerxes thought it convenient "to order his army and to number it throughout;" and Herodotus (vii, 59) tells how he did it, by marching troop after troop into an enclosure estimated to hold ten thousand men. The army filled it one hundred and seventy times. So, having given us the total and explained how it was reached, Herodotus sets forth in many pages what nations were there, sixty-one several peoples in all, equipped in some seventeen or eighteen styles from the full armour of the Greek vassals to the camels of the Arabs, the wild-ass chariots of the Indians, and the lassoes of the Sagartians (iii, 60-99). Taken with his accounts of the satrapies of the Persian Empire and of the Royal Road, it is our best authority for the ethnography of the Ancient East.[1] Whatever his ultimate authorities, it is a remarkable pageant, and it is a sure indication of the tastes and interests of the historian. He enjoyed it as he enjoyed his travels and his inquiries, seeing the cities of men and learning their minds.

We have already seen how Egyptians and Persians appealed to him, and we shall at a later point

[1] How and Wells on vii, 61; G. B. Grundy, *Great Persian War*, pp. 218-220.

return to his study of the religious ideas of the world. Here we shall be concerned with the picture that he made for himself of the world as he saw it and heard of it, with his views of climate and soil as affecting human life, with his interest in wild animals and the strange things of nature, and above all with the minds of savage men as reflected in their customs. At no point will our treatment be exhaustive, for he was not writing an encyclopaedia; that task he left to the duller ages of antiquity and to the modern world. But, when we are trying to learn the mind of a man, it is more significant to get the range of his interests than to ascertain how often he was accurate. A man's accuracy depends on two things: on his own conscience in describing "what he has himself seen and what he has learnt from others by the most careful and particular inquiry"[2] and on the conscience of others who report to him of what he could not see and what he cannot verify; and here, as we have seen, a man who has gone outside the ordinary round of experience is less apt to be incredulous than men of a narrower sphere subjected to fewer surprises.

Herodotus had not seen all the lands and peoples of which he speaks; he makes no such claim.[3] Here and there he says definitely that he has seen such and such things; "he went to see them," he says, and he did, at Tyre (ii, 44). Elsewhere he alludes to monuments or dedications that "were there till my time," which would seem to imply a visit in the case of a man so conscientious—as at Cyrene (ii, 181), where other indications suggest the same conclusion

[2] Thucydides, i, 22.
[3] On the range of his travels see Macan, *Herodotus* iv-vi, Vol. I, p. xciv; and also p. xcix for references that prove his knowledge of south Italy; and on book iv, 124 as to Scythia.

(ii, 192, 199). Now and then he describes the general look of a land. "When the Nile overflows the land, the towns alone are seen above it, most like of all things to the islands in the Aegean Sea. The rest of Egypt becomes an open sea, the cities alone stand out. So when this happens folk are ferried about not, as is their wont, in the course of the stream, but clean over the plain" (ii, 97). Another and more complicated comparison implies similar sight of his own eyes. He speaks of the so-called Rough Peninsula, inhabited by the Tauri; "This ends in the Eastern Sea [Azov]. For the sea to the south and the sea to the east are two of the four boundary lines of Scythia, even as the seas are the boundaries of Attica;" he compares small things, Sunium and the demes, with great; "but whoever has not coasted along that part of Attica, I will show it him in another way. It is as though in Iapygia some other people, and not the Iapygians, were to dwell on the promontory [the heel of Italy] within a line drawn from the harbour of Brentesion [Brindisi] to Taras [Tarentum]. Of these two countries I speak, but there are many others of a like kind which Tauris resembles" (iv, 99). That passage surely implies personal familiarity with all three promontories, though it is hardly the language of science. The Black Sea is "a sight worth seeing" (iv, 85) from the headland by the Cyanean rocks, it is so vast. His acquaintance with Colchians and his discussion of their physical characteristics suggest that he also saw the Black Sea from the eastern end of it (ii, 104),[4]

[4] See H. F. Tozer, *History of Ancient Geography*, p. 84 f. on the contrast of his elaborate account of Scythia with his slight knowledge of western Europe and on the implication of personal travel on the Hypanis (Bug) iv, 52, 81.

though a modern may find it hard to accept his theory that Colchians and Egyptians are one people. He speaks of information gathered by himself in Scythia (iv, 76, 81). He knew Thasos (vi, 47) and he seems to describe the lake dwellers of Lake Prasias from personal knowledge (v, 16). His migration to Italy is one of the few points in his own history generally attested by antiquity. But did he go much farther afield? He says, and Sayce denies, that in Egypt he reached Elephantine or Yeb (ii, 29); the Oxford scholar is good enough to hope that the word αὐτόπτης is an interpolation. Herodotus says that what he could tell about grain in Babylonia would be wholly disbelieved by those who have never visited the country (i, 193), which certainly suggests that he had been there himself. Perhaps he also saw Susa (vi, 119), though he does not definitely say so.

Twice at least he makes it clear that he has not himself visited regions to which he refers. If he had himself travelled in southern Gaul he would not have let the Danube cut across the Rhone, nor would he probably have missed the Rhone altogether (ii, 33). There he was speaking by report and depending on men who knew the Danube only from the Balkan end. When he says that for the Indians "the sun is hottest at dawn, not at midday as elsewhere, but from sunrise to the hour of market-closing," and that "as it grows to afternoon the sun becomes to them what it is to other men at dawn," (iii, 104) it is very certain that he never saw the sun in India. His statement that with the sinking of the sun the Indian day grows cooler, is less disputable, and his concluding clause that "at sundown it is very cold indeed" is at least relatively true in the Panjāb winter, as one finds at

Delhi, for instance, and on the night trains. His doubt as to a sea to the north of Europe is well based; "it is plain that none have obtained knowledge of its eastern or northern parts so as to say if it be encompassed by seas" (iv, 45); and "of the extremities of Europe toward the West I cannot speak with exactness" (iii, 115), so he lets them alone. Even Carthage appears to have lain outside his travels.[5]

II

His account of the Indian sun shows that he does not always stick to his rule, for it is obviously deduction from known fact rather than known fact, and here the known fact is wrong; experience had so far convinced men of the flatness of the earth over which the sun moved (v, 92, a); the inference followed and was also wrong.[6] He ridicules the circular world that others sketched: "I laugh to see how many have drawn maps of the world ($\gamma\hat{\eta}\varsigma\ \pi\epsilon\rho\iota\delta\delta o\nu\varsigma$) ere now, not one of them showing the matter reasonably; for they draw the earth as round as if fashioned by compasses [or, with a lathe], with Oceanus running round it, and Asia and Europe of like size" (iv, 36). But he himself falls into the same sort of temptation and makes the Nile and the Danube a good deal more symmetrical than they are; "as I guess" he adds, "reasoning as to things unknown from visible signs, the Nile takes its rise from the same measure of distance as the Danube" (ii, 33). He refuses to be-

[5] See How and Wells on vi, 181; Macan, iv-vi, Vol. II, p. 273.
[6] See Gomperz, *Greek Thinkers* (English translation), Vol. I, pp. 269-271; H. F. Tozer, *History of Ancient Geography*, p. 78.

lieve in Hyperboreans for two reasons: "if there be men beyond at the back of the North wind, then there are others at the back of the South wind," and this in the very chapter where he laughs at the round world (iv, 36). This reason does not seem very strong, but it follows a valid one. He has noticed that the Scythians and the northern peoples really know nothing of Hyperboreans; Hesiod speaks of them, and Homer (if Homer wrote the *Epigonoi*); but the people of Delos tell much more about them than does anybody else (iv, 33).

On astronomy he is very weak. Even arithmetic sometimes overtaxed him, as well it might with Greek systems of notation and nothing but the *abacus* to manage addition or subtraction. He is not very clear as to the true length of the year and the nature of the Greek systems of intercalation. Probably, like most of us, he let other people provide his almanack. In Solon's talk with Croesus he puts in an extra month every two years, and manages to get so many days into seventy years that with that month each year would have 375 days (i, 32). The Egyptians, he says (ii, 4), working from the stars, as they told him, made twelve months of 30 days and added five days every year—total 365. He knows that Thales foretold an eclipse (i, 74), but it is doubtful if Herodotus could have explained it. He rejects the Phoenician circumnavigation of Africa on astronomical grounds, which for a modern go far to prove it (iv, 42). He lays it down as a law that "after snow has fallen there must needs be rain within five days" (ii, 22), as English rustics say the weather breaks with the moon's changes. And, finally,

[7] See E. Meyer, *Geschichte des Altertums*, IV, 107, 108.

strangest notion of all, he thinks it may be possible that in winter the sun is driven by storms from his customary course (ii, 24).

With these theories, and quite untravelled himself in the interior of Russia, he will not believe in the Polar night, or, as he puts it, that "there are men, who sleep for six months of the twelve" (iv, 25). Of course, he is so far right, they do not sleep.[8] The Polar night goes, with the Northern Sea; and he will not have Ocean, in spite of Kolaios' voyage to Tartessus outside the Pillars. "The man who talked about Oceanus carried his tale into the unseen and needs no disproof; for I know of no one who has seen any river Oceanus, and I suppose that Homer or one of the poets before him invented the name and brought it into poetry" (ii, 23). Kolaios did not get into the unseen, but that there is a waterway to Tartessus does not prove an Oceanus running round the whole earth, nor give any clue to the extent of what we call the Atlantic. With Oceanus and the Northern Sea, he throws over two other famous western tales.

I do not believe there is a river, called by barbarians Eridanos, issuing into the Northern Sea, from which the amber is said to come,[9] nor have I any knowledge of Cassiterides (tin islands) from which tin comes to us. The very name Eridanos betrays itself as Greek and not barbarian and invented by some poet. Nor, though I took pains over it, can I hear from any one who has seen it that there is a sea beyond Europe. Anyhow the tin comes to us from the end of the earth (or of Europe) and the amber too (iii, 115).

[8] I venture on this very obvious remark, to have a chance of recommending Harry Whitney's fascinating book, *Hunting with the Eskimos*; where the author describes how busy that long night really is, particularly when the moon is full and makes hunting possible.

[9] Cf. Strabo, v, C. 215 τὸν Ἠριδανόν, τὸν μηδαμοῦ γῆς ὄντα.

As to the Cassiterides, British or Spanish, we need say nothing; Herodotus had no evidence as to their existence.[10] Legend brought tin and amber from the unknown, and just so much he concedes. He will allow that gold may be found in the most distant parts of the earth; he knew that to the north of Europe it was far more abundant than elsewhere; but that does not prove that one-eyed Arimaspians steal it from Griffins; one-eyed men, so planned by nature, have to be proved (iii, 116; iv, 27).[11]

So turning back to the world that men really do know, we find that for Herodotus it was amazingly full of interests; there are people, and places, and climates, and, what is more, there are the relations between men and their climates. Hellas, he holds, has the kindliest climate of all (iii, 106); Ionia, as we saw before,[12] is free from the cold and the drought of northern and southern lands, and is "the fairest spot we know of for sky and seasons" (i, 142). Cyrene is almost as favoured, with three climates, and three harvests covering eight months, on the sea level and the higher regions inland; "so that the latest fruits of the earth are coming in, when the earliest is already spent by way of food and drink" (iv, 199). Egypt next after Libya has the healthiest inhabitants;[13] "the reason of which to my thinking is that the climate is in all seasons the same, for changes are the chief causes of sickness for men, specially changes of seasons" (ii, 77). Confirmation

[10] See T. Rice Holmes, *Ancient Britain*, pp. 483-488; H. F. Tozer, *History of Ancient Geography*, pp. 37, 38, 80.

[11] Cf. pp. 40, 157, 177.

[12] Cf. p. 6.

[13] See Breasted, *History of the Ancient Egyptians*, p. 10, on the Climate of Egypt.

of the ill effects of change was to be seen in the death rate of Xerxes' army on the march. On the Hellespont "they had distributed to them an allowance of food more abundant than they had had by the way, and from satisfying their hunger without restraint and also from changes of water there died many" (viii, 117). The best medical opinion of the day was the same; "the changes of the seasons above all engender disease," wrote Hippocrates,[14] who also held that differences in the source and taste of waters have very great influence on health. But whatever the reason, climate or a peculiar treatment of their children, the Libyans are really the most healthy of men; that, he says, is a fact (iv, 187).

Northward it is another story; the country of the Scythians

is excessively cold; for eight months of the year there is frost unbearable. You will not make mud then by pouring out water, but by lighting a fire you will make mud. The sea freezes and all the Cimmerian Bosporos; and the Scythians, on this side the fosse, lead armies over the ice and drive wagons across to the Sindi. So winter lasts eight months and it is cold for the other four.[15] Their winter is different in character from the winters in other lands, for in the season for rain scarce any rain falls, and all the summer there is rain unceasing (iv, 28),

and so with thunderstorms. "An earthquake, whether in summer or winter, is counted a portent in the Scythian country. Horses are able to bear this winter, but mules and asses cannot bear it at all, though in other lands horses standing in the frost are frost-bitten while asses and mules endure it" (iv, 28). He has the Cossack ponies in view; but in Greece and

[14] See How and Wells on ii, 77, and viii, 117.
[15] The passage recalls the quip about the Far North West, where they "have the four seasons all right—June, July, August and Winter."

Asia Minor horses were kept too delicately; "the pampered jades of Asia" could not be hardy. He has other curious observations on mules.[16] He doubts the alleged swarms of bees north of the Danube, for bees are intolerant of cold;[17] "to me it seems that the regions which go up towards the pole are uninhabitable by reason of the cold climate" (v, 10).

The cranes of course fly south from the wintry weather of Scythia to Ethiopia, where the swallows live all the year round,—a clear proof that the Nile owes nothing to the melting of snow, as the colour of the Negro is another; "the men of that country are black as a result of the heat" (ii, 22). We have already noticed another effect of the sun, which caught his attention on the field of Papremis (iii, 12); the skulls of the Persians were very brittle, a pebble thrown at them would break them; you could pound an Egyptian skull with a stone and not break it. The Persian in life wears a felt tiara; the Egyptian shaves his head, and as a result he never goes bald and the sun thickens the bone. The mummies, it is said, confirm the fact he states, and it is attested (or was till lately) by the capacity of the Egyptian head for being beaten in life by the Turks. The explanation may not be so ready. Heredity plays a smaller part in Herodotus' speculations than in ours; his causes get to work more quickly, and characteristics are more rapidly acquired.

But, once more, it is of importance to us to note the readiness of observation of this Greek traveller

[16] No mules are born in Elis, iv, 30.

[17] Bees were not in Utah, in spite of the Mormon name Deseret, when settlement began. So at least Sir Richard Burton says.

and his Greek way of wanting to understand and
explain what he observes. "From soft lands," says
Cyrus, "come soft men; it does not belong to the
same land to bear wondrous fruits and good warriors" (ix, 122).[18] Yet Greeks lived among the
Scythians on the northern shore of the Black Sea,
among the Egyptians at the Nile's mouth, and among
the Libyans at Cyrene, and they remained Greeks.
Herodotus raises no question as to how soon nature
may re-mould them in the native likeness. Mean-
while, they adopt all sorts of customs and cults without ceasing to be Greek, while within the period of
Greek memory they have made Pelasgian, Carian,
and Ionian Hellenic too. But we must not insist on
his having realized all the implications of his many
thoughts and many reflections. Once at least he
shows how nature was too much for a tribe; the
change of climate may indeed have been due to other
causes, but the result would not have been different.
In Libya was the land of the Psylloi, some of whom,
as other authorities tell us, continued to exist and
were snake charmers; but, says Herodotus,

the force of the south wind dried up their water tanks, and
all their land (lying within the region of the Syrtis) was
waterless. They took counsel together and marched
southward (I tell the tale as the Libyans tell it), and when
they were now in the sand, the south wind blew and buried
them. So they utterly perished, and the Nasamones have
their country (iv, 173).

We may turn now to some of the regions of which
he speaks. In discussing the influences of Egypt and
its antiquity upon him, we saw how he believes

[18] See the discussion by J. L. Myres in *Anthropology and the Classics*,
pp. 146-152, and his references to Hippocrates and the effect of the
climate of Phasis and its marshlands on its people.

Egypt itself to be the gift of the river (ii, 5) busy for thousands of years (ii, 11). He gives his grounds for so thinking, which modern observers confirm:

I have seen that Egypt projects in the sea beyond the neighbouring land, and shells are plain to view on the hills, and the ground exudes with salt to such an extent as even to injure the pyramids; and I noticed also that there is but a single hill in all Egypt where sand is found, namely the hill above Memphis; and further I found the country to bear no resemblance either to its borderland Arabia or to Libya, no, nor even to Syria (for the seaboard of Arabia is inhabited by Syrians). It is a land of black and crumbling earth, as being alluvial, and deposit carried down from Ethiopia. But we know that the soil of Libya is reddish and rather sandy, and Arabia and Syria have more clay and rock (ii, 12).

Even a full day's run from land, the sounding line brings up mud at eleven fathoms, which shows how far out the deposit is carried (ii, 5). The Nile has no tributaries, he says (iv, 50), nor has it north of the Atbara, which is six degrees of latitude to the south of his southernmost point, Elephantine (lat. 24°). "There is no rain at all in the upper parts of Egypt, and at that time (when Cambyses invaded the land) a mere drizzle fell at Thebes" and was counted a wonderful sight (iii, 10). Indeed the Egyptians, on hearing that Greece depended on rain, expressed the expectation that "some day they would be deceived in a great hope and starve miserably" (ii, 13). The Nile does everything for Egypt with its constant loads of silt and its regular overflow; the peoples of the Delta

get the fruits of the land with less labour than any other people in the world or the rest of Egypt. They have not the toil of ploughing up their land into furrows, nor of hoeing, nor of any other work which other men must do for a crop. But when the river rises of its own accord and spreads over their fields and waters them and after watering them goes back again, then every man sows his field and turns swine into it to tread down the seed, and after that he waits for the harvest. The swine also serve him to thresh his grain, and so he garners it (ii, 14).

The cause of the Nile's overflow occupies him, as it did all the ancients. Did not Caesar, according to Lucan, turn the talk at Cleopatra's table to this question?[19] Why the Nile should overflow at all, and above all in summer, when rivers elsewhere run dry, he "was eager to hear;" but "neither from the priests nor anybody else could I learn anything" (ii, 19). Why further do no airs blow from it as from every other stream? Some of the Greeks, however, "wishing to be remarkable for wisdom," have put forward three opinions, two of which Herodotus would not even mention but to show what they are. One would have it that the etesian winds, by stopping the outflow of the Nile, cause the annual flood; but it comes whether they blow or not (ii, 20). Another explanation was that "the river effects what it does because it flows from Oceanus, and Oceanus flows round the world" (ii, 21). The third assigns as cause the melting of snows; but where are the snows in the hottest of lands (ii, 22)? His own idea is that the summer flood is the really normal Nile, but that in winter when the sun is driven by winds over the inland parts of Libya, evaporation is greater and the Nile is less (ii, 24-26). As for the source of the river, only one man offered him any information; and he took it to be jest. The recorder of the sacred treasures at Sais said that the Nile welled up from

[19] Lucan, X, 137, Cleopatra *immodice formam fucata nocentem*; 190, Caesar asks as to the Nile, *nihil est quod noscere malim*; 193-331, the answer of Achoreus.

holes of fathomless depth between the hills Crophi and Mophi,[20] that lie between Syene and Elephantine (ii, 28), but Herodotus himself saw Elephantine (ii, 29) and found there was no end to the Nile beyond it. Forty-four days away lies Meroe, and beyond that the land of the Deserters,[21] four months away upstream from Elephantine; and "beyond this none has clear knowledge to declare; for this country is desert by reason of heat" (ii, 29-31).

At this point Herodotus' story achieves one of its most interesting additions, at third hand but probable. Certain men of Cyrene had been at the oracle of Ammon, and Etearchus the king there told them of a visit from Nasamonians, Libyans of the Syrtis region, who had a remarkable story. Five young men of their people, sons of chiefs, set out to see what lay in the heart of Africa.

They journeyed first through the inhabited country, and after passing through this they came to the region of wild animals; thence through desert westward, and after crossing a wide region of sand in many days they saw trees growing in a plain. When they reached these and began to pluck the fruit, little men came upon them, of stature smaller than common, and took them, and led them away. The Nasamonians knew nothing of those men's speech, nor did the men leading them off know that of the Nasamonians. They brought them through very great swamps, and after passing these they came to a city where all the people were of the same stature as their escort, and black. A great river ran past this city from the West toward the rising sun; and crocodiles could be seen in it (ii, 32).

The little people were all wizards (ii, 33). King Etearchus guessed that the river was the Nile, and Herodotus thinks it a reasonable view. The Nile

[20] If the tale was jest, or a misunderstanding as Maspero suggests, he shows that the names of the hills are genuine and old Egyptian.

[21] For the Deserters, see Herodotus ii, 30.

"runs from the West and the sunset," he has previously said; and between latitudes 21° and 23° N the Nile undoubtedly flows to the northeast, and, though a degree or two higher upstream the course is quite different, Herodotus' knowledge may not have reached so far. And the crocodiles made it likelier still; even Alexander, a century or so later, dreamed that the Indus might be the Nile, because of the crocodiles.[22]

The explorations of Du Chaillu, Schweinfurth, and Stanley have given a new value to the Nasamonian story. There are pygmies in central Africa, and they are black; they are not quite so small as Homer said, they are bigger than your fist. But what Herodotus says of their height does not clash with modern discovery. Perhaps Mr. Tozer's quiet verdict will serve: "On such a subject as the identification of the river it is hazardous to speak with confidence, but the direction which was followed by the Nasamones suggests the probability that the stream which they reached was the Niger, which lies to the southwest of the Sahara."[23]

Now suppose for a moment that Herodotus had been a person of normal intelligence. He would assuredly have been too shrewd to incur laughter with a tale of pygmies; and it was true. It is this interest in the regions beyond, this triumph over the matter-of-fact, that gives Herodotus his greatness. African exploration—was it germane to Persian invasion? It depends on what we mean by history.

[22] Cf. page 17.
[23] H. F. Tozer, *History of Ancient Geography*, p. 97. How and Wells, *ad loc.*, confirm the swamps, but say the city was not Timbuctoo, which is modern (about 1000 A.D.)

If we mean incidents, perhaps it is not relevant; but if the theme of history as of tragedy is the development of the human spirit, the clash of instincts and temperaments, the struggle of mind and disposition and tradition, then to the last sentence on Libyan savagery, it is all relevant.

The Libyan section of his book will concern us more at a later point, when we consider the Anthropology of Herodotus.[24] But while Geography still occupies us, the story that he preserves, but does not believe, of the circumnavigation of Africa is of great import.

Necos, King of Egypt, the Pharaoh Necoh who overthrew and killed the Jewish Josiah,[25] dug again the canal from the Nile to the Red Sea. (The term is here used to cover the Arabian Gulf.) It was first made by Sethos I (1326-1300 B.C.), who commemorated it in a picture at Karnak. Necos designed it to be of a breadth to allow two triremes rowed abreast. Herodotus says it was four days' voyage in length, that it cost 120,000 lives, that Necos abandoned it in consequence of an oracle that he was labouring for the barbarian; and that Darius finished it (ii, 158, 159).[26] Monuments have been found which Darius set up on its completion. Necos, however, built ships of war on the Arabian Gulf; and then, we read at a later point (iv, 42), he sent Phoenicians in ships (southward), charging them to sail back past the Pillars of Heracles until they reach the Northern Sea (the Mediterranean) and so come to Egypt. So the Phoenicians set out from the Red

[24] For geography of Libya, see How and Wells on iv, 181.
[25] 1 Kings xxiii, 29.
[26] See How and Wells, *ad loc*.

Sea and sailed the Southern Sea. Whenever autumn came, they would put in and sow the land, wherever they might be in Libya on their voyage, and await the harvest, and, after reaping their crop, they would sail on. After two years, and in the third, they rounded the Pillars of Heracles and came to Egypt. "They [i.e. Herodotus' friends] told me what I do not believe but another may, that in sailing round Libya they had the sun on their right hand," i.e., to the north of them.

Herodotus did not believe this, nor did Polybius, nor Strabo; but "others may," and many modern readers do believe it. The voyage was quite feasible; for currents would be favourable all the way, the monsoon on the east coast, the trade wind on the west. As to the statement about the sun, which he did not believe,[27] to say nothing of the equator, south of Syene the sun at times might be seen to the northward. It has been suggested that this supplied the point of the story, and doubters remark that Herodotus says very little about that south country. Such an argument from silence is surely worthless. He was not obliged, as he says elsewhere, to mention everything; and it is likely enough that he knew no more of that voyage. But he knew, and he tells us, of other attempts.

He says that the Carthaginians claimed to have made the voyage again (iv, 43); and he quotes in another connexion a Carthaginian story of the Atlantic coast of Africa which may belong in the first instance to this expedition, though he implies that they habitually went so far. It is "the dumb

[27] See How and Wells, *ad loc;* G. Rawlinson *ad loc;* and Meyer, *Gesch. der Altertums,* Vol. iii, p. 60.

commerce" of the African that he mentions, and that modern travellers have seen (iv, 196). Finally, he tells of a Persian attempt to circumnavigate Africa from the west. Sataspes went for months down the coast of Africa, and came to a country of small men, who wore palm-leaf raiment but fled to the hills whenever he and his men came ashore. Beyond this "the ship could not move forward but was stayed" (iv, 43). Xerxes would not believe this, and inflicted on him the penalty from which success was to free him. The stoppage is not explained at all, though other ancient writers have tales of "masses of mud and seaweed;" but the modern explanation confirms Sataspes. If he reached the coast of Guinea in the early summer, he met the southerly trade wind, which modern sailors avoid by sailing all but to South America. This an ancient would not think of attempting; they habitually coasted. The trade wind blows for months without ceasing; and Sataspes might well despair.[28] Hanno's contemporary attempt Herodotus does not mention, the record of which has many points of interest,—notably savage people at one place, "most of whom were women, whose bodies were covered with hair; these the interpreters called Gorillas. Three women we caught, but they refused to accompany us, and scratched and bit those who conducted them. So we killed them and flayed them, and brought their skins to Carthage."[29] To this passage the anthropoid ape owes its name, rightly or wrongly. But, women or apes, Herodotus omits them.

[28] See G. Rawlinson, *ad loc*; H. F. Tozer, *History of Ancient Geography*, p. 103.

[29] See H. F. Tozer, *History of Ancient Geography*, pp. 104-108; Hanno, *Periplus*, 17, 18.

III

Turning eastward again, we have a good deal of
information from Herodotus as to the Ethiopians,
but some of it is myth and some of it may be fact
dislocated. Some of them were actually subjugated
by the Persians. Among subjects, "on whom no
tribute was laid but who rendered gifts instead, were
firstly the Ethiopians nearest Egypt whom Cambyses
subdued on his march toward the long-lived Ethiopians" (iii, 97). Their gifts were every two years two
quarts of pure gold, two hundred blocks of ebony,
five Ethiopian boys, and twenty big elephant tusks.
The "long-lived" branch of the race make a good
story—"the tallest and most beautiful of men;" and
their king was tallest of them all. He thought purple
garments full of guile, and wheat a poor diet if
longevity were an object; he lived on milk and roast
meat (but liked the Persian's gift of wine); he fettered
his prisoners with gold, and ruled a people who
habitually lived to a hundred and twenty. The army
sent against them never reached them (iii, 20-25).
The conquered Ethiopians, however, contributed a
contingent to the expedition of Xerxes, clad in skins
of leopards and lions, armed with great bows, and
small arrows with stone heads, with spears that bore
a gazelle's horn for a point, and with clubs; and half
of his body every man would smear with white chalk
and half with red ochre, when he went to battle
(vii, 69).

Of Arabs Herodotus has little to say. There are
no men who respect pledges more; their only gods are
Dionysus and Aphrodite; they clip their hair round

the head and shave their temples like Dionysus, whom they call Orotalt; and Aphrodite they name Alilat (iii, 8). In the last name he is almost surprisingly right. Their land, and no other, yields frankincense, myrrh, casia, and cinnamon, as we have seen; and "airs wondrous sweet blow from that land" (iii, 113). They were not made subject by Darius, but "became his friends" (iii, 88) and gave him a thousand talents weight of frankincense year by year (iii, 97). They too sent a contingent with Xerxes.

On India Herodotus is peculiarly interesting, though, as we have already seen, he had not been to the country. Of all men then known, of whom anything reliable was said, the men of India lived farthest to the east, nearest the sunrise, and beyond them all is desert because of the sand (iii, 98),—the Rājputāna desert, H. G. Rawlinson says.[30] In India all living creatures, fourfooted and flying, are larger than those of other lands, except the horses, which are smaller than the Median (iii, 106); and the ants, that guard the gold, are as large as foxes, an echo, it is said, of Indian legend and of "ant-gold," *Paippīlika*. He distinguishes, or perhaps confuses, the Indian tribes, of which there are many, none speaking the same language as the rest. Holdich writes that a generation ago the tribes just over the northwest frontier were hardly better known than in Herodotus' day, but some still surviving bear witness that some real knowledge of them had reached the west by the fifth century B.C. Herodotus is the first European to write of Indian ascetics. "There are

[30] H. G. Rawlinson, *Intercourse between India and Western World*, pp. 21-27.

other Indians, again," he says, "who kill no living
creature, nor sow, nor are wont to have houses; they
eat grass, and they have a grain growing naturally
from the earth in its calyx, about the size of a millet-
seed, which they gather, and then roast and eat,
calyx and all. Whosoever of them falls sick, he goes
into the desert and there he lies; and none takes
thought of him, dead or sick" (iii, 100). Lassen says
these are Brahmans; H. G. Rawlinson suggests that
he refers to Buddhists, and points out that Gautama
died in 488 B. C., four years before Herodotus was
born. Northward of the rest of India dwells a tribe
in manner of life like the Bactrians, of all Indians
most warlike,—"the paler refined Aryans of the
Kaspapura and Pakhtū districts, whom he appro-
priately compares to their Iranian kinsmen of
Bactria."[31] Others farther south,[32] now classed generally as Dravidian, he tells us, were savages—
dwellers in marshes, eaters of raw fish, wearing
clothes made of rushes and sailing about in dugouts,
black as Ethiopians, and ignorant of elemental
decencies; others again he mentions who themselves
devour their aged and sick kinsfolk (iii, 98, 99, 101).
Sanskrit literature speaks even less kindly of these
primitive peoples. Herodotus notes the cotton
clothes of India (iv, 107), and says the Indians in
Xerxes' army rode on horseback and drove chariots
harnessed with horses or wild asses (vii, 86). For
all he tells us of India, Herodotus is believed to have
drawn on Persian sources, and but for a loose grouping
which appears to class the ascetics with the primitive
tribes and to distinguish them from the warriors, he

[31] H. G. Rawlinson, *India and Western World*, p. 21.
[32] Obviously still in north India and not in the Deccan.

is praised for his "admirable sobriety" and the truth
of his statements.

The Scythian section of Herodotus' work is very
full;[33] he was obviously interested in these savage but
effective peoples,[34] who baffled Darius in having no
cities that he could attack, no houses nor fortunes
that he could destroy. If Darius went on this expedition, as Professor Bury long ago suggested,[35] in the
hope of getting control of gold mines, he failed altogether. No one, Herodotus says, has penetrated to
the lands beyond the Scythians (iv, 16), but traders
from among the Scythians and even Greeks went a
long way, and he speaks of business done "with seven
interpreters and in seven tongues" (iv, 24). He
learnt something too of Scythian folklore. He tells
us their story of the three brothers, whose grand-
father (they say, but Herodotus does not believe it)
was Zeus himself, and how the youngest of them,
Colaxais, alone, was able to approach the plough, the
yoke, the sword, and the flask of burning gold that
fell from heaven, and so he became king (iv, 5).
That third son was the first of many third sons who
have thrilled us by excelling their elder brothers,
marrying princesses and becoming kings. But
Lipoxais and Arpoxais also became founders of
clans. Another tribe were were-wolves; every year
every one of them is turned into a wolf for a few days;
so say the Scythians and the Greeks settled in
Scythia; "they say it, but they do not persuade me;
but they say it all the same and swear to it" (iv, 105).
He tells also the tale of the Amazons raiding the

[33] H. F. Tozer, *History of Ancient Geography*, pp. 84-88.
[34] On their cleverness, iv, 46.
[35] *Classical Review*, Vol. XI, 1897.

Scythian country and what came of it. Stricter
chronology might have reminded him that the
Amazons belonged to the age of Herakles and
Theseus before the Trojan War, while the Scythians
only reached their present land and drove out the
Cimmerians long after that war, in the reign of the
Lydian Ardys, in good historic times (i, 15),—though
the Scythians say they were there a thousand years
before Darius' crossing (iv, 7). Modern students
have been as perplexed as he says the Scythians were
by these warrior women. Were they priestesses of the
great Goddess of Asia Minor? or were the beardless
invaders, so skilled in horsemanship and archery,
men after all, not unlike the Huns?[36]

Herodotus gives the length of the Black Sea
incorrectly, making it almost twice as long as it is.
He explains how the measure was reached; "a ship
will for the most part accomplish 70,000 fathoms in a
long day's voyage, and 60,000 by night. Granted so
much, to Phasis from the mouth (Bosporus), which
is the greatest length of the sea, it is a voyage of nine
days and eight nights; that means 1,110,000 fathoms
or 11,100 furlongs. Thus have I measured this Pontus" (iv, 86). Various explanations are given of the
error,—a conclusion from a single voyage, a double
reckoning of the nights, forgetfulness that a long day
means a short night; and it is pointed out that the
Massiliot explorer, Pytheas, made almost the same
over-estimate of the south coast of England.[37] But we
may note how Herodotus speaks of his estimate, and
ask whether he had made the voyage himself. As we

[36] See J. L. Myres, in *Anthropology and the Classics*, pp. 138 ff., an
interesting discussion of the stages of discovery indicated by the data.
[37] See How and Wells, *ad loc.*

saw, Sayce always finds him guilty of pretending knowledge he had not. In this passage, he may be construed as indicating (but no more than that) that he had made the voyage; one feels that, if Sayce's language were to be justified, Herodotus should have spoken out more sweepingly. But large claims are not in his style; if he lies as to what he saw, it is open to dispute whether he does it with deliberate art, concealing his art, or simply badly. For my own part, he makes on my mind the impression of truth. Here, for instance, he may be calculating from what he has been told; but neither here nor, as a rule, elsewhere, unless he has the special purpose of giving grounds for a belief or an observation, does he put forward his own claim to be a great traveller. He certainly speaks quite naturally, and, I am convinced, straightforwardly.

His geography of Scythia is a great deal fuller than we might have expected, but Ionia had long been interested in the Black Sea trade, and Herodotus with others of his day was concerned with a problem of some theoretical import, which was o bear on conduct and life. Were morals nature or convention? There was only one way, really, to settle such a question; and that was observation. But first a word or two more on Geography.[38] He pictures Scythia as a sort of square region intersected by the lower waters of the Russian rivers, Dniester, Bug, and Dnieper; but eastward of the Dnieper he is less informed. The Volga (running into the Caspian) he omits altogether, and it escaped the other geographers down to Claudius Ptolemy, about 150 A.D. The other three run into the Black Sea, with the Danube; and

[38] See H. F. Tozer, *History of Ancient Geography*, pp. 85, 340.

here what he says of the Danube is significant. If summer increases the Danube's waters with rains and the melting of snows, "the sun draws more water to himself in summer . . . and these opposites keep the balance true, so that the volume of the river appears ever the same" (iv, 50). He is said to be right about the summer rains of Rumania, to exaggerate the evaporation, and to miss the explanation of the absence of floods on the lower Danube because he does not know that Hungary gets them instead, above the Iron Gates, near Belgrade.[39]

His chief triumph in Scythian geography is that he is right against Strabo and other later geographers, who thought that the Caspian was a gulf of the Northern Sea. Herodotus was not convinced that there was a Northern Sea, and he says that the Caspian "is a sea by itself, not joined to the other sea" (i, 203). Here I shall do better to quote the recent investigations of Mr. Stanley Casson[40] than to offer conjectures of my own. He explains the absence of any reference to the Sea of Aral in Herodotus, and generally in authors before the seventeenth century, by the probable union of that sea with the Caspian in a series of marshlands and archipelagoes. The Oxus (the Araxes of i, 205) thus flowed into a united sea, which Herodotus calls the Caspian (i, 202); if it does not flow into the Caspian, it appears to have changed its course three times since 500 B.C. The tribe, called Budini, live, says Herodotus, in a country thickly wooded with every kind of tree; "in the depth of the forests there is a

[39] See How and Wells, *ad loc.*
[40] *Annual of British School at Athens for 1918-1919*, "Herodotus and the Caspian."

great and wide lake with marsh land and reeds round it. In this otters are caught, and beavers, and certain other animals with square faces" (iv, 109). The square-faced animals Mr. Casson identifies as seals, and places the tribe on the north end of the Caspian, fixed there by their seal-fishing. Herodotus, he says, got the direction of the Don too northerly to begin, but, as he goes, corrects it toward the east, and this must be allowed for in his placing of the tribes.

Once again we are impressed with the range of the historian's interest and of his knowledge. He is not always right in his information; but to know what to look for is of more importance than to find it. The one may depend on luck, good or bad; the other gives a clue to the man.

Finally, and we shall leave Geography. Herodotus, as we have seen, has several allusions to maps; the brass map that Aristagoras showed to King Cleomenes, when he forgot that Spartan geography was so very local and gave himself away with an offhand suggestion of a three months' march from the sea (v, 49); and the too round map, which made the historian laugh, in which Europe and Asia were made of one size (iv, 36) though Europe is so much longer and probably broader (iv, 42). But when one begins to meddle with maps, the temptation comes to draw one; and here, as Mr. Tozer says, we discover "the more scientific side of Herodotus' mind; for in attempting to draw an imaginary line from Egypt to Cilicia, and thence by way of Sinope to the Ister, he is evidently feeling his way towards a meridian of longitude."[41]

[41] H. F. Tozer, *History of Ancient Geography*, p. 79; and Herodotus iv, 34; for other attempts see Tozer, pp. 177, 342.

IV

Wherever Herodotus goes, he is apt to notice the strange animals of the land; and where he does not go but depends on inquiry, he asks about them. He will not describe the camel's appearance to the Greeks, for they know it (iii, 103); and one presumes that more familiar things he omitted in the same wise spirit of economy. But he found much to surprise. In Egypt, as we saw, nothing is quite like other lands. The lizard of Greece is small; the crocodile is another story.

No mortal creature known to us grows from so small a beginning to such greatness, for its eggs are not much bigger than goose eggs, and the young crocodile is of a bigness answering thereto, but it grows to a length of seventeen cubits and more. It has eyes like a pig, and great teeth and tusks answering to the size of its body. It is the only creature that has no tongue,[42] nor does it move the lower jaw. . . . It has strong claws and a scaly hide impenetrable (ii, 68).

He tells of the sandpiper that picks the leeches from the crocodile's mouth, though all other creatures flee from it, and he describes how it is caught, and how the Egyptians make a god of it. The hippopotamus was also sacred in the province of Papremis, a beast "four-footed with cloven hoofs like an ox, blunt-nosed, with a mane like a horse, with tusks that show, a horse's tail and the voice of a horse, big as the biggest ox; and his hide is so thick, that, when it is dried, spearshafts are made of it" (ii, 71).

[42] Plutarch repeats this, and uses it to justify the Egyptians worshipping the tongueless crocodile as a symbol of god; *de Iside et Osiride*, § 75, p. 381 B.

Otters in the Nile and other things he mentions and passes by, to describe the phoenix, which "I myself have never seen, but only pictures of it" (ii, 73).

We have already seen a number of the animals which he notices—the great beasts of India, where for some reason he quite omits the elephant; the Cossack ponies; the seals of the Caspian. For north Africa his list is a long one, with some data that may need examination—in the nomads' country gazelles, asses ("not the horned asses, but those that never drink"), antelopes as big as oxen, foxes, hyaenas, porcupines, wild rams, the *dictys* and the *borys*, jackals and panthers, land crocodiles three cubits long, ostriches and one-horned serpents (iv, 192). Farther west are huge snakes, elephants, bears, asps, horned asses; and, they say, the dogheaded men and the men without heads but with eyes in their breasts, the wild men and wild women, "and a great many other creatures that are not fabulous" (iv, 191). And yet there are those who tell us that he believed everything without criticism! Ctesias has fuller information as to the dogheaded; they are a tribe 120,000 strong; they cannot speak, which is what one might expect, but they understand when spoken to. Some of the Garamantes have cattle that go backward as they graze, as their horns curve forward (iv, 183).

More probable than some of these tales, which he quotes from the world's edges, are his stories of the Persian king's great stables and his kennels of Indian dogs (i, 192; vii, 187); the Nesaean horses that quite eclipsed the Thessalian (vii, 196); the little shaggy ponies of the Sigynnai north of the Danube, whose hair is five fingers deep, little horses, blunt-nosed, not equal to carrying men, but very swift when yoked to carts (v, 9); the wild white horses that graze round the lake whence flows the Hypanis (the Bug) (iv, 52); the wild cattle of Thessaly with huge horns (vii, 126);[43] and the lions of Thessaly, which attacked Xerxes' camels, beasts they had never seen before, and left the other baggage animals alone, for some reason that Herodotus cannot guess (vii, 126). Some moderns have ridiculed lions being in Europe at that day; but Xenophon, Aristotle, Pliny, and Pausanias believed it, and Homer abounds with similes taken from the creature's life in the wild, which naturalists praise as well as men of letters.[44] Herodotus finds the working of Providence in the reproductive habits of animals, though perhaps not all his data are as reliable as the superfetation of the hare appears to be (iv, 108). Later naturalists went much farther, and Christian apologists drew on a strange collection of still more improbable animal stories to prove that the taboo lists of the Jews were to be taken spiritually and not literally.[45]

[43] Hornless (really shorthorned) cattle of the Steppes, iv, 29.

[44] See T. D. Seymour, *Life in the Homeric Age*, p. 372, who says there are 62 references to the lion in the poems, about 30 similes in the *Iliad*. Xenophon, *Cynegeticos*, 11, 1, says lions are caught near Pangaeus and Cittos above Macedonia.

[45] Barnabas, 10.

V

But as Herodotus' friend, Sophocles, said—and
he might have been hearing the historian when he
wrote the song in his *Antigone* (c. 441 B.C.)—"Many
are the wondrous things and nought more wondrous
than man." The poet surveys man's mastery of sea
and land, the multitude of his inventions; from his
early and successful warfare with birds and animals,
the snaring of the wild beast, the taming of the
horse, the yoking of the bull, to the building of the
house and "all the moods that mould a state," and
speech and wind-swift thought.[46] The air was full
of speculation as to the origin of man. If man had
been such as he is now, born incapable of helping
himself, how could he have survived? they asked.
Then how did he come? Was the first man produced
inside (say) a fish or something of the kind and there
lodged till mature? So asked Anaximander.[47] Others
fancied that single parts of animals might have arisen
separately, heads without necks, eyes without fore-
heads, and hence centaurs and other odd combinations. More serious was the origin of civilized life.

Herodotus does not in Anthropology, as in
Geology, go back before the beginning of years; he
has none of these quaint speculations. He starts
with man ready made, but not in a Golden Age; and
he observes and collects facts that may bear on the
real history of the development of culture. Here, as

[46] Sophocles, *Antigone*, 332-360.
[47] Diels, *Vorsokratiker*, Vol. I, Anaximander, § 30, from Plutarch,
Symposiaca, viii, 8, 4, p. 730 E; E. E. Sikes, *Anthropology of the Greeks*,
p. 48.

in other parts of his "inquiry," he is bound to be
dependent on hearsay. He tells at third hand—and
says so—of the pygmies of the Niger; much else that
he received, or that any traveller receives, must be
at the same distance from the actual, with chances
of misunderstanding and even falsification at every
stage of transmission. Again and again he cautions
us that he is repeating what he has been told, and
we have already seen that we are the gainers for his
doing so, even when he did not himself believe what
he repeats. But with time[48] strange things happen
and all lands are not Ionia;[49]—"in what way they
[the Sigynnai] have come to be colonists of the
Medes, for my part I cannot conjecture, but everything is possible in the course of ages" (v, 9). So,
without explaining what his precise object is nor if he
has one, without spinning theories as to origins,
Herodotus goes to the actual and records the ways
and customs of living men over a very wide area,—
at least as far as he can ascertain them. Once more,
as in other fields, we may note his caution, the
shrewdness of his judgment, his wide range of
inquiry, and above all his instinct for the sort of
thing that matters most.

What real attention he paid to the story of Psammetichus' experiment to discover who were the first
men, he does not betray; he tells it and alludes to
idle variants (ii, 2). He knows of many races more
primitive than the Phrygians, even if they are admitted by the Egyptians to be the older people. We
have seen that he does not really accept the dogheaded, the headless, and the wild people who are
said to dwell west of the Libyans "besides other

[48] Cf. ii, 12.   [49] Cf. iv, 195.

creatures not fabulous" (iv, 191); and with them he rejects the one-eyed (iii, 116) and the goat-footed (iv, 25). But he recognizes some of the great famous types that anthropologists know. He is familiar with the nomad, of whom in classical days the Scythian was the standard example (iv, 19, 46, 106). He notes the Ethiopian cave-dweller, the troglodyte, who lives on snakes and lizards and such like creeping things, who has a speech like no known tongue in the world, more like the squeaking of bats, and is reputed the fleetest footed of men (iv, 183); and modern travellers have identified the tribe from his account of it.[50] He gives the oldest known description of lake-dwellings, now found all over the world from Glastonbury to New Guinea,—the platform set on lofty piles in the middle of the lake, driven in by all the community working together, the narrow bridge from the mainland, the trapdoor and the fishing from it, and the children tied by the foot for safety (v, 16). He knows of the type that lives by hunting (iv, 22) and of man-eaters "of all men the most savage in their manner of life; they know no justice and obey no law," who dress like the Scythians but are by no means Scythian (iv, 106; 18).

In the days of Herodotus great Athenian poets wrote tragedies turning on the question, then much discussed, whether man was nearer akin to his father or to his mother. Among other great aspects of life it was bound to be debated whether marriage were a matter of Nature or Custom; is its stability mere convention? Is it in nature that man should be monogamous? Herodotus, as usual, discusses marriage in the abstract as little as he does anything else.

[50] See How and Wells, *ad loc.*

But he notes cases of savages who appear to have no real marriage at all, where the intercourse of the sexes is as promiscuous apparently as that of the animals—some remote Scythians (iv, 104) and several North African tribes (iv, 172, 176)—and as open (i, 203; iv, 180). He notes curious usages,—the right of the chief (iv, 168), and the strange tradition of the Sauromatai that a girl, before she can marry, must kill a man of some hostile tribe (iv, 117). There is polygamy to be found round Mount Pangaion (v, 16). The Lycians "take their names not from their fathers but from their mothers," a practice so strange that he expounds it more fully; "When one is asked by his neighbour who he is, he will say he is the son of such a mother, and recount the mothers of his mother. Nay, if a woman of full rights marry a slave, her children are counted pureborn; and if a man, a citizen and the first of them, take a stranger as wife or concubine, his children are no citizens" (i, 173). This "Mother-right" survives notably among the Nairs in southwest India, and one of them has actually served as judge in the High Court of Madras and been Minister of Education for all India. Herodotus does not mention whether the inheritance goes with the mother,—as in India, to the sister's children. The Mahārājā of Travancore must leave his throne to his sister's son, and the right of adoption conceded to semi-independent princes by the sovereign power had in his case to be modified to let him adopt not sons but sisters. Herodotus also records the survival among Babylonians of the single act of sacred prostitution in the temple (i, 198, 199) and the loose ways of the Lydians (i, 93). The sale of girls for marriage in the market of Babylonia is famous (i, 196), and the Thracians also buy wives (v, 6). He seems to have some inkling of marriage by capture, or at least he tells of something that may preserve its memory among Pelasgians (vi, 138), and perhaps at Sparta (vi, 64), where there is other evidence of the same sort. The Bacchiads at Corinth might, or would, marry only within their own clan (v, 92, β) and the Persian king only in certain families (iii, 84). The Issedones, who eat their dead parents, are otherwise so unusually modern that "the women have equal power with the men," whatever that means (iv, 26). Every one of his strange marriage customs is thus, as Professor J. L. Myres says, representative of a widespread type of observance; and he believes that it is not accidental,—"he is not simply emptying an ill-filled notebook on to the margins of his history."[51]

Wherever there is any diet, peculiar to a tribe, or connected with its particular environment, Herodotus pauses to notice it; and this too can hardly be accidental. G. B. Grundy in his *Thucydides* and W. E. Heitland in his *Agricola* have shown us that, both in the Greek world of Herodotus' day, and in the Roman Empire later on, the food problem was more serious than earlier readers of the great historians had gathered. Herodotus particularly notes the regimen of the Egyptians, their monthly purges and emetics, their bread of coarse grain, the "drink made of barley" in a land without vines, their use of fish sun-dried or preserved in brine, of quails and ducks and small birds salted and raw, and of other fish and birds roasted or boiled; and of course their climate helps to make them the healthiest of

[51] J. L. Myres, in *Anthropology and the Classics*, pp. 153-156.

men (ii, 77). They also eat the lotus root (ii, 92) and use castor oil, *kiki* (ii, 94). He remarks three tribes in Babylonia that eat nothing but fish, dried in the sun and pounded (i, 200); and eaters of roots and dried fruits, who perhaps smoke hemp, on the Araxes (i, 202); the Scythian diet of wheat, onions, garlic, lentils, and millet (iv, 17); the cherry concoction of the Bald Argippaioi (iv, 23); and the various Libyans who eat locusts and dates (iv, 172), or monkeys and artificial honey (iv, 194); and the Massagetai who eat fish and live stock and the aged, and drink milk (i, 216); and lice-eaters (iv, 168). With food, we may include food taboos. The nomad Libyans from the same reasons as the Egyptians will not touch the flesh of cows, and they rear no swine; the women of Cyrene also, because of Isis, think it wrong to eat cows' flesh, and the women of Barca reject swine's flesh as well (iv, 186). We may recall that, for a similar religious reason, long forgotten, Anglo-Saxons will not eat the horse.

The dress of one tribe and another we have already incidentally noticed. The Scythians, or some of them, use hemp to make clothing (iv, 74) and practise the use of the hot vapour bath, digging a pit under a tent, throwing into it stones, red-hot from the fire, and sprinkling hemp on them; and they howl with delight when they take it (iv, 73, 75). Several times he calls attention to the peculiar ways in which the Libyans cut their hair, shaved to a crest on top (iv, 175), or long behind (iv, 180), or long on the right side and close-shaved on the left (v, 191). He notes burial usages, from the elaborate devices of the Egyptians to the funeral games of the Thracians (v, 8); the killing of the favourite wife by way of honour over a man's grave in the country above Creston (v, 4); and the odd belief of the Getae that on death they go to their god Salmoxis, or Gebeleizis as some call him, and their way of sending a messenger to their god at times, by hurling him aloft and catching him on their spear points (iv, 94); the grave of the ancestor as the one thing that Scythians will fight to defend (iv, 127); and the habit of the Nasamonians who bury their dead in a sitting posture (iv, 190). What is there that does not catch the eye of this Greek whom men have supposed to be simple? What does not start within him trains of reflection, which in modern days men have followed up with wider opportunities of learning, but hardly keener zest? Tattooing (v, 6), the collection of the heads of enemies (iv, 107) or their scalps (iv, 64) or skulls for drinking cups (iv, 65), and the law-abiding character of savages who will eat their dead (iv, 26), and the dishonour of tillage (v, 6)—"many are the wondrous things, and none more wondrous than man!"

Wherever you go in this world so full of strange and interesting people, every tribe prefers its own customs, each is persuaded that its own are best. King Darius, we are told, once asked the Greeks who were with him what price would persuade them to eat their fathers' dead bodies; and they said there was nothing that would make them do it. Then the King summoned those Indians, called Callatiai (perhaps Black from the Sanskrit *Kala*), who eat their parents, and he asked them in turn—and the interpreters explained it all to the Greeks—what would make them willing to burn their fathers when dead; and the Indians cried out aloud and bade him not speak evil. "Such are men's customs, and I think Pindar was right when he said that Custom is King" (iii, 38).

Custom is King. Down to a certain date the Egyptians were as great a people in their way as the world knew and they would not hear of adopting any new custom from a foreigner (ii, 79), they would not associate or eat with the foreigner, nor kiss him. But the world had two peoples of another mind, who were willing to learn, and the Persian mastered the Egyptian; he tried to master the Greek, but the Greek was perhaps better at learning or knew something that the Persian could not learn; and victory rested after all with the men of the most open mind. Herodotus does not say all this in so many words; but somehow it seems to follow from what he does say, as he rambles and thinks; and perhaps it is not far from his own conclusion.

What it was that the Greeks learnt and understood, and the Persians as a people (though with exceptions) could neither understand nor achieve, it will be our next task to discover.

CHAPTER VI

THE RISE OF FREEDOM

I

The paradox of Greek excellence is that the Greeks, at least for a while, united things that for most races were in antithesis. The outlying barbarians of the ancient world apparently enjoyed freedom, though perhaps not quite so thoroughly as the Cyclopes in the *Odyssey*.

> An undiscerning people, void of art
> In life, and tramplers on the sacred claim
> Of laws which men for civil uses frame.
> Scorners of common weal, no bounds they keep,
> Nor learn with labours the rude earth to tame;
> Who neither plant nor plough nor sow nor reap;
> Still in the gods they trust, still careless wake and sleep.
> . . . . . They no councils know
> Nor justice, but for ever lawless go.
> Housed in the hills, they neither buy nor sell,
> No kindly offices demand or show;
> Each in the hollow cave where he doth dwell
> Gives law to wife and children as he thinketh well.[1]

If Worsley has expanded the few compressed lines of Homer, he brings out the picture of a way of life wholly free, and of what it costs. On the other hand, as we have seen, the Egyptians lived under ancient rules; "they keep," says Herodotus (ii, 79), "the ordinances of their fathers, and add none others

---

[1] *Odyssey*, ix, 107-115. See Plato, *Laws* III, 680, who calls it not liberty but δυναστεία.

to them." For the modern the contrast is patent if we compare the rigidity of Egyptian, Assyrian, and Hindu sculpture, on the one hand, and the ugly freedom of some very recent schools, on the other ("whose names I know but I do not speak them"), with Greek art. To none but to the Greek would one give the name "art," except by an extension of its meaning till it means nothing. The Greek work is plastic and alive, the eastern is dead, the new western style is the chaos that cosmos came to order and to end. In poetry it is the same. Sappho can be lyrical and adhere to laws of rhythm and sound. In short, Greek art is the child of the impossible union of incompatible loyalties, and justifies its parents and their marriage. Stone and speech and paint have their laws, made by Nature, and not by Convention. The Greek would discover and obey them; and, when by obedience he has drawn the utmost from them, he will transcend them, he will "soar" as Milton loves to say, and achieve a freedom that shows his rivals as mere slaves of tradition or whim.

But can this union of law and freedom be achieved in the ordinary lives of men and women? in the state? Or does it ask for more than Plato's dream of a community of philosophers,—a community of artists? Artists! "the very word is like a bell to toll us back" to the life of hugger-mugger, to chaos financial, social, and moral. The Greek state was assuredly no community of artists in our modern sense, nor the Greek himself the least like the modern aesthete. He was not precious; he was a man of the world, but one who thought and felt, and tried to understand and to grasp the whole. He thought intensely and profoundly about politics and their relation to life.

It was not idly that a shrewd Canadian in a new province made Plato's *Republic* in English the text-book of the College of Education. We are still wrestling with the problem which the Greek started. Can *we* combine law and freedom, and make them work together,—not by turns or in spasms, but stead-ily and harmoniously together in the life of a modern city, of a modern great state? Or is it a dream, too? The Greek tried a great many experiments and the modern says that they all failed. But what of ourselves? Is France a land of law or of freedom? Germany chose law, we say, and America freedom; and both evolved types of life which men of spirit and education, approximating to Greek ideals, have found odious, fatal to beauty and to sound thinking, to say nothing more. Russia under Czars and under Bolsheviks has tried various experiments—law first and then something else in isolation; and both have been failures, as all quiet people see, each for want of the opposite principle and of the thought that should unite them. Let us turn once more to the Greek and learn what he made of it,—this problem of popular and personal life, difficult to handle beyond wood and stone, evasive as sweet sound and subtle word are not.

Here once more, as we are told in other connex-ions, the extreme simplicity of the language and the style of Herodotus tends to conceal the amount of thought that he put into his work. Here and there he tells of things about which he "wondered." But to an attentive reader it is plain that he won-dered about many more and did not say so. He shared the many speculations of his race and of his day and let the reader take them for granted. He is not a professed philosopher, but he is a thinker. From time to time he makes clear his own position; he is an enthusiast for Freedom, and points out with satisfaction what effects it has in the life of a community (v, 66) and how beautiful is its very name (iii, 80). But he, like other Greeks of his day, is familiar with the discussion of types of government, he knows the antitheses; and the dream that the ideal state should combine them was not far off.

Here are two illustrative passages, to a certain degree in antithesis each to the other, and both fundamentally to Persian thought. The exiled Spartan king, Demaratus, is asked by Xerxes, if the Spartans will fight. They will indeed fight, rejoins the exile and he gives the reason:

they are free, but not in all things free; over them is a master, even Law, whom they fear much more even than thy men fear thee. It is certain at least that they do whatsoever that master commands; and he commands ever the same thing, he suffers them not to flee out of battle before whatever multitude of men, but will have them abide in their rank, conquer or die (vii, 104).

Here is what Herodotus says of the growth of Athens after the expulsion of the Pisistratids:—

So the Athenians increased in power; and it is plain, not from one instance only, but everywhere, that Equality is a good thing. For the Athenians, when ruled by tyrants, were no better in war than any of those who dwelt about them, but rid of the tyrants they became by far the first. This then proves that, when subjects, they would not do their best, because they were working for a master, but, when set free, every man of them was eager to achieve something for himself (v, 78).

The difference is not after all very sharp, yet it is there; and the blending of the two ideas is to be felt in both passages. In each case the controlling law is unwritten; it is partly, with the Spartans, custom, and "customary laws have more weight and relate to matters of more weight than written laws;"[2] there are unwritten laws the breaking of which brings admitted shame.[3] Hippocrates felt with his neighbour of Halicarnassus that "men self-governing, seeing that they face dangers on their own account, are eager and ready as they go into peril. . . . thus their laws produce a good state of soul."[4]

Xerxes held the opposite; how could the Greeks hope to bring a thousand or ten thousand or five thousand against him, if they were all equally free and not under one ruler? If they were under one ruler in the Persian way, they might under compulsion and the lash, and contrary to the promptings of their nature, face the Persian host that outnumbered them by a thousand to one (vii, 103). Xerxes does not believe that individuals, left to themselves, will face certain death in any numbers; he assumed that they would most of them be what Plato describes in "the democratic man"—they would lack moral control of themselves, would act on the impulse of the moment, and in this case run.

The Greek was a practical man, and what Xerxes surmised did not escape him. Self-rule is the ideal, that is liberty; but some people, not responsive quickly to the unwritten law, nor to what later writers call the law within, need the stimulus of law laid upon them from without,—not the crude prompting of the Persian's lash, but its equivalent; and this not only in battle but in daily life. Liberty,

---

[2] Aristotle, *Politics* III, 16, 9, p. 1287 b.
[3] Thucydides, ii, 37.
[4] Hippocrates, *de aere*, 23 (How and Wells).

the Greek felt, was a good thing, as Herodotus said; he would be autonomous to the extremest verge of political subdivision; but the point comes where the other man at last must be brought to realize law somehow, the point where it might frankly be good for oneself as well. Then can you combine law and liberty?

Thinkers found instances where law and liberty had been more or less blended. "There are," says the Athenian in Plato's *Laws*,

two mother forms of states from which the rest may be truly said to be derived; and one of them may be called monarchy and the other democracy: the Persians have the highest form of the one, and we [Athenians] of the other; almost all the rest, as I was saying, are varying mixtures of these. Now if you are to have liberty and the combination of friendship with wisdom, you must have both these forms of government in a measure; the argument emphatically declares that no city can be well governed which is not made up of both. The state which has become exclusively and excessively attached to monarchy or to freedom has neither of them in moderation; but your states, the Laconian and Cretan, have a certain moderation; and the Athenians and Persians, having had more at first, have now less. . . . There was a time when the Persians had more of the state, which is a mean between slavery and freedom. [5]

Aristotle quotes people who say the same of Sparta, maintaining

that the best constitution is a combination of all existing forms; and they praise the Lacedaemonian because it is made up of oligarchy, monarchy and democracy, the king representing the monarchy, and the council of elders the oligarchy, while the democratic element is supplied by the ephors; for the ephors are selected from the people. Others however declare the ephoralty to be a tyranny, and find the element of democracy in the common meals and in the habits of daily life. [6]

[5] *Laws*, III, 693 D, Jowett's translation.
[6] Aristotle, *Politics*, II, 6, 17, p. 1265 b (Jowett).

He also quotes opinion attributing the same sort of merit to Solon's legislation at Athens:

As to Solon, he is thought by some to have been a good legislator, who put an end to the exclusiveness of the oligarchy, emancipated the people, and established the ancient Athenian democracy, making the constitution a good mixture. According to their view, the council of Areopagus was an oligarchical element, the elected magistracy aristocratic, and the courts of law democratic. The truth seems to be that the council and the elected magistracy existed before the time of Solon and were retained by him, but that he formed the courts of law out of all citizens, thus creating the democracy, which is the very reason why he is sometimes blamed.[7]

By the fourth century the legislators were indeed sometimes blamed, and still more those who developed their work. Isocrates is evidence enough for the general Greek conviction that the Spartan government was the very ruin of Greek liberty, and for the Athenian conviction that unmixed democracy was not real equality or freedom. Plato's "democratic man," whose mind is a democracy of impulses and passions all as equal as Athenian citizens, was unhappily not pure parody; it was unjust as a description of daily Athenian democracy, but there was proof sooner or later to be found here or there for nearly every detail. His old acquaintance Alcibiades might have sat for the portrait.

[7] Aristotle, *Politics*, II, 12, 2, p. 1273 b.

II

But in the times of which Herodotus writes, the sad decline of government and of principle, which the fourth century recognized, had not come. He writes not of the evening twilight of Democracy, but, at its noon, of its glad confident morning. Law was the despot that tempered the freedom of Sparta; Freedom was the impulse that nerved the Athenian heart, that opened the Athenian mind, that built up the Athenian state. And Plato confirms him, when he makes his Athenian all but quote him, in a passage that shows an interesting blend of the language of the idealist and the phrase of the practical statesman.

Entire freedom and the absence of all superior authority is not a little worse than moderate government by others. At the time when the Persian attack was made on the Greeks, or rather perhaps on all the inhabitants of Europe, we had our ancient constitution and a type of rule on the basis of four property classes. Reverence was our Queen and Mistress, and made us willing to live in obedience to the laws of that time.[8]

Pericles in the great funeral speech would have it that the same spirit survived to his day, and was embodied in every true Athenian; and we might believe him, if we could forget Cleon and some of the pictures which Aristophanes draws. But Cleon's day was not in the sixth century, and to that we must return.

The task of Herodotus was to tell of the Persian War, that the memory of the past may not be blotted out from among men by time, nor the great and wonderful deeds of Greek and barbarian, nor the reason for which they warred one with another (i, 1).

---

[8] Plato, *Laws*, III, p. 698 A.B., δεσπότις ἐνῆν τις αἰδώς.

Loyal to his task, loyal to his avowed plan of reporting faithfully what was told him and his tacit plan of letting the story tell itself with as little as might be of comment from the writer, he leaves us in the main to collect for ourselves from his work what may elucidate the reason underlying the war. At one point he tells of dreams sent from God which drove Xerxes into the fatal expedition (vii, 12-18). But perhaps the reason for which they warred is not to be so easily reached. Happily Herodotus did not take refuge in our abstract and impersonal nouns as the true causes of war. But we can hardly use any other language; and we gather from data which he gives here, and from stories told there, that there was a fundamental difference between Persian and Greek outlooks, between the silent theories on which the two peoples severally based life. His Greek readers, or some of them, had a far wider knowledge than we of the antiquities and histories of the Greek states, as Aristotle's *Politics* lets us see; and into this great range of story Herodotus plunges almost in the Homeric way, as if we knew it already. Much as he tells us, there was much he did not need to tell his contemporaries; and his tale, like Pindar's, had meaning for such as understood. We have to collect its sequence and its gist for ourselves. His method sometimes recalls what Charles Lamb wrote of Gilbert Burnet: "Truth and sincerity staring out upon you perpetually in *alto relievo*. None of the cursed Gibbonian fine writing, so fine and composite. None of Mr. Roscoe's sage remarks, all so apposite and coming in so clever, lest the reader should have had the trouble of drawing an inference."[9]

[9] Charles Lamb, Letter to Thomas Manning, 1 March, 1800.

First then, and foremost, we have perpetually to remind ourselves of the variety of that Greek world. In the fifth century the Peloponnesians went to war with Athens, and after ten years of war there was peace, because the Peloponnesians would no longer hang together. Corinth had got them into the war, as Corinth in 440 and in 506 had stopped their embarking on war; and Sparta by 421 or even earlier was weary of war and perhaps uneasy as to its continuance. Athens was a unit and a big one, a Confederacy nominally; but the advice of Pericles to "keep your allies well in hand" is the obverse of Thucydides' statement that the allies were all of them fidgeting and hoping for autonomy; and tribute lists show that at one time and another there were two hundred and fifty "states" in the Confederacy. To all of these the Peloponnesian official programme promised autonomy; they should be, it was understood, as they had been before the foundation of the Confederacy of Delos, before the Persian advance had made the loose array of small but entirely sovereign powers impossible. Autonomy was promised, but all that was achieved was "autonomy convenient to the Spartans," a very modified autonomy indeed, so entirely under the control of the harmost in Europe, and of the satrap in Asia, that it did not seem to be autonomy at all.

Before the Persian came, there had been real autonomy in all or most of those two hundred and fifty communities, and a varying degree of autonomy among the Peloponnesians too. That world, with its hundreds of sovereign autonomies, is the world that Herodotus shows us.

> The little town by river or sea-shore,
> Or mountain-built with peaceful citadel,

is the English poet's dream of it. It was not very
far from the dream of the later Greek, who resented
the brutal facts of his day,—the Persian menace never
absent and the inevitable hegemony of one power
or other which was the only alternative—inter-
ference either way and never a peaceful citadel. But,
as Xenophon shows us in the *Hellenica*, the little
town, when left to itself, was rarely peaceful for
very long; and Herodotus implies a state of things
not very different. "Full of scandal which all true
history is. No palliatives; but all the stark wickedness, that actually gives the *momentum* to national
actors." So Lamb wrote of Burnet; and Greek
history admits of much the same description whoever
wrote it—before Plutarch. Mountains and arms of
the sea kept the Greek states apart; the sea at the
same time was often their only or their easiest means
of communication. Whether or not there was among
the Greeks (the form of expression is vague) from
the first that tendency to subdivide every community, which kept every state small and every
state the uneasy prey of faction, who shall say?
But their lands, west and east of the Aegaean, developed it to the utmost, if they did not produce it.
The food supply that these small districts could
produce must have been scanty at all times. Greece
is not a land for cattle, and of its surface only about
twenty-two per cent is today under cultivation.[10]
Megara, we are told, was mostly stones, and an
invading army soon deleted its home produce. Few
Greek citizens could see the invasion of the town's

[10] G. B. Grundy, *Thucydides*, pp. 58, 59.

lands by neighbours without instant recourse to battle; and where all were liable to go short, neighbours were always a danger. Inside the towns there was the same jealous watchfulness between fellow-citizens. When Themistocles after Salamis tried to get money out of the Andrians—whatever the origin of the story may be[11]—and told them quite bluntly that two great deities stood with the Athenians in their demand, Persuasion and Force, they replied to him that they also had two deities on their side, who could not be induced to leave the island, namely, Poverty and Inability.[12] Like Apollo who said one thing to Dorians in Delphi and another to Athenians on Delos, these divinities must have had many homes to which they clung as faithfully as to Andros, but unlike Apollo they always said the same thing. If Greeks meant to live and the land failed them, there remained the sea.

To the sea they turned, sometimes to find new and broader lands beyond it, as about Cyrene, in Sicily, and in Italy. There the mass of warm Mediterranean water produced a climate which they liked, which fitted their idea of life in the agora, which permitted them to grow the olive. Or they went to the Black Sea and planted themselves down on the sea fronts of the great wheat lands, with a shallow sea not far off, half bay, half river-mouth, and rich in fish; and wheat and dried fish they sent to warmer lands in exchange for olive oil. The Adriatic they avoided; it was colder; and the heavy rainfall on the

[11] See Grundy, *Great Persian War*, pp. 416, 417; see also the charming book of J. Irving Manatt, *Aegaean Days*, who has much to say of Andros, and tells us that these two old divinities still reign there.
[12] Herodotus, viii, 111.

eastern shore, and the lack of good harbours on the
west side, the Italian coast, and the barbarous and
trade-less hinterland northward told against it as
land for settlement. But always, whether colonies
were planted or not, it was to the sea that the Greek
must turn. Even the Peloponnese in the fifth century drew its food, its wheat, from the western
colonies.[13] Herodotus' story implies the sea and the
full and familiar intimacy with it that Greeks had.
Once more we may recall the adventure of Kolaios,
and all it involved of seamanship, skill, daring and
triumph; of astronomy and exploration and sea-
knowledge. Where gifts of these kinds develope in a
race, manhood and independence develope with
them; and the sea made for Democracy in the long
run. The Greeks saw it. "The sea," writes Plato,[14]
"is pleasant enough as a daily companion, but has
also a bitter and brackish quality; filling the streets
with merchants and shopkeepers, and begetting in the
souls of men uncertain and unfaithful ways." And
other factors in Greek life also made for Democracy.

Now and again Herodotus pauses to notice developments in metallurgy; twice he speaks of the art
of Theodorus of Samos who made the great silver
bowl at Delphi (i, 51) and the far more famous ring
of Polycrates, the emerald signet set in gold (iii, 41),
and he tells us how the Lydians invented coin
(i, 94). Once more the extraordinary skill of the
craftsman must have made him a man of ideas among
his people, and perhaps by and by a man of some
degree of wealth. He might at last be a man of

[13] At all events during the war, Thucydides, iii, 86.
[14] Plato, *Laws*, IV, p. 705 A.

obviously more substance than the landowner himself. But in those early centuries the advance of metallurgy affected politics more simply and directly by cheapening armour, by taking from chief and noble the monopoly in war which made them alternately the great bulwark of the community and its invincible masters. Others rose to speak on more equal terms with them. But the invention of coinage was a more subtle solvent of old society. The age of barter, of rents paid in produce, passed; and that long period of the world began, through which the price of grain has risen and fallen, making and breaking by turns tenant and landlord, but, whichever of these was for the moment in the ascendant, always enriching the dealer.[15] Of changes in society produced by a currency, not the least was the movement which it accelerated in the break-up of clan-life, in the transformation of clansman and chief into tenant and landlord, in the supersession of old ties by the cash nexus. Time saw a rough agricultural canton change to a city with lands about it, the city now the centre and full of tradesmen and craftsmen and seafaring men, of new capacities, new ideas, new demands, a town democracy. The townsmen came to have a clear majority over the farmers, who were no longer the mainstay of the state but an adjunct to the city people.

The Greek was thus more and more committed to Democracy and town life. Herodotus saw the drawbacks or at least had the opportunity of learning them from Greek and foreign critics. We have seen

[15] See the witty talk of Socrates on men who were "lovers of wheat" and took it wherever men valued it most highly; Xenophon, *Oeconomicus*, 20, 28.

what Cyrus said of the agora and its place in Greek
life (i, 153). When Demaratos warns Xerxes not
to hope that the Spartans will yield to him without a fight, the King's brother Achaemenes de-
nounces him as a typical Greek; " in truth the
Hellenes delight in such a temper; they envy good
fortune and hate what is better than themselves."
Xerxes admits this more or less, but hints it is a
feature of Democracy; "citizen envies citizen in
good fortune, and shows ill will in silence, nor if
his townsman asked advice would a citizen tell
him what seemeth him the best, unless indeed he
were far advanced in virtue; and such men are few"
(vii, 236, 237). The Greeks knew this well; did not
Hesiod "four hundred years before my time" (ii, 53)
say, "Potter has ill will at potter, carpenter at
carpenter; poor man envies poor man, and singer
singer?"[16] "It seems," says Herodotus, "it must
be easier to hoodwink many men than one—if
Aristagoras failed to hoodwink Cleomenes the
Lacedaemonian, one man, and then succeeded at
it with thirty thousand Athenians" (v, 97).

The struggle for life, the social dislocation that
trade and coin involved, the break-up of old clan
bonds, the modernization of society, and the old
envies that never die in a small community where
people are nearly equal but not quite,— the crowd's
readiness to be humbugged,—here was a world where
faction would flourish. Herodotus shows that it
did. "When there was *stasis*, or faction," he says,
"between the Athenians of the sea coast and the
Athenians of the plain," Pisistratus, "aiming at
tyranny, raised up a third party. He collected

16 Hesiod, *Works and Days*, 25.

partisans and pretended to be champion of the hillmen" (i, 59). The hillmen, we are told today, may
have been a mining population, but they seem in any
case to have been poor. Elsewhere we get glimpses
of similar things. Theagenes became tyrant of
Megara after "slaughtering the cattle of the wealthy,
which he found by the riverside, where they had put
them to graze,"[17]—a brief story that tells of many
difficulties in a growing urban civilization, shortage of
water for everybody, shortage of pasture, and perhaps insistence on ancient privilege antedating the
city's growth. The creation of the Athenian water
supply, the fountain of Enneacrounos, was one of
Pisistratus' contributions to the city's welfare.[18] The
tunnel through the hill on Samos for a conduit is
another illustration of the water problem; it was
perhaps the work of Polycrates.[19] All these indicate
social change widely spread. Another source of
tyranny was dissension in the noble house that had
ruled a clan once, and still wished to rule what was
now a city. A changing community and an un-
changing family dynasty gave an opening to the
ambitious or expelled nobles; and so Cypselus
ruled Corinth in succession to the Bacchiads of whom
he came.[20] "Most of the ancient tyrants were originally demagogues," says Aristotle.

Professor P. N. Ure has recently raised some
interesting questions as to tyranny in the Greek
cities of the period we are studying. How far can a
modern party leader manage to control either a great

[17] Aristotle, *Politics*, V, 5, 9, p. 1305 a.
[18] Thucydides, ii, 15, who says it was done by "the tyrants."
[19] Herodotus, iii, 60.
[20] Herodotus, v, 91.

nation or a city unless he has party funds? He may
go a good way with very little capital under certain
conditions; but any kind of campaign means money,
as King Archidamus told the Spartans; "war is an
affair of money;"[21] and party war—perhaps one
should except Mexico and Central America here—
party war is in the same case. Mr. Ure urges that
the tyrants, at least the founders of the dynasties,
were one and all first-class business men, rulers who
made reforms and innovations in currency, devised
and carried through great public works, enacted laws
bearing upon labour, thought out enlightened
colonial policies which they supported with com-
mercial alliances.[22] Such interests, he holds, taken in
conjunction with their control of funds and main-
tenance of mercenary forces, point not so naturally to
demagogues of the agora as to the new man, increased
in goods and pushed to the front by the new conditions of the world. No doubt, after power was once
attained, confiscations served the tyrant's purpose.
The land policy of Pisistratus in Attica, his allot-
ments of small holdings, would hardly have been
possible if he had left his well-to-do enemies in undis-
turbed possession of what for Attica were large
estates. Polycrates was of another type, and got his
funds in another way; he was a wholesale pirate,
as Herodotus shows—"all his warlike enterprises
prospered. An hundred fifty-oared ships he had,
and a thousand archers, and he harried all men
alike, making no difference; for, he said, he would get
more thanks if he gave a friend back what he had
taken than if he never took it at all" (iii, 39). But

[21] Thucydides, i, 83.
[22] P. N. Ure, *Origin of Tyranny*, pp. 300-301.

Polycrates too was up to a certain point, on the same showing, a shrewd observer of the Mediterranean world and its balancing powers.

Some well-known verses of Solon indicate yet another origin of tyranny. In the confusion which new developments of trade and currency and new conceptions of life and liberty brought about in a Greek city, sometimes fighting and murder were avoided, as in modern industrial strikes, by recourse, to a species of arbitration. Some man was chosen who had the public confidences, he was to be *aisymnetes*; he was charged to produce cosmos out of chaos, and the conflicting factions covenanted to abide by his decision. Herodotus does not himself tell the story of Solon's legislation, though he alludes to it (i, 29), and in particular commends his adoption of the Egyptian census, "the law that every Egyptian should every year declare his means of livelihood to the ruler of his province (*nomarch*); and, failing so to do, or to prove that he had a just way of life, be punished with death. Solon the Athenian got this law from Egypt, and established it among his people; which may they keep for ever! for it is a blameless law" (ii, 177). Miletus, Herodotus tells us, ended its factions by getting men of Paros to reconcile them; the Parians came, surveyed the land and noted down owners who farmed well, and to these they awarded the ruling of the city; the rest should obey them (v, 29); and no doubt it answered for a time. Solon, however, says himself that some of his friends thought him a simpleton, because once in the saddle he did not stay there; he could have been tyrant and he preferred not to be—a simpleton indeed, but such was his preference.

Plato in his old age put forward the view that there neither is nor ever will be, a better or speedier way of establishing an ideal polity than by a tyranny.[23] One must not say abruptly that he held the view, but Isocrates his contemporary held it. Isocrates praised the rule of Evagoras in Cyprus, conscious as he did so that in Athens the democratic man had very different ideals and very different success. In his old age Isocrates called on Philip of Macedon to unite Greece—of course, it involved force—and to lead a united Greece against the source of all its divisions, the guilty Persian Empire. Herodotus belonged to an earlier day and he did not like monarchy; but, as usual with him, this dislike did not in the least prevent his having a very human interest in the men themselves who held tyrannies.

III

The three tyrannies of longest duration according to Aristotle were that of the Orthagorid family at Sicyon which lasted a hundred years, the rule of Cypselus and his family for seventy-three and a half years at Corinth, and the broken but renewed sway of Pisistratus and his house at Athens, thirty-five years in all. Hiero and Gelon between them at Syracuse had only seventeen or eighteen years, and in fact most tyrannies were of quite short duration.[24] It is interesting to contrast how Aristotle and Herodotus deal with the three great houses who reigned long. The men are far more interesting in Herodotus' story, incomparably more, and he stands, one may

[23] *Laws*, IV, p. 710.
[24] Aristotle, *Politics*, V, 12, 1-6, p. 1315 b.

be sure, a good deal nearer popular tradition; but
Aristotle a hundred years later can rescue relevant
political facts.

The Orthagorids ruled so long, says Aristotle, because they treated their subjects with moderation
and in general observed the laws, and they won the
favour of the people by taking care of them. Cleisthenes was respected for his military ability, and, it is
said, once crowned a judge who decided against him
at the games. Diodorus Siculus found it recorded
that Orthagoras, the founder,[25] had been a cook.
Herodotus at once makes Cleisthenes a personality,
a great figure, a man with strong racial prejudices and
(to our minds) very original ways of giving expression
to them. He did not approve of Dorians in general,
from which modern scholars take it that the tyranny
embodied a reaction of the original inhabitants
against their Dorian conquerors, and this they link
with Aristotle's remark about the care the family
took of their subjects; peasants and husbandmen
and workers generally must have been the bulk of
the population, and of the old stock. And of Dorians,
Cleisthenes, like a true Greek, disliked particularly
his neighbours at Argos; for Argos was perhaps still
the predominant power of the Peloponnese, though
shortly after Cleisthenes' death Argos began to
decline as Sparta rose. Few would think it possible
to tell the story better than Herodotus, so a page
shall be taken from him intact, a page as full of
history as it can be, and yet light and bright as every
story that Herodotus tells (v, 67, 68).

Cleisthenes, when he went to war with Argos, first
stopped in Sicyon the contests of the rhapsodes [the re-
citers of Homer] by reason of the poems of Homer, for in

[25] Herodotus, vi, 126, calls him Andreas.

them Argives and Argos are hymned almost everywhere.
Then, secondly, since there was—and there is still—in the
market-place itself of the Sicyonians a hero-shrine of
Adrastos the son of Talaos, Cleisthenes desired, seeing he
was an Argive, to cast him out of the land. So he came to
Delphi and asked the oracle if he should cast out Adrastos;
and the Pythian prophetess answered him saying that
Adrastos is king of the Sicyonians, and Cleisthenes but a
stoner of the people. When the god did not grant this, he
went away home and took thought to devise how Adrastos
shall get gone of himself. And when he thought the way
was found, he sent unto Thebes in Boeotia and said he
desired to bring into his own city Melanippos the son of
Astakos; and the Thebans gave him leave [apparently, to
remove the bones]. Cleisthenes then brought Melanippos
to Sicyon and gave him a sacred precinct in the *prytaneion*
itself and planted him there in the strongest position.
Now the reason why Cleisthenes brought in Melanippos
(for I must tell this also) was that he was the bitterest foe
of Adrastos, seeing Melanippos had killed both his brother
Mekisteus and his son-in-law Tydeus. And when he had
appointed for him the precinct, he took away the sacrifices
and festivals of Adrastos and gave them to Melanippos.
For the Sicyonians had been accustomed to honour
Adrastos exceedingly, since their land was formerly the
land of Polybos, and Adrastos was daughter's son of
Polybos, and Polybos dying without son gave his kingdom
to Adrastos. The Sicyonians then not only gave other
honours to Adrastos but, what is more, honoured him with
tragic dances referring to his sorrows; and this honour they
gave not to Dionysos but to Adrastos. Cleisthenes be-
stowed the dances on Dionysos, but the sacrifice on
Melanippos.
    Such were his acts regarding Adrastos, and moreover
he changed the names of the Dorian tribes, that Sicyonians
and Argives might not have the same tribes. And therein
he mocked the Sicyonians to the utmost, for changing the
names he took them from pig and ass and hog and added
the tribal ending to them, except in his own tribe, to which
he gave a name from his own rule. These were called
Archelaoi (rulers of the people), and the others of one tribe
Hyatai (Pig-folk), of another *Oneatai* (Ass-folk) and of the
last tribe *Choireatai* (Swine-folk). These names of the
tribes the men of Sicyon used both while Cleisthenes ruled

and, when he was dead, for sixty years more. Then however they took counsel together and changed them to *Hylleis*, *Pamphyloi* and *Dymanatai*, and to these they added a fourth, calling them *Aigialeis* after Aigialeus the son of Adrastos.

In this story we have gleams of much that stirred in that century,—struggles of non-Dorian populace and Dorian nobles, the inrush of Dionysiac religion, the beginnings of drama, and a state of religious belief that is almost unintelligible to people trained for a thousand years, or at least four hundred, in monotheism. The oracle, it is suggested,[26] was ungrateful, for Cleisthenes fought for the god on the side of the Amphictyons against Cirrha not unsuccessfully[27] and joined in the re-instituted Pythian festival;[28] or else the response was made up later on in days when the Dorian—the Spartan—controlled god and oracle at Delphi. As for Melanippos, the story that Herodotus tells of the bones of Orestes and how the Spartans recovered them from Tegea (i, 68), explains exactly what Cleisthenes did. Cimon, the Athenian, in Herodotus' own day did the same for Theseus,[29] and Sophocles long years after wrote his *Oedipus at Colonus* with a similar motif.

At a later point (vi, 126-130) Herodotus returns to Cleisthenes, and gives his pedigree,—Andreas, Myron and Aristonymos,—and tells the splendid tale of the Wooers of Agariste, his daughter. Cleisthenes wished to find out the best man of all the Hellenes and give her to him to wife. So when the Olympic games were being held, and Cleisthenes was victor in them with a

[26] By How and Wells.

[27] Pausanias, ii, 9, 6.

[28] Pausanias, x, 7, 6, Cleisthenes won the chariot race, 582 B.C.

[29] Plutarch, *Theseus*, 36; *Cimon*, 8; Cimon and his colleagues were allowed that year to award the prize for Tragedy; they gave it to Sophocles, and Aeschylus in vexation left Athens for Sicily.

four-horse chariot, he caused a proclamation to be made, that, whosoever of the Hellenes thinketh himself worthy to be son-in-law of Cleisthenes, he shall come to Sicyon on the sixtieth day or before; for Cleisthenes will conclude the marriage within a year reckoning from the sixtieth day. Then all those of the Hellenes who had pride either in themselves or in their country, came as wooers; and for them Cleisthenes had a running course made and a wrestling ground and kept them for this very end.

Herodotus gives a long list of young men of renown who gathered to Sicyon, some of them bringing with them sore perplexities for chronologers, but all as happy as the athletes and demigods that Pindar hymns; indeed the whole atmosphere is much the same. Cleisthenes inquired of each one of them first his native land and his family, and then for a year he made trial of them to test their manhood and disposition as companions singly and together; the younger he watched in the gymnasium and particularly at the banquet, and he entertained them magnificently. But he misjudged; for preferring the two Athenians, he chose Hippocleides "who surpassed all other Athenians in wealth and beauty."

Here comes in curiously a tale told in the Orient of another lost bride[30]—the fable of the Dancing Peacock, who for his beauty won the Royal Goose's daughter—her own choice, and then overflowing with delight, in breach of all modesty, began to spread his wings and to dance and expose himself, whereupon cries his host:

Pleasant is your cry, brilliant is your back,
Almost like the opal in its colour is your neck,
The feathers in your tail reach about a fathom's length,
But to such a dancer I can give no daughter, sir, of mine;

[30] Macan, *Herodotus*, iv-vi, Vol. II, appendix xiv. See also H. G. Rawlinson, *Intercourse between India and the Western World*, p. 25.

and the peacock covered with shame suddenly flew off without a word. Herodotus, as might be expected, tells a better tale.

When dinner was over the wooers began to vie with one another in music and in speeches. And as the drinking went forward, Hippocleides, now far outdoing the rest, bade the flute player play a dance measure for him, and the flute player obeyed him, and he danced. And he pleased himself marvellous well with his dancing; but Cleisthenes eyed the whole business with disfavour. After a while Hippocleides bade one bring in a table; and when it came he danced on the table first Laconian figures, and after that Attic also; and, thirdly, he placed his head on the table and made gestures with his legs. Now Cleisthenes, while he danced the first and the second, hated it that Hippocleides should yet become his son-in-law, because of his dancing and his shamelessness; but he refrained himself, unwilling to break out upon him. But, when he saw that he had made gestures with his legs, he could no longer restrain himself, but said: "O son of Tisandros, thou hast however danced away the marriage." And Hippocleides caught him up and said "No matter to Hippocleides." And the word became a proverb οὐ φροντὶς Ἱπποκλείδη.

So Agariste was given to Megacles "son of that Alcmaeon who went to Croesus,"[31] and she bore him a son, the legislator, Cleisthenes—a son worthy of both the great houses of which he came. But whether the story of the Peacock came westward to Herodotus, or the story of Hippocleides drifted eastward, there is neither chronological nor other proof to show. The story is sixteen hundred years old, we know, in the East, and twenty-four centuries old by now in Herodotus, and there we must leave it.

[31] See chap. IV, p. 124.

IV

Next after the Sicyon tyrants Aristotle puts the house of Cypselus as successful in maintaining themselves. Of the means by which Cypselus became tyrant Herodotus tells us nothing but he gives us a hint. He puts the story into the mouth of the Corinthians, when the Spartans called the Peloponnesians together to restore Hippias to Athens. His expulsion, the Spartans say, had proved already a mistake; a thankless people is increasing in power; some have learnt, and some may yet learn, that they had blundered in freeing Athens; so Hippias is here to be restored. The majority of the allies disagreed, but kept silence, till the Corinthian Socles protested, and told at length of the Corinthian experience of tyranny (v, 92). The speech shows, as Mr. Macan says, the contrast between Herodotus and Thucydides, contemporaries as they are; even here Herodotus is a story-teller. But it is conceivable that the story of Cypselus was told at the conference, if not so well; for standards of relevance have varied with ages and civilizations. Abraham Lincoln was criticized by more cultured colleagues for telling irrelevant little stories, but his stories solved a great many problems. The tale told by Socles was not irrelevant.

Corinth had been an oligarchy, Socles says, or Herodotus says it for him; the oligarchs were a noble family, the Bacchiadai, who married among themselves. One of them had a lame daughter, known as Labda, from the Greek letter Λ, because she was so crooked; and none of the Bacchiadai cared to marry

her. So she was given to an outsider, and she bore
him a son. The coincidence of two oracles warned
the Bacchiadai, and they sent men to destroy the
child. Labda supposed it was friendship that
brought them to see her baby and fetched him.
"They had planned on the way that the man who
first received the child should dash it on the ground.
So when Labda came with the child, by divine
chance the child smiled to the man who took it, and
he saw, and pity seized him and stayed him from
killing it, and in compassion he handed it to the
next," and it went round and back to Labda; and
they left. But she heard their talk at the door and
hid the child in a chest (*cypsele*) and when they
returned to kill it, they could not find it. So Cypselus
came by his name, and by that sense of inequality,
which, we learn from Aristotle, produces revolutions.[32] He grew to manhood and became tyrant,
"and many of the Corinthians he drove out, and
many he deprived of their substance and very many
more of their lives." And Periander his son succeeded him.

When Periander became tyrant, he was at first
milder than his father; but he sent a messenger to ask
Thrasybulus, the tyrant of Miletus, what course
would be safest for him in government. Thrasybulus
led the man into a field of growing corn and kept
asking him why he had come from Corinth and, as
he asked, striking the heads off the taller ears, till he
had destroyed the best part of the crop. Periander
understood the message, and "whatsoever Cypselus
had left undone in killing and driving into exile, this
Periander finished." Aristotle tells it the other way;

[32] Aristotle, *Politics*, II, 7, 10, p. 1266 B.

it was Periander's advice to Thrasybulus. Aristotle justifies it so far as "a policy not only expedient for tyrants or in practice confined to them, but equally necessary in oligarchies and democracies;"[33] and he reminds his readers that the Athenian ostracism which "disables and banishes the most prominent citizens" is a measure of the same kind.

Periander's most famous outrage illustrates the beliefs of the day, so aptly that it has sometimes baffled commentators. He had killed his wife Melissa (iii, 50), perhaps accidentally, though her family took it ill. It so fell that he sent to consult the oracle of the dead on the river Acheron among the Thesprotians; and Melissa came up from the dead, possessed of the knowledge he wanted, but she would not reveal it, "for she was cold and naked; the clothes he had buried with her were of no use at all, for they had not been burned." So Periander called all the women of Corinth to a festival in the temple of Hera. They came in their fairest raiment, and he had them all stripped, free and slave alike, and burnt their clothes, praying the while to Melissa; and after that Melissa told him what she knew. "Such a thing, then, ye see, O Lacedaemonians, is tyranny and such are its deeds." (v, 92.) Elsewhere Herodotus tells of the sad quarrel between Periander and his younger son, who bitterly resented his mother's death; and how he had to send the boy to Corcyra out of his sight; "for Corcyra, too, was subject to him;" and how later on he tried to have him back reconciled, as he himself grew old; how the sister pleaded with the youth not to cure ill by ill, not to punish himself and see their father's house

[33] Aristotole, *Politics*, V, 10, 13, p. 1311 a; III, 13, 17, 18, p. 1284 a.

plundered. "There be many" she said, "that set reason before righteousness; and many ere now have sought what was their mother's and lost what was their father's. Tyranny is a hard thing to come by, and many are its lovers; and he is old and past his youth; give not thine own blessings to others." But the boy would not hear; he would never return while Periander lived; and shortly after the Corcyraeans killed him (iii, 50-53).

The older commentators were sorely puzzled by the story of the burning of the clothes. Was it to get the gold out of them? asks Rawlinson, with some recent Indian parallel in mind. Was it to diminish the resources of powerful families, or is it a perverted account of a sumptuary law? Modern students of folklore have less difficulty; they know more about ghosts among primitive peoples, and the ways of communicating with them and sending presents to them. Once more Herodotus has preserved for us a story that some historians would have disdained to chronicle; and he has shown us the thoughts that really lived in the age.

V

Of tyrants perhaps the Pisistratids are the most famous. Pisistratus with his supporters from the hills, and, so the story says, his bodyguard, becomes tyrant; and twice expelled, as Herodotus and Aristotle both say, he twice returns, and he dies tyrant, and regretted. He was plainly one of the most remarkable men of his age, a born leader of men, genial, kindly, and tolerant. The best story of him is in the Aristotelian *Republic of Athens*—the story of the "taxless farm." He saw a man hard at work "digging stones," and sent a slave to ask what he got out of it. "All the troubles and pains there are," says the man, "and of these troubles and pains Pisistratus has got to take the tenth." The tyrant, charmed with his outspokenness and industry, said the farm should be free of all taxes. He had an agrarian policy, and men looked back to his days as "the reign of Kronos," the Golden Age; he had a system of international alliances and a colonial outlook; he built a water supply; he got his name connected with Homer somehow, and more intelligibly with other poets still living; and he founded festivals. He was a ruler thoroughly alive to his age and its requirements; he acted vigorously, and he laid the foundations of Athenian greatness—of empire and trade and culture alike. In exile or in Attica, he was always equal to life and not afraid of it. Herodotus dwells chiefly on his expulsions and returns, his alliance and his quarrel with the Alcmaeonid Megacles, and the pageant of Athena in person bringing him home,—but in truth, men said afterwards, she was just Phye of the Paeanian deme, 5 foot 10 inches tall and fair to look upon, especially in such armour as Athena wore.[34]

Of the sons of Pisistratus he tells us rather more (v, 55-65). They keep coming into his narrative. He sets forth the story of Harmodius and Aristogiton, and incurs Plutarch's wrath[35] by saying that these famous (if not very creditable) liberators were of Phoenician descent, which leads to a capital di-

[34] For Pisistratus, see Herodotus, i, 59-64.
[35] Plutarch, *De malignitate Herodoti*, 23, p. 860 E.

gression on the alphabet (v, 58, 59). Then the Alcmaeonids come again into the tale, and bribe the Pythian priestess, to whom they had access, seeing they had restored the burnt temple of Delphi and made it beautiful beyond their contract with a front of Parian marble. So the Spartans were egged on to free Athens and at last they came; and by a fluke, just as they were abandoning the siege of the Acropolis, the children of Hippias fell into their hands, and Hippias capitulated and went into long exile. For twice the Corinthians stopped the Spartans from reversing their policy, and Hippias, long "familiar with oracles more exactly than any other man" warned them of days to come when they would assuredly regret above all' others the loss of the sons of Pisistratus. Hippias next induces the Persians to intervene, but even so Athens would not have him back (v, 94). But after long years he did get back for a day, and the battle of Marathon wrecked his last hope (vi, 107). But his sons carried on the intrigue, and went up to Susa to induce Xerxes to restore them (vii, 6). For a Greek must be in his own land to be permanently happy; and Herodotus shows in the terrible tale of Samos to what lengths a Greek would go to be at home—Samos is ruined, "the Persians swept it clear and delivered it to Syloson, empty of men" (iii, 149), the reward of a red cloak given long before to Darius at Memphis (iii, 139).

We need not perhaps survey other Greek tyrannies of which Herodotus speaks, but may attempt a general view of the results to be gathered from his picture of Greece in the age of the tyrants and down to the beginnings of Persian aggression. The personal aspect comes first. Whatever Herodotus has to say of tyranny—and that awaits us—it is impossible quite to dislike his tyrants; author and reader are too much interested in them. Polycrates plunders and harries everybody whom his corsairs meet on the sea—a pirate, a ruffian, and one of those who, as Thucydides says, kept Greece divided and weak,[36] a conqueror of Greek islands and mainland towns (iii, 39). But romance and something Greek hang about it all. He made his *coup d'état* in Samos with fifteen men at arms (hoplites) and remained lord of the island (iii, 120). Herodotus does not say it in so many words, but it looks as if Polycrates might be the author of "the three greatest works of all the Greeks"—the water channel designed by Eupalinos and driven through the hill, the mole twenty fathoms deep round the harbour, and the greatest temple that Herodotus has seen (iii, 60). At all events, "saving only the tyrants of Syracuse, not one of all the other Greek tyrants is worth comparing with Polycrates for magnificence" (iii, 125). He is the hero of the famous tale of the ring thrown into the sea and brought back inside the fish (iii, 41, 42), and the victim, at the end, of Persian treachery and cruelty (iii, 125). After all, the reader is somewhat inhuman who does not love every man that interests Herodotus.

VI

When Darius and his six friends had put an end to the Magian usurper,—whom Herodotus calls Smerdis and Aeschylus calls Mardos,[37] both attempt-

[36] Thucydides, i, 17.

[37] Aeschylus, *Persae*, 774, πεμπτὸς δὲ Μάρδος ἦρξεν, αἰσχύνη πάτρᾳ, θρόνοισί τ' ἀρχαίοισι.

ing the Bardiya of the rock of Behistun,—they debated, the historian says, on the government that Persia ought to have, "and words were said incredible to certain Greeks, but they were said all the same" (iii, 80). "The Greek readers of Herodotus," says Sayce, always ready with a charge of lying,

displayed a wise incredulity, since the sentiments expressed were those of Greeks, not of Persians. The Behistun inscription implies that Darius succeeded to the throne by birth. . . . Herodotus does not tell how he knew these speeches were spoken although he had not travelled in Persia, and was unacquainted with the Persian language.

One may remark that elsewhere, when, like Professor Sayce here, Herodotus uses the plural in a generalization about a race and its thoughts, it is with some critics enough to discredit him; Professor Sayce, however, may generalize sweepingly without being called a liar. How Herodotus came by this story of the debate, which he re-asseverates at a later point (vi, 43), it is not so hard for a close student of him to divine. He had not indeed been in Persia, and he clearly did not speak Persian; we have seen so much. But that Persians were to be found outside Persia, we know on other evidence than that of Herodotus. Even Aristophanes can joke about the possibility of their coming to Athens,[38] and Thucydides himself speaks of Persian envoys coming westward,[39] even if we suppose there were no satraps in that century in Asia Minor. But we have seen already the strong probability of intimate intercourse between Herodotus and Persian nobles; and that the family of Zopyrus, who stood for phil-Hellen ideas

[38] Aristophanes, *Acharnians*, 91.
[39] Thucydides, iv, 50, envoy to Sparta.

and therefore probably for a more liberal way of life, would put the case strongly for the supporters of Democracy among the Persians, is at least as probable a supposition as the well-worn theory of lying, to be used whenever anything unfamiliar to the reader occurs,—or as the fancy of Maass that Herodotus simply took the story from Protagoras. "That," says Eduard Meyer who knows Herodotus with some intimacy, would "make him a *Dummkopf*," and by now we hardly think Herodotus a *Dummkopf*.[40]

But whether the sentiments are Greek or Persian, the evidence behind them can be multiplied at will from Greek and Persian history, from the story of Rome and the records of Islam, and perhaps elsewhere. The great elemental passions are the same everywhere; black women love their children, and yellow men love their wives. So let us at least hear what Herodotus was told that Otanes said for his proposal to give the government to the whole Persian people, and not forget how Plato tells us[41] (and probability is with him) that "there was a time when the Persians had more of the state which is a mean between slavery and freedom. . . . the nation waxed, because there was freedom and friendship and communion of soul among them." To something like this, we are told, Otanes would have wished to return.

"I hold," he said,

that no single one of us should any longer be monarch. For it is neither pleasant nor advantageous. You saw the insolence (ὕβρις) of Cambyses and how far it went; you

[40] Meyer, *Forschungen*, I, pp. 201-202. Busolt, *Griech. Gesch.*[2] II, 619n agrees with Meyer.

[41] Plato, *Laws*, III, 694 A; cf. Herodotus, i, 126-129, on Cyrus as liberator of the Persians from Median rule.

had your share in the insolence of the Magian. How could monarchy be a well-ordered thing, where the ruler can do what he will and not be called to account for it? For indeed the best of all men, once in such a position, would be set outside the ordinary thoughts [a very striking and Greek picture of it]. For insolence grows in him out of the blessings he has; and envy from the beginning is native to man. And he that has these two (insolence and envy) has all wickedness. For, sated by insolence, he does many shameful things, and others from jealousy. And yet a man that is a tyrant should be without jealousy, seeing that he has already every blessing. But it is the opposite of all this in his dealings with his citizens; for he envies the best men that they live and are safe, and he rejoices in the worst of the townsfolk and is himself best at listening to slander. Nothing is so hard to fit in; if thou wonder at him in moderation, he is vexed that he has not utter service, and if one serve him to the utmost he hates him for a flatterer. The worst yet I have to say. He alters the customs of the country, he does violence to women, and he kills men without trial. But the rule of the many— first, its name is of all most beautiful, to wit *isonomy*, equality before the law; and, next, it does none of the things that a monarch does. The offices are assigned by lot; no man has rule without being accountable; and it carries all counsels to the general assembly.

So he votes for Democracy.

So votes Herodotus, and he sees in the progress of Athens after the attainment of liberty a proof of Freedom's value. He knows what men say of Democracy,—how much easier it is to humbug a multitude than one man (v, 97), how jealous the vulgar are of one another (vii, 237), how Gelon the tyrant of Syracuse sold a whole people into slavery because he counted "a demos an ungracious thing to dwell with" (vi, 156), how Megabyzos retorted to Otanes upon the folly and violence of a useless mob, its insolence worse than the insolence of a tyrant because less informed, its ignorance of what is best, and its unwillingness to learn, its headlong sweep, like a river in spate, into business without reflection (iii, 81). He knows all these things; and they are all very largely true, as Plato saw, and as others have seen and said in our own day. Yet liberty, equality, fraternity, in spite of the crimes done in their name, are beautiful things, as he says. Herodotus, exile, wanderer, and lover of men, sticks to the most daring of all faiths, that at bottom you can trust the people. Athens grew great on Freedom; and, grown great, she above all others saved the Freedom of all the Greeks (vii, 139), and he loves her for it above all other Greek cities, as we all do.

CHAPTER VII

THE PERSIAN WARS

I

For two hundred years and more the Greeks had been developing the sense of freedom, the taste for it, and the instinct for self-government. Noble families had yielded place to tyrant dynasties and they to one kind and another of democracy. Perhaps by 500 B.C. the tradition was not so well established as later on that each community of Greeks ought ideally to be independent of every other, but the Greek leaders, who had to secure the coöperation of all Greeks if the Persian was to be driven back, would bear witness that the passion for independence was their chief difficulty. It was carried as far as it could be with safety to the Greek world. Greeks must be free, that was an axiom. Barbarians were cast in another mould. "After the reign of the priest of Hephaestus" says Herodotus, "the Egyptians were made free; but they never could live without a king" (ii, 147). What a people! And King Amasis, "held at first in little esteem as a man that was but one of the people and of no high family," made himself their master and "brought them to consent to be his slaves" (ii, 172, 173). Such were barbarians; and even the Persians would prostrate themselves before their Great King and try to force Greek envoys to do the same; but "they said they would not be pushed down by them head first; for it was not their custom to prostrate themselves to a man, nor had they come for this" (vii, 136). "Ich kann nicht mit Proskynesis dienen," said Bismarck of William the Second. Let the Persian do it, the Greek would not; he was not planned by Nature, as the barbarian was, to be any man's slave.[1]

But it is one thing to believe oneself entitled to freedom, and another thing to achieve and keep freedom. "The price of liberty is eternal vigilance," and Greek freedom was not exempt from the constant dangers that beset high ideals. On the whole the difficult transition from an age of clans and cantons to one of cities, from primitive pastoral and agricultural life to one of far more intricate and complicated economics, had been made successfully. The incubus of old noble families was removed, tyranny for the time was no urgent danger, nor had Democracy yet become a parody of itself. The individual was still free to be himself, and was still conceivably capable of managing the affairs of the state. Greece had not yet reached what later on was bitterly called the equality of the unequal.[2] The question, however, was to rise, which rises in all democracies; the citizen, reasonable enough where domestic problems were concerned, intelligent of existing conditions—is he capable of a sudden expansion of outlook and the realization that all the familiar conditions hold no longer or only by a

1 Aristotle, *Politics* i, 2, 4, p. 1252 b. "Among barbarians no distinction is made between women and slaves, because there is no natural ruler among them; they are a community of slaves, male and female." Cf. Euripides, *Iph. Aul.*, 1266.

2 Cf. Isocrates, *Areopagiticus*, §§ 20 ff.

jeopardous tenure? The Pennsylvania Quaker managed well enough with his local Indians—that fact has been sufficiently announced; the testing time came when he and the local Indian were the merest details in a much larger problem, involving Quebec, and the West, and Europe. Democracy of one sort and another was achieved or in sight in most of the Greek cities of which we know anything. But Lydia had shown the limitations of a city democracy; for five generations Greek cities had fought in loose order against organized monarchy and had in general succumbed. Now it emerged that such monarchies as Lydia itself were mere units struggling in vain with a world power, not only markedly superior in force to themselves but greatly advanced in all the arts of government beyond any mankind had yet seen. Darius would seem to have had a clearer and more powerful brain than any other king of antiquity who had anything approaching his responsibilities and opportunities. Cyrus had made a great empire: Darius inherited it at a bad time when an incompetent successor, a usurper, and a series of rebellions had shaken Persian rule everywhere. He had restored the empire once more by force of arms, and then welded it into the system, which, in spite of weak rulers and disorderly satraps, made it the predominant power in the world for nearly two centuries, —limited only, as we remember, in the waters of the Mediterranean by a tacit compromise with a city which owned a fleet upon that sea. Darius was the real menace to Greek democracy, and it was a question how far the democratic leaders of the three hundred communities understood his significance.

This is the story which Herodotus has to tell,—
interesting enough, whoever told it, as a narrative, an
episode in ancient history. But it was far more than
an episode; it was a turning point in the development
of mankind, that struggle of Greece with Persia, a
crucial case of Democracy on trial. For us it has a
new interest. The American Civil War once more
saw Democracy on trial; it survived the test, and for
half a century the faith was far and wide securely
held that a democracy is equal to any strain put upon
it. The very name was beautiful, as Herodotus says;
and it was to prove the easiest thing in the world
to turn Irish and Italians into good Americans and
to endow Bengalis with all the virtues bred by a
thousand years of struggle in the Anglo-Saxon.
Today few thinking people are quite happy in their
faith in Democracy; and those who cling most to it
realize how far are the ideals sketched by Pericles
from Bengali, and Irishman, and Spanish American.
Men may cling to the ideal of Democracy, but if they
think at all about it, they realize sadly that it is not
easy of achievement but the most difficult and
dangerous of all ideals, not yet achieved—a Celestial
City, the pilgrims toward which need all the hope
and faith that God and History can wake in them.
"I have known all along" said Cleon, "that a democracy cannot rule an empire;"[3]—and Cleon was the
favourite son of a democracy, its own peculiar prod-
uct and pride, whose very name became a perpetual
hissing for every enemy of democratic government.
Incapable of governing others, incapable (as Plato
felt) of governing itself, incapable of anything but
weltering down to suicide, Democracy perished in

[3] Thucydides, iii, 37.

Greece and in Rome, and none too soon in either case, as even enthusiasts must admit. Democracy failed in antiquity, but not till it had done certain things. It failed at last, the victim of its own ideals of autonomy and individualism, but in the meantime it had given the world everything that we call Greek; it bequeathed to us nearly everything that makes life human—ideals of freedom, a great literature, a great art, a splendid tradition. Its story is itself like the vision in Plato's *Phaedrus*, where the soul, a charioteer with two horses—reason the controlling power, spirit and passion the impulses—rises into the ideal world, and there beholds the wonders of God, eternal beauty and eternal wisdom, and the great procession of glorious and blessed spirits,—a vision that will haunt and inspire a man for ever, but cut short by the plunging of the horse called Passion,—a gleam unsteadily seen, but enough to quicken him who sees. That the horse called Passion has lost for us of late the vision of the pattern laid up in the heavens, most thoughtful democrats will own.

II

At the critical hour Greek democracy met the test and survived it; it did not succumb to the invader, and the great story had a great historian; and there mankind are happy. For certain other great and formative periods in old-world history we have no great historians. The work of Alexander and the rise of Rome we know in part, but not from writers of the supreme gifts of Herodotus. Polybius saw and understood, but he stammered in the telling of it, and men cut his story down and saved authors far less valuable.

But in the story of the Persian War, which after all is more signal, more crucial, in human history, we have no such lament. For, to recall and to sum up what we have already discussed, Herodotus had all or nearly all the qualifications that could be asked. He knew the Greek world from the Black Sea to Italy; he knew the Persian and the Egyptian, one might almost say every barbarian except the Carthaginian; and he liked the Greek and the barbarian too well to fail in sympathy; he was *philobarbaros*, as we have seen. Not every statement in his pages can be taken as absolutely true; he was fallible, and men misled him, consciously or unconsciously. But no one can read him long and often, and know him intimately without being convinced of his essential fairness; "malignity" is the last vice that an ordinary reader of intelligence would attribute to him. He had his attachments, his prejudices, as even moderns have; he was influenced, as we all are, by contemporary views, by the estimates that become established, the legend to which a great man will grow.[4] But he was one of those whose passion is to know the truth.[5] An age which had no printed page and knew no footnotes neither permitted our modern consultation of records nor allowed an author to flaunt his pains. But how carefully and thoroughly he prepared for the writing of his history by close and accurate survey of the ground, notably at Thermopylae and Plataea, was not guessed by ancient or

[4] Surely in the case of Themistocles he chose not to follow the legend.
[5] G. B. Grundy, *Great Persian War*, p. 559.

modern, till G. B. Grundy, as we saw, did the same
and found that Herodotus was before him. And
further to recall what we have seen already, Herodotus took pains to learn from men who had
been in the actions; and it is brought out that their
data, not always complete and often from men not
in possession of the headquarters' plans, again and
again give the modern military expert the clue that
the historian himself had missed. He compared and
he criticized what men told him;[6] sometimes he would
give discrepant versions; sometimes, as in the story
of the Ionic Revolt, he left gaps in his narrative.
"A dishonest historian," as Mr. Grundy adds,[7]
"would have been sorely tempted to round off the
tale; an unscrupulous one would not have hesitated
to do so." There are men who do less criticism as
they understand it better; and Herodotus repeats
that his part is to tell the story and let the reader
judge.

We have already discussed the sort of sources to
which he had access; it remains to notice another
limitation which his environment put upon him. He
was, though he does not look it, a pioneer in the
writing of History, making his own method, finding
out as he went how it ought to be done. One feature
of all successful writing is that the writer shall not
forget that men are to read what he writes. Herodotus wrote for an age that was not accustomed
very much to historical writing; he had not the sort
of public to which Polybius appealed, nor the security
of survival that print gave to E. A. Freeman. Hence
the taunt of Thucydides, whose "strictly historical

---

[6] Cf. Herodotus, v, 85, 86; vii, 214.
[7] G. B. Grundy, *Great Persian War*, p. 559.

narrative might be displeasing to the ear," but who does not write a show piece to be heard, or read, and then forgotten.[8] Herodotus meant to please the ear, as Macaulay did, yes, and as Shakespeare did. He shared the interest of ordinary men in the marvellous, the strange coincidence, the hint of other worlds than ours. If he had not yielded to his interest here, our own picture of historic Greece would have been far poorer. He loved a good story, as most men do; and his stories give us the very breath and pulse of Greek life; they are far more valuable to us than they were to his listeners and his earliest readers. His audience was interested in battles; military manoeuvres pervade the histories of the ancients; Thucydides, Tacitus, Arrian are packed with battles, surprises and movements. But surely the fact that Herodotus of all ancient historians tells the tale of mankind's most famous war with a minimum of military detail, with far less of it proportionately than any other great historian of antiquity, is a measure of his greatness. From a military point of view the story of the Persian invasion is interesting; conceivably Xenophon's retreat might be from that point of view more interesting; I do not know. For the historian, Herodotus' method and his treatment of his material are far more valuable. It was the war of one half of the world against the other, and the belligerents were of more moment than Salamis itself. Even a layman is surprised at the brevity with which that great action is settled. But here the digressions are the story; and, whatever else we miss or would wish, we come to know Greeks and Persians with a rare degree of intimacy, and our

[8] Thucydides, i, 22.

historian never gets his perspective wrong. He has throughout the sense of the grandeur of his theme, its bigness, its dignity.

Aristotle contrasts Tragedy and History in his *Poetics*, and speaks somewhat slightingly of History and of Herodotus. Not in a spirit of mere revenge, but surely with a certain right, with Herodotus before us, we may borrow some of his great phrases about Tragedy. Tragedy, he says,[9] reproduces an action serious, complete, and of a certain magnitude; it is an "imitation of life," it depends on plot and character; the plot must have sequence and connexion, beginning, middle and end, and the characters must be above the common level, true to life but more beautiful. Now may not much of this be applied to History? May it not be as "serious and philosophic" as Tragedy, without losing its own proper character? May we not say that Herodotus reproduces, "imitates," or gets the real life of, an action, with real antecedents and real consequences, with a plot that hangs together and becomes more and more intelligible as he unfolds it, and that his characters have the dignity, the moral value, which they should? All these words are liable to trivial use, but is it not true that, as one grasps the real significance of the Persian War, one grows more sure that Herodotus' treatment of it is worthy? And what higher praise can poet or historian ask?

9 Aristotle, *Poetics*, 6, p. 1449 b.

III

To show the Persians for what they are, the historian goes back to their rise, to the days of Cyrus and the shattering of the power of the Medes. He brings out, as we have seen, and shall see, their fine character, not without hints of that change which Plato afterwards noted. A race that teaches its sons to ride, to shoot with the bow, and to tell the truth, that wears leather breeches and drinks water, comes down into the battle ground of the old empires. With less avowal of design than Polybius, Herodotus shows how in half a century the Persian did what the Roman did afterwards, mastered the known civilized world, the Greeks of the mainland and of Italy and Carthage excepted. First the Mede fell, then Babylon, then Lydia, then Egypt, till the Persian ruled from the Aegaean to the Satlej. What a story he unfolds! It is as Aeschylus summed it up, when he described their march against Greece:

Heroes?—none is so heroic as to stem that warrior-flood!
    Not their strongest dams shall bide
    Such resistless ocean-tide:—
Nay, Persia's valiant myriads shall in no wise be withstood.
For the God's doom all-controlling had decreed this long
    ago.
    Persia's sons shall win renown,
    Beating hold and tower down,
In the clash of charging horsemen, and in cities' overthrow.[10]

Beyond Asia they had already gone; Egypt and Cyrene were theirs, and Darius had attempted to conquer Thrace and the lands across the Danube.

[10] Aeschylus, *Persae*, 87-92; 101-107 (A. Way, with some alteration).

So far the Danube remained the frontier, but the Persian had a firm foothold on Europe already. But it was plain that genuine peace on the Asiatic shore of the Aegaean would be impossible so long as a kindred race on the farther shore was always ready to send ships and hoplites to the Ionians in any attempt they made against the Imperial government. Order on one side of a frontier and disorder on the other is an impossible combination; something will happen to the frontier, and a serious governing power will sooner or later carry order out into chaos.

Other considerations moved Persia forward, less cogent in modern eyes. There was the example of the kings before, who had advanced the frontier and enlarged the Empire—a consideration that seems historically to have weighed with most of the conquering dynasties of the Orient. Persia, like other powers, had imperial destinies. There were also Greek exiles, whose friends and countrymen perhaps overestimated their influence; but their influence, whatever it was, told in favour of Persian advance. Demaratus from Sparta, the Pisistratids from Athens, did what they could, with a view to their own return to their countries, to secure Persian ascendancy. "The sons of Pisistratus," says Herodotus, "sat at the Persian's elbow and brought charges continually against the Athenians, while at the same time Darius himself wished to use this pretext and subdue those nations of Hellas, which had not given him earth and water" (vi, 94). That was between the Ionic Revolt and Marathon; and it went on afterwards in the reign of Xerxes. The Aleuadai, the royal house of Thessaly, were pressing the King to come against Greece (vii, 6); and the

Pisistratids in person at Susa, with Onomacritos, an Athenian oraclemonger (and not above suspicion, as they well knew), were doing all they could to move the King. They told him great things of Onomacritos as a prophet; and he in turn quoted all the oracles he knew (or perhaps could adapt) which implied the subjection of Greece; he even foretold that it was prophesied the Hellespont should be yoked by the Persian with a bridge; but, Herodotus adds, there were oracles that he suppressed (vii, 6). And when Xerxes marched, the Pisistratids went with him; and they did their best to get Athens to surrender when the Persian troops besieged the city (viii, 52).

Herodotus' narrative of the Ionic Revolt is involved and difficult, and it has gaps. It is only by inference that the modern reader gathers how serious a struggle it was, and how much more sturdily the Ionians maintained it than Herodotus' critical attitude toward them would lead one naturally to suppose. It took Persia nearly seven years to crush these desultory fighters, who would not practise rowing in their triremes but preferred to sit in the shade on the shore (vi, 12). The suggestion conveyed by this story clashes with the general trend of the narrative, and Mr. Grundy uses the contradiction to elucidate a point in Herodotus' method. The historian cannot be supposed, by any who know him intimately, to have invented this refusal of navy practice; whence then did he borrow it? Who told him of it? Mr. Grundy traces it to Samos, where, as we know, the historian lived for a while, and where he learnt the many stories of Samos that enrich his book. But the Samians, after fifty years, had things to explain as to their conduct in the war; men said they had deserted, while the battle at Lade was still raging (vi, 14) as a result of overtures from the Persians through Aiakes the son of Syloson (vi, 13), and that this was why the Persians spared their famous temple, the Heraion (vi, 25). Herodotus records the apology of his hosts; their fathers, when approached by the Persian, were already dissatisfied with the conduct of the war and foresaw that it would be a fiasco (vi, 13). Yet even so, eleven Samian ships refused to retreat, and to their commanders later on a monument was erected in Samos, which, Herodotus says, is in the agora (vi, 14). Anyhow, he says, there are accusations all round about that battle of Lade, and he cannot say who fought well or ill (vi, 14). Mr. Grundy emphasizes the value to us of a historian who can leave his tale with loose ends and contradictions, but who preserves the contemporary evidence in the form in which he received it.[11]

The story is woefully incomplete; the seven years seem telescoped, and the names of men, who must have fought with a courage to match Thermopylae and Salamis, are lost. It was, says Mr. Grundy,[12] "one of the glorious pages in the history of the Hellenic race. Nature had so placed them in the world that their struggle against the great empire was from its very outset a desperate, a hopeless venture."

Several things contributed to make the revolt possible and to prolong it. The Ionians were not alone; Caria and Cyprus were also in revolt. The Carians, as we have seen, were a fighting race,

[11] G. B. Grundy, *Great Persian War*, pp. 126-131.
[12] G. B. Grundy, *Great Persian War*, pp. 131, 132.

though in the end they were subdued somehow; it is not clear how; but they kept their own royal dynasty, and its representative stood high with Xerxes. Plutarch, trying to be caustic, says that Herodotus makes his fellow-citizen, Queen Artemisia, more gifted than Themistocles.[13] The history of Cyprus, though difficult to follow, is significant in the record of Greek and Persian relations, whether it be war or diplomacy. A century later the reign of Evagoras reveals how serious a menace to Persia an independent Cyprus could be. Cyprus was the key of the Levant.[14] Mr. Grundy finds the precipitating cause of the adhesion of Cyprus to the Ionians in a victory gained by the Ionian fleet off the Pamphylian coast in 498, which would account for the Phoenician fleet being out of action. Of this victory Herodotus perhaps had not heard, but Plutarch indignantly accuses him of leaving it out on purpose.[15]

But far more significant for the history of mankind was the fact that the Athenians supported their kinsmen in the fight for freedom and sent them twenty ships; "and these ships," adds Herodotus (v, 97), "were the beginning of evils for Greeks and for barbarians." "He tells about Sardis," says Plutarch,[16] "and does his utmost to spoil and slander the exploit; the ships, which the Athenians sent to help the Ionians when in their revolt from the King, he dares to call the beginning of evils, because they endeavoured to set free from the barbarians Greek cities so many and so great." How and Wells

[13] Plutarch *De malignitate Herodoti*, § 38, p. 869 F.
[14] G. B. Grundy, *Great Persian War*, p. 105.
[15] Plutarch *De malignitate Herodoti*, §24, p. 861 B.
[16] Plutarch *De malignitate Herodoti*, § 24, p. 861 A.

call this comment at once just and patriotic, and Macan says the historian's phrase is "an exaggeration, used with epic force to dramatize the story."[17] Herodotus, however, does not express this view once only. "After this," he says at an earlier point (v, 28), "there was for no long time an abatement of evils, and then again evils began the second time to fall on the Ionians, arising from Naxos and Miletus." "Evils began to come to pass for the Ionians from these cities on this wise" (v, 30), and he tells how Aristagoras, ruling at Miletus, wished to restore certain exiles to Naxos, and persuaded Artaphrenes to send ships to take Naxos, and thence to subdue the Cyclades and go on to Euboea; how the expedition failed and Aristagoras conceived that his only safety was in revolt. Histiaeus, of course (with the man who had the message tattooed on his head), was in the plot; and, when all came to ruin, the Ionians "asked him why he had so eagerly charged Aristagoras to revolt from the king and had done thereby so great evil to the Ionians" (vi, 3). Dr. Macan does not believe that the Ionians put such a question at all, but "Herodotus fully endorsed the shallow view that the Ionian revolt was a huge mistake." Mr. Grundy takes strongly the view that "the revolt had saved Greece."[18] But this was hardly the view of Herodotus.[19]

The Revolt failed after seven years of war,—battles, sieges, and death in every form, and Miletus wiped out (vi, 19-21); and it left, to all seeming,

---

[17] Professor Bury (*History of Greece*, p. 244) puts the remark down to "the solemnity due to the historical significance of the moment." This is to ignore the other passages.

[18] G. B. Grundy, *Great Persian War*, p. 132.

[19] See also Eduard Meyer, *Forschungen*, II, p. 200.

everything as it was before, Persia triumphant all round, Greek cities enslaved (even if Mardonius did come down from the King and clear out the tyrants and set up democracies), Cyprus reduced, and the Carians again a subject people. What was more, it was now certain, as it had not been before, that the Persians would make the attempt to conquer European Greece, and indeed Europe. It is very well for moderns to say that Persia would inevitably have attempted this in any case. "Inevitable" is a dogmatic word; and, if Thucydides is to be trusted,[20] it is not wise to be dogmatic where war is concerned. Flukes and chances are many, and the inevitable may be postponed till it is forgotten. The inevitable war between England and Napoleon III did not come; Antiochus Epiphanes did not extinguish Judaism. But after the Ionic Revolt it was fairly plain to everybody, with an outlook on the whole world, and beyond his canton, that the Persian would come, and that he would find once more what he found in Ionia, divided counsels, mistrustful confederates, and so many leaders that nobody could lead at all. It was not to be counted on that Caria and Cyprus would again hold up the course of events and postpone destruction another seven years. Nor could anybody foresee what Thucydides almost alone recognized in retrospect— that two factors would wreck the Persian undertaking, the presence of Themistocles among the Greeks, and the supreme command of the Persian forces in the hands of Xerxes. "Themis-

[20] Thucydides, i, 78, the inscrutable nature of war; i, 80, Archidamus, with experience of many wars, will not allow war to be "either a safe or a good thing." So, too, Hermocrates, iv, 59.

tocles," he says (i, 138), "by natural power of mind and with the least preparation was of all men the best able to extemporize the right thing to be done," and "the Barbarian miscarried chiefly through his own errors—he fell over himself" (i, 69). The English commentators whom I quote wrote before the European War, and Herodotus had seen a good deal more of the evil effects of war.

On the other hand, if we grant Mr. Grundy's contention that the blow would have fallen on European Greece in any case, there is more to be said for his point that the struggle would have been "waged without the aid of that factor which was decisive— the great Athenian fleet." But if there had been no Themistocles, would there have been that fleet? But such inquiries are too like the speculations as to what the world's history would have been if Cleopatra had had a nose of another type, or if Alexander could have had a stiff dose of quinine at Babylon.[21]

The Ionians failed, as Greeks failed again and again in antiquity, and as Slav and Greek peoples have failed, and the concert of Europe itself has failed, before the Asiatic enemy—through division. In the first round between Democracy and Monarchy, the honours rested with the King, though they had cost him something; for the "evils," as Herodotus quite plainly says, were not solely reserved for the Greeks, though our critics hardly notice this.

The Athenians of the twenty ships had landed on Asiatic soil, had marched inland and taken and plundered Sardis, which Mr. Grundy counts a brilliant stroke if, as he thinks, Sardis was the

[21] The latter was the not unnatural question of Sir Clements Markham, who domesticated quinine in India.

Persian base. The town had been burnt in the process. The famous anecdote, which Herodotus records (v, 105), tells how Darius, on hearing of it, asked first who the Athenians were, as if the Ionians did not matter, and then shot an arrow into the air with a prayer for vengeance. When once the Ionic Revolt was over, vengeance did not delay. But the King, as before among the Scythians, began by under-estimating the difficulties of the conquest of European Greece. His first attempt, with fleet and army working in conjunction, was shattered in the storm off Mount Athos (vi, 44). The fleet was large, for Herodotus was told that three hundred ships were lost; and the plan of keeping so large a fleet in so uncertain a sea dependent on the rate of the army's progress was proved dangerous.[22]

IV

The next attempt left a far more signal landmark in history—Marathon. The experts tell us of the general clearness with which Herodotus sets out the main tactics employed in the battle, how "that honest old historian has winnowed out nearly all the chaff from the crop of legends,"[23] even if he has lost a little good grain in the process, and even if, from general lack of interest in constitutional or official detail, his account of the precise position of Calli-machus as polemarch is somewhat uncertain. After all, the gist of the story is not the method of electing

[22] G. B. Grundy, *Great Persian War*, p. 153.
[23] *Ibid.*, p. 193.

archons in that day, nor the official status of Callimachus. The hero of the day was Miltiades, of whom
Grundy says that "never again, until Leuctra, did any
Greek general display such ability for command,"[24]
and as the story was told—and whatever the detail
the main point would not be wrong—Callimachus
supported Miltiades. Whether Marathon was to be
the point from which the real attack was coming, or
whether the landing were only a feint, it seems clear
that the resolution to which Miltiades brought his
colleagues was right—a battle, and a battle at once;
and victory confirmed the resolve.

There remain a number of questions about the
Persian plan of campaign and the possibility of some
understanding between the Persian commanders and
a party in Athens. It was the fashion before the late
European war to call the defence of the Alcmaeonidai
made by Herodotus against the charge of signalling
to the enemy a flimsy and inadequate attempt, and
to regard it as equivalent to proof that the Alcmaeonidai were in communication with the enemy.
Perhaps the experience which we had in England of
similar charges may allay some of the suspicion
against the great Athenian house. It was widely
believed, when the first Zeppelins came over, that
they were guided through England by automobiles
with suspiciously strong headlights. Responsible
people doubted this, and later on we learnt more
about Zeppelins and nobody mentioned the theory
again. But it reminded me of the shield-signalling
which was charged against the Alcmaeonidai,—a
thrilling story, useful in political strife, but quite
probably untrue. Of course the criticism commonly

[24] *Ibid.*, p. 195.

passed upon the defence made by Herodotus is true enough; he is naïve and argues *a priori*. But how else could anybody meet such a charge, or prove a negative, in a case forty years old? The story may be true that the family had political reasons for wishing a great change, as modern historians hold; but the evidence is flimsy. The report about the signalling may quite as well have been falsehood as truth;[25] such things are not even yet outside the range of politicians. Herodotus has been accused of naïveté elsewhere, and has often proved sounder than his critics.

Marathon must have done for all Greeks what Shiloh and Corinth, with the emergence of Grant, did for the North in the American Civil War. The Persian had conquered one continent, and held of a second all that was worth while; it was only likely that Europe would collapse before him. The first naval attempt had miscarried through a storm at sea. The Scythian expedition had been a war against geographical conditions. The Thracian and Macedonian proceedings were what could have been expected. Marathon was the first real trial of strength on European soil, a battle against Greek soldiers and on land. Athens had, as Herodotus says, greatly improved her position in Greece since the expulsion of the Pisistratids; Athenians had beaten other Greeks in battle. But the Persian was another story altogether. Lydia and Egypt, the greatest powers of which Greeks knew anything, had fallen before him. And now in overpowering strength, after

[25] G. B. Grundy, *Great Persian War*, p. 191, "The *details* of the shield incident hardly admit of discussion. The incident itself is obviously a historical fact." Nevertheless, 1915 makes me doubt it.

triumphantly blotting out Eretria (vi, 101), the Persian descended on Attica, landed, and in the open plain met the Athenian hoplite in battle—and was beaten, and the expedition was an ignominious failure. Whatever temptation to exaggeration might flush a Greek victor, the bare fact here was amazing enough; the hoplite had beaten the Persian, on good ground, the Persian outnumbering the Greek army. "The battle of Marathon," Plato makes one of his characters say in ¹he *Laws* (707), "was the beginning and the battle of Plataea the completion of the great deliverance, and these battles made the Hellenes better"—which he denies of Salamis and Artemisium. Marathon was a forewarning, just as the Retreat of Xenophon and the Ten Thousand was a forewarning, that Persia would one day fall before Alexander the Great.

But Alexander was still a century and a half away; and, signal as the victory of Marathon was, it did not finally decide the issue. The Persian would come again. It may have been—we can hardly do more than guess—that the impressive character of the victory of the foot soldier led some in Greece to undervalue Themistocles' foresight about the navy. Certainly, Herodotus, as we have seen, met and listened to men who had little admiration for Themistocles; but all that is involved in the narrative unfolded by Herodotus confirms the judgment of Thucydides as to the genius of Themistocles. It is not brought out in any clear or satisfactory way by Herodotus that Themistocles virtually conceived and created the Athenian navy; but it is plain that to him belongs the credit for its creation as for its supreme service at Salamis.

V

The Persian took his own time for returning. Philip of Spain let thirty years pass before he made his decisive attempt to subdue England. Darius had to deal with a revolt in Egypt,[26] but died before he could do it; "and thus he did not succeed in taking vengeance either upon the revolted Egyptians or upon the Athenians" (vii, 4). It was left to Xerxes, the handsomest man among the Persians (vii, 187), to add Greece to the Empire. The last three books of Herodotus cover the expedition of Xerxes and end with the decisive victories of Greek soldier and sailor.

Herodotus tells us of the years spent both by Darius and by Xerxes in preparation, but he says little of the detail of the arrangements made. Perhaps they were not recoverable; probably they would have been of much less interest to the Greek than to the English soldier. For, in any case, an army so large and operating at so great a distance from its own countries and sources of supply, if it had never been dreamed of before, was never likely to be seen again. There might be little practical interest in an account of plans and means that nobody would ever have to use. A Roman general two or three centuries later would have read it, perhaps, and probably with interest; but Herodotus foresaw neither English nor Romans, and he wrote what would engage his own people. They found the bridge over the Dardanelles a thing to excite the imagination (vii, 36). The shade of Darius questions Atossa about it in the play:

[26] Herodotus, vii, 1.

DARIUS: Yea?—but how did hosts so mighty cross afoot from shore to shore?
ATOSSA: Hellê's sea-gorge with his engines bridged he, stretched a highway o'er.
DARIUS: And he wrought the deed, to bar the gates of mighty Bosporus?
ATOSSA: Even so; some daemon was it helped him, when he purposed thus.[27]

The cutting of the canal across the neck of Athos also impressed the Greeks. Herodotus tells a curious story of the double trouble it caused many of the workers (the Phoenicians excepted), which historians might not have expected, but which four years of War Office work leave a great deal more intelligible to English readers, possibly to Americans, also. "It seems to me," so writes Herodotus (vii, 24),

so far as I can conjecture, that it was from love of magnificence that Xerxes bade dig the canal; he wished to display his power and leave memorials of it. Without any trouble at all, they could have drawn the ships over the isthmos; yet he bade dig a channel to the sea, so broad that two triremes might sail through with their oars spread. To the same men on whom he laid this digging, he gave orders to bridge the Strymon also.

In this connexion his two hints at commissariat are found, apart from the tale of rivers drunk dry and towns ruined by providing one meal for the great army.[28] Somewhere near Athos was "a meadow where they had an agora and a market, and great quantities of wheat from time to time came to them from Asia ready ground" (vii, 23). "He charged the Phoenicians and Egyptians to lay down food for the army, that the army might not hunger nor the baggage animals, driving on to Greece" (vii, 25).

[27] Aeschylus, *Persae*, 721 (A. S. Way).
[28] Herodotus, vii, 58; 108; 109; 118; 120.

To the modern military student, what Herodotus omits or never learnt would be very interesting. The means by which the various contingents were massed at Sardis, the arrangements for feeding them in detail on their tribal and traditional diets, the moving of an army so vast and of so many languages,—even if we set the total figure a long way below the estimated five millions of the historian,—the effective coöperation of fleet and army, which was the secret probably of the victualling, and on which the whole campaign depended—all these are matters which imply an extraordinary degree of thought and experience.[29] So much the late war brought home to us. But not even Thucydides stops to tell us of the feeding of the troops at Syracuse, though (truth to tell) many incidents of the Peloponnesian War have less interest. The Greek's mind was elsewhere. When he built a city, as Strabo tells us, his thought ran on beauty and a fair land and harbours, while the Roman thought out paving and water supplies and sewers and other tedious things.[30] Once Herodotus does just glance at the Persian medical service and sufficiently reveals the backwardness of the Greeks on that side. There was an Aeginetan on a ship, who "fought till he was hacked all to pieces;" the Persians took him alive, however, and in admiration of his valour "used all diligence to save him alive, both tending his wounds with ointments of myrrh, and also wrapping him up in bandages of linen cloth" (vii, 181).

[29] Cf. G. B. Grundy, *Great Persian War*, p. 222, who holds that the organization for food and transport necesssary to bring so great a force so far and to place it in efficient condition on the field of action is convincing proof of ability of no ordinary kind.

[30] Strabo, v, 8; C. 235.

But other aspects of the struggle interest Herodotus more, and particularly the attitude of the
various Greek states. The doubtfully Greek kingdom
of Macedon was, of course, under Persian control,
though the quite Greek royal house (v, 22) had a hero
prince, Alexander, whose sympathies were with the
land of his ancestors, and whose help was ready on
occasion, though necessarily not too openly (ix, 44).
It is remarked that Alexander is a favourite with
Herodotus; and his full information about the prince,
and his liking for him, are taken to show personal
friendship and perhaps residence at his court long
after the war. The Thessalians, who lay next on the
King's path, were divided. The princely house of the
Aleuadai "were the first of the Hellenes who gave
themselves over to the king" (vii, 132). They had
urged the conquest of Greece from the first (vii, 6).
But other Thessalians took another view; and before
the King arrived in their country, they urged the
Greeks in congress at Corinth to hold the pass by
Olympus; they would themselves aid, and in this
way the war might be kept out of Thessaly and out
of Greece; but a large force would be needed, and
"if you shall not send, be assured that we shall make
agreement with the Persian; since it is not right that
we, standing as outposts so far in advance of the rest
of Hellas, should perish alone in your defence"
(vii, 172). A force was sent, and then for reasons not
very clear it was withdrawn. Herodotus says that
Alexander advised them to depart and "not remain
in the pass and be trodden under foot;" the Greeks
discussed the message and thought it good advice,
the word of a man friendly to their cause, and they
went away (vii, 173). But Herodotus thinks the real

reason was fear, when they learnt that there was another way into Thessaly, which Xerxes actually used. Another story preserved by Diodorus was that, in spite of the Greek army, the Thessalians were beginning to surrender to Xerxes, perhaps a consequence of their knowledge of the other pass. It has again been suggested that the Greeks were none too sure of the Boeotians. In any case Mr. Grundy notes the military insight of Herodotus, who tells the story of Alexander, but gives himself the one cause sufficient by itself, the discovery that they could be assailed from the other pass.[31]

Plutarch's feminine quality makes itself felt in his comment here. "He need not have trampled too much on those of the Greeks who Medized—a man, counted by others a Thurian, but attaching himself to the Halicarnassians, who, Dorians as they were, marched with the *harem* against the Greeks."[32] He is particularly angry with Herodotus for saying "in so many words" that "the Phocians alone of men in that region did not Medize, and for no other reason at all, as I conjecture, but hatred of the Thessalians. But, if the Thessalians had supported the cause of the Hellenes, then, I think, the Phocians would have Medized" (viii, 30). Yet few things are so evident in Greek history as the strength of local jealousy as a political motive. It was not a thing on which a hero worshipper would look back with pleasure, but the allusion to it does not prove Herodotus either malign or a liar, even if elsewhere some of these local enmities were sunk, as Plutarch says. But the real sin of Herodotus was that he had

---

[31] G. B. Grundy, *Great Persian War*, pp. 228-231.
[32] Plutarch, *De malignitate Herodoti*, 35, p. 868 A.

written a book in which, in indelible letters, that no time would ever blot out, he had told of the treason of the Boeotians, especially the Thebans "Medizing greatly and keen for the war" (ix, 40). The Theban defence is given by a Boeotian speaker, who, in the pages of Thucydides, maintains that at the time Thebes was ruled by an oligarchy, a cabal very like a tyranny, who, to keep the people down, brought in the Persian.[33] Some support is found for this in the story told by Herodotus (ix, 86-88) of the general Greek demand after Plataea that Thebes should surrender the Medizing party, two leaders being specially named.

Argos was another Greek city that supported the Persian. The Greeks had a story, confirmed by what happened, they said, when Callias was in Susa about 448 B.C. "on other business," to the effect that Argive envoys had been there before in the time of Xerxes and made friends with him. So says Herodotus (vii, 151) and his curious reticence on the "other business" is noted; it was not perhaps quite in tune with his main theme. Or else Xerxes had approached the Argives (vii, 150). In any case the Argives preferred "to be ruled by the barbarians rather than yield at all to the Spartans," whose "grasping selfishness they could not endure" (vii, 149). They had reason to prefer the enemies of Sparta; for, fourteen years earlier the long struggle for the land of debate between them, the Thyreatis, had been settled by the battle of Sepeia (494 B.C.) in which Argos "was widowed of men" and lost (it was said) six thousand soldiers. She had great trouble with her Perioikoi,—slaves Herodotus calls

[33] See E. Meyer *Forschungen*, II, pp. 211, 212; Thucydides, iii, 62.

them,—and intestine war went on for long (vi, 77-83). Argos never really recovered for a half-century, and if any city had a right to weigh its own title to existence, Argos had; the Persian could not be worse, from an Argive outlook, than the Spartan. Moreover, Delphi gave them an oracle, which they understood, very justly, to warn them against Greek alliances (vii, 148, 149). Herodotus' own comment is interesting; he gives no opinion as to relations between Xerxes and Argos,

but I know this at least, that if all men were to bring their own troubles into the midst, to exchange them with their neighbours, when they had looked into the troubles of their neighbours they would gladly carry back their own. Thus it was not the Argives who have acted most basely of all. But I am bound to say what is said, but I am not bound entirely to believe it—let this hold good for all my story; for this further is said, that, in fact, the Argives were those who summoned the Persian to Greece, since the spear stood ill with them against the Spartans, and they preferred anything to their present pain (vii, 152).

So the Argives "sat out of the midst; and, if I may speak freely, by sitting out of the midst, they Medized" (viii, 73).

Who it is that the historian hints at as baser in conduct than the Argives, we have to guess for ourselves. Whether Delphi sent this message to Argos or not, "terrible oracles" were sent to Athens (vii, 139). No amount of subsequent editorial care could get rid of the fact that the Delphian god foresaw a Persian victory and Medized; perhaps, as Mr. Grundy suggests, from a notion that Athens alone was the real objective of the king. Even if Spartan pressure helped to steady the god a little, there was no concealing that the god took the wrong side, as he had done before when Croesus was so courteous to

him. He expected Athens to share the horrible fate
of Miletus and Eretria.

The outlying powers had their own doubts and
dangers. Sicily was threatened with a Carthaginian
invasion, which actually came (vii, 165-167). Herodotus records so much; but he does not connect
that movement of the Oriental in the west with the
Asiatic attack on the older Greece of the Aegaean.
The Greeks had, in the meantime, applied to Gelon
of Syracuse for aid. He offered large forces and
abundant wheat supply for all the Greek army, pro-
vided he were made commander of all Greek forces
engaged against the barbarian (vii, 158). In view of
the struggles recorded later on among the Greek
captains, there is something to be said in excuse of
Gelon's idea of unity of command; and it is also
intelligible that the Greeks refused the offer, possibly thinking there might be little difference between one autocrat and another. It may of course
be that Gelon added the condition to his offer to
secure its refusal. With Gelon's taunt that they were
likely to have plenty of leaders but not many to be
led, the negotiations ended. A Venetian proverb, of
medieval or later date, said: "Every five Greeks,
six commanders."[34] So careful of the type is Nature.

The other great western power of the Greek
world, Corcyra, halfway to Sicily, and not threatened
by Carthaginians, a city practised in neutrality, as
Thucydides shows us,[35] found it difficult to decide
what to do. The Corcyraeans promised and shuffled
and planned to wait on events, and that was all they
did. It was not glorious; and they had to explain

[34] William Miller, *Greek Life in Town and Country*, p. 7.
[35] Thucydides, i, 32, 37.

that etesian winds off Cape Malea had stood between them and glory (vii, 168). At a later date they
had to confess that "the policy of not making alliances, lest they endanger us at another's bidding,
instead of being wisdom, as we once fancied, has now
unmistakably proved to be weakness and folly."[36]
It is indeed difficult to do without the rest of the
world. "To himself, no doubt," wrote Mr. Grundy
in 1901,[37] the Corcyraean (in 480) "appeared the
honest man; but to his contemporaries of larger view,
he seemed, as it were, 'the man with the muckrake' of
Greek politics, over whose head the crown of patriotism was held in vain."

In view of the event—the failure of Xerxes, the
two generations of Persia's acceptance of Greek
lordship of the sea, and the later predominance of
Persia—it is plain enough to us what the Great King
should have done, with a divided Greece ready to his
hand. Herodotus tells us that there were Greeks who
told him the true policy for the invader. Demaratos,
with whose house we have seen reason to believe
Herodotus well acquainted,—Demaratos, whose children counted him to be in a sense author of Xerxes'
succession (vii, 3), told the King not to be in any
hurry to fight at Thermopylae; let him send three
hundred ships round to the Peloponnese and take
that island of Cythera, which a wise Spartan had
wished below the waves; he would have no Spartans
left to fight and the rest of the Greeks would crumple
up. (vii, 235). Before Salamis, Queen Artemisia
bade Xerxes not risk a sea battle; he can disperse
the Greeks easily enough without that (vii, 68); and

[36] Thucydides, i, 32; the Corinthian comment is in i, 37.
[37] G. B. Grundy, *Great Persian War*, p. 242.

Themistocles had, as the story shows, all he could do to prevent the Greeks doing as the queen predicted. Before Plataea, the Theban leaders told Mardonius to send money to the party chiefs in the Greek cities, and Greece would break up and fall into his hands (ix, 2). Artabazos a little later said the same to Mardonius; money without stint, especially to the chief men in the cities, and they would quickly hand over their freedom (ix, 41). Mardonius tried to bring Athens to terms (viii, 140), but that was not the right place at which to begin. The great-grandson of Arta-bazos[38] saw the plan carried into effect, and Greece abased before the Great King; and once more the advice was given by a Greek who knew his nation, Alcibiades in exile.[39] But Xerxes and his captains had to learn by experience. They fought the three battles. They took Thermopylae with the aid of a Greek traitor, and they ruined themselves at Salamis and Plataea.

VI

Let us now turn to the Greek states which stood for freedom. Delphi kept sending "terrible oracles" to Athens, which it took all the adroitness of Themistocles to interpret; and then "those Hellenes, who had the better mind for Hellas, gathered together and exchanged proposals and pledges, and there it seemed to them well, first of all things that their quarrels and the wars they had with one another should be

[38] The Pharnabazos who is so pleasing a figure in Xenophon's *Hellenica*.

[39] See Thucydides, viii, 46, who probably learnt from Alcibiades himself, as he learnt much else, that he had given this advice.

brought to reconciliation" (vii, 145). The most notable of these wars was that between Aegina and Athens, and for the time the breach was healed and they fought side by side at Salamis. Sparta also, as we know, played her part in the war in the deliberate and unpunctual way in which she did everything in that century. "Of all Hellenes, you Spartans," say the pungent Corinthians in Thucydides (i, 69), "are the only people who never do anything; on the approach of an enemy you are content to defend yourselves against him, not by acts but by intentions. . . . .We all know that the Persian made his way from the ends of the earth against Peloponnesus before you encountered him in a worthy manner." So the Athenians thought, and so thought Thucydides. Herodotus, perhaps rather amenable to Athenian opinion but not unfriendly to Sparta, says that the Spartans "did not expect that the fighting at Thermopylae would be so soon decided, and so merely sent Leonidas and his three hundred—for the Carneian festival stood in their way, and they meant to do more when it should be over" (vii, 206). By and by they did more—"the Carneian festival was over" (viii, 72). Next year it was the same again. When Mardonius began his campaign, the Spartans were keeping another festival, the Hyacinthia, and "they counted it of utmost importance to attend to the affairs of the god; and at the same time their wall, that they were building across the Isthmos, was beginning to get its battlements on" (ix, 7). Eduard Meyer speaks of Herodotus' "light irony" for the Spartans, and perhaps he is right. Perhaps too it was the best style in which to treat their slow ways of understanding and acting. They could not, apparently, take in the idea, which the Athenians understood well enough, that a hostile power with so great a fleet would never be kept off by a wall across an isthmos. The Corinthians were more sensible, and they perhaps may claim, more justly than the others whom Plutarch champions, that they did better in fact than Herodotus supposed from the Athenian account of the war. But the glory of the war rests with Athens; so the historian believed and so he has taught mankind to believe with him; and, if in these lectures anything has been done to make good his title to be called a true and just historian, Athens deserved the glory. I must not repeat at length what I have already quoted[40] from him as to the great service of Athens,—"but, if a man were to call the Athenians the saviours of Hellas he would not miss the truth" (vii, 139).[41]

Thermopylae, Salamis, Plataea! What a story they make! The bare facts, the very names, are inspiration; but the art, the sympathy, the grace of Herodotus have given them such a setting as no other three battles in human history have had. In the words of Polybius (ii, 35), "he made no small contribution to the struggle of the Hellenes for their common freedom," and, we may add, to those who in every age have believed in Freedom and stood for it. "Most Homeric of men," he has written an epic—the eternal epic of human freedom, never to be read without a deepening of our belief in man and his idealisms, and of our faith in the triumph of the highest.

[40] See Chap. I, pp. 34, 35.
[41] Cf. also Herodotus, vii, 144; viii, 143, 144.

But a question remains. "I am compelled by necessity," says Herodotus in the passage just cited, "to declare an opinion odious in the sight of most men" (vii, 139). Was Athens the saviour of Greece, the author of freedom? Athens the tyrant of the Confederacy of Delos, Athens whose yoke men sought to break in another great war? Was it freedom after all? The Persian invasion was over fifty years before the book was published. The enthusiasm of the boy of Halicarnassus carried him through, and he achieved his epic. Touches here and there[42] remind the reader that he was working at it down to the Peloponnesian War, still loyal to the great purpose of his boyhood, to the great ideal of freedom for which Athens had fought. Men, grown old while he remained young—realists in every sense with which realism and *Realpolitik* can darken life as they darken intelligence—had not his enthusiasm. Was it Freedom?

It was clearly not the old freedom of the days before the struggle, when nearly every Greek state outside the Peloponnese was autonomous. The war had killed the old dream of every city being independent, in every particular, of every neighbour. That dream had come near being the ruin of Greece outright; autonomy for each had all but meant slavery for all. Some unity of command had been proved necessary during the war; Salamis had itself been the fruit of the peculiar activities of one man. The victory had been followed by the Confederacy; the Confederacy in fifty years became an Empire

[42] These are collected by R. W. Macan, *Herodotus* iv-vi, Vol. I, pp. lxiii; xcii; and vii-ix, Vol. I, p. 51; also How and Wells, Vol. I, p. 51. See too Busolt, *Griechische Geschichte*,[2] II, p. 612.

(ἀρχή), and from an Empire it became, as Pericles and Cleon both say in Thucydides,[43] practically a tyranny, to end which was the avowed war cry of the Peloponnesian War. From the retreat of Xerxes onward, the small city and the island town are progressively mere units, or items, in great combinations. Thought and poetry and art are centred as never before in one place, Athens. The courts of the tyrants had of old drawn their poets from islands and little home towns; artists, poets and physicians wandered the world over. From 480 till the foundation of new cities by Alexander and his successors, only Archelaus of Macedon or a Sicilian tyrant could offer attractions comparable with those of Athens, and even so only a second best. Herodotus himself had his intellectual home in Athens. With the political independence died the life of intellect and literature in the little places. They produced at times men of ability, but not as they once did; they had not the background or the stimulus; they had become good places to leave, and such spots contribute little to the fullest life. Greece had to be federated somehow. Any form of federation is liable to imply a centre, and a human centre is apt to starve the circumference. But Greece never much liked any form of federalism, and most of the experiments in that line she thoroughly disliked. The small places hated to be swamped in huge unions and struck for independence, and every fresh blow struck for it showed how futile was the aspiration. Many Greeks of the century might be found to endorse the much criticized view of Herodotus that the twenty ships which the Athenians sent to Ionia were the begin-

[43] Thucydides, ii, 63, Pericles; iii, 37, Cleon.

ning of sorrows; after all Lydian suzerainty had not been so very bad, and Persia had established democracies (vi, 43).

But Herodotus believed that Freedom was a good thing and that the story of Athens proved it; and perhaps he knew that his story of Persia proved it, too. He is taunted by Plutarch, as we have seen, with having been too fair to the Persian. It will repay us to see what Persian rule meant, as he saw it. Individual Persians he clearly liked; but when one recalls the famous description of the monarch who changes customs, does violence to women and kills men without trial (iii, 80), and compares what was done by Persia, we may once more draw a conclusion as to his mind. We may begin with the destruction of Miletus (vi, 19) and Eretria (vi, 101, 106), the killing of their men and the slavery of their women and children—events that clearly shocked Greek sentiment, though it is notorious that, in the days after Herodotus, Athens did the same to Melos, Torone, Scione and other small places, and feared the like herself, after the battle of Aegospotami.⁴⁴ But when one unrolls the tale of savagery that Herodotus records as attendant on Persian monarchy, we get into a region "outside the ordinary thoughts" of democracies and good men. Cambyses to prove himself no drunkard shot the son of Prexaspes, and "laughed with delight" when the arrow was found in the boy's heart (iii, 35); he sought to kill Croesus, and, though glad that the Lydian was saved, killed the men who saved him (iii, 36); he had the unjust judge flayed, and set the man's son to sit as judge and do justly, with his father's skin covering the

⁴⁴ Xenophon, *Hellenica*, ii, 2, 3.

cushion on the bench (v, 25); he insulted Egyptian
religion (iii, 37). Cambyses was perhaps mad—very
mad Herodotus thinks him (iii, 38); but, mad or not,
he was king. Xerxes rewarded the genial Pythios,
who wanted one son not to go on the great expedition,
by cutting the son in two and letting his army march
between the halves of his body (vii, 39). Even
Darius had done something similar for the same
reason to all the sons of Oeobazos (iv, 84, 85).
Persian nobles and governors did the same sort of
thing: Intaphernes mutilated the doorkeepers of
Darius (iii, 118); Oroites impaled Polycrates (iii, 125),
and killed the messenger from King Darius (iii, 126).
They were served by castrated boys from the Greek
islands (vi, 32); they made men do forced labour
under the lash (vii, 22); and Xerxes thought to make
good soldiers of them too with the lash (vii, 103).
They buried children alive (vii, 114); their princesses
mutilated their rivals (ix, 108-113), and their
generals their fallen foes (vii, 238). Neither body,
nor life, nor wife was safe under such a régime; in
truth all were slaves save one. From all this Greece
was kept free, and the Athenians were the saviours
of Greece.

Freedom may be a very negative thing, but Greek
freedom was creative. Let a man read the great
funeral speech of Pericles as Thucydides gives it and
say whether such an ideal of democracy and manhood
is anything, whether any monarchy or republic of
the modern world has achieved anything like it, or
even can claim to pitch its ideals so high. Amid that
democracy which Pericles described Herodotus lived,
and he knew something of Pericles and admired him.
Freedom *is* a good thing, he says, living in that

community of free men without peers in the ancient
or the modern world. At the heart of these great
ideals was the sense of power, proved by all those
victories over sea and soil and sky that Herodotus
describes in his story of the development of Greece,
and clinched by the conquest of wisdom and the
defeat of the great invader. Democracy and Freedom
stood justified by their achievements, and the
achievements gave to the ideals basis and substance.
Athens had saved not Greece only, but the world—
and for no Spanish-American version of liberty, but
for all we associate with Athens and for all we have
learnt to call Greek.

Herodotus knew this. He dreamed aright when he
conceived of the book which should secure "that the
memory of the past may not be blotted out from
among men by time, nor the great and wonderful
deeds of Greeks and barbarians lack renown, nor the
reason for which they fought one another" (i, 1).
He achieved his purpose, and he wrote a book where
History comes clad in delight and explains what she
has seen and why it means so much.

CHAPTER VIII

THE GODS AND THE LIFE OF MAN

I

Herodotus has been described of late as "the intellectual ancestor of the modern anthropologist and student of comparative religion."[1] Few studies of mankind are so seriously maintained today; and that such a title should be given to Herodotus is a hint that older verdicts begin to be obsolete which emphasized his extreme innocence and credulity, and that a more modern one, crediting him with irony and almost with persiflage[2] in his treatment of religion, may also have to be discarded. We have seen already the intense interest which Herodotus took in the "inquiry" which we call Anthropology. It remains to see how closely interested he was in Religion and in the great questions that it implies.

Here, as in all other regions of human life, he "wished to know." He tells the tale of Psammetichos and his experiment to discover the earliest language, and he continues:

I heard also other things at Memphis, in converse with the priests of Hephaistos; and I visited Thebes also and Heliopolis too, for this very purpose, because I wished to know if they would agree with tales told in Memphis; for the people of Heliopolis are said to be the most learned of the Egyptians. Such stories as I heard about the gods,

[1] L. R. Farnell, *Outline History of Greek Religion*, p. 9.
[2] J. B. Bury, *Ancient Greek Historians*, p. 49.

I am not eager to relate, saving only the names of the gods, for I think all men have equal knowledge about them; and I will say no more about them than what I am constrained to say by my story (ii, 3).

Later on, he adds that "wishing to know something certain from them from whom I could, I sailed to Tyre also in Phoenicia, where I heard there is a holy temple of Herakles. . . . Then I went to Thasos also" (ii, 44). Here we have travels with a purpose avowed, and the purpose is the attainment of real knowledge on religion. We have only to recall his inquiries into the beliefs and cults of all the savages he could hear of, and his interest in Persian religious thought, and it is plain that here lay one of the serious preoccupations of his life.

As we go on, we shall note that, though in the passage just quoted and in others he is very reticent, he does not hesitate to inquire. "Were I to declare the reason for the dedication [of sacred animals in Egypt], I should be brought to speak of things divine, which I especially seek to avoid telling; so far as I have spoken of them in passing(or allusion), it has been under the constraint of necessity" (ii, 65). "The Egyptians have a story about this, but, though I know it, it is fitter I should not tell it"[3] (ii, 47). He takes pains to know, and he is willing to let his reader learn that there is knowledge to be had; but the reader can go to the original sources. Once he ventures perhaps a little farther than he intended, in drawing an inference, or rather in recording the inference he drew; "and as to this, so much said, may gods and heroes be gracious to me!" (ii, 45). This is no "graceful genuflexion," and no "irony," unless

[3] Cf. also ii, 46; 61; 86; 132; 170; 171, for this reluctance to speak of Egyptian religion.

we detach it altogether from the whole mind of the man—a procedure which is not historical criticism. He obviously inquired intensely and acutely, eager to learn all that really could be known; he inquired everywhere; and he remembered and compared what he heard. Inquiry, comparison, and inference are a historian's trade; and the habits of mind, the methods, practised and developed in the whole course of his general "inquiry," remained with him when he dealt with religion. Perhaps gods and heroes may draw other inferences or have fuller knowledge; in that case may they feel no displeasure! He hopes they will feel none, and devotes himself to discovering so far as he can the real truth about the gods; and he uses considerable freedom of mind, and methods more scientific than some of his readers suppose. Most of them would say he is no philosopher, and probably most of the philosophers of his century would sustain the criticism. Mr. Grundy, however, whom I have quoted so often on things military, holds that "by predilection Herodotus was almost as much a philosopher as an historian."[4] He is a thinker, but unlike his contemporaries, the Sophists, he is apt to prefer the procedure *a posteriori*. If this is a limitation, it is one that attaches to historians in every age; and when they transcend it, their usefulness as historians is past.

One drawback or advantage, as one may regard it, of this method of procedure is that it leaves a man who cares for evidence at times very uncertain of his conclusions. At different points his mind will react to evidence not quite uniformly. Now he will lean rather more to one conclusion, and again to the

[4] G. B. Grundy, *Great Persian War*, p. 195.

other. Critics, as we have seen,[4a] have contrasted the tone of the last three books with that of the second, the Egyptian book, and tried to make out some scheme of dates for his writing. They decide that he was more pious when he wrote his *Flavit deus et dissipati sunt*, more sceptical when he inquired as to the relations between the Greek and Egyptian pantheons. Such a distinction, shows, I think, a certain superficiality in the critics, a certain naïveté. They have not always been men peculiarly interested in religion, and they miss the point that piety is not in antithesis to a stringent demand for certainty; on the contrary it frequently goes with sterner canons of truth. To some readers it may seem that we forget Herodotus when we discuss stern canons of truth; an author so pleasant, so easy, so full of good stories, as men have always seen, yes, and, as we have learnt, a peculiarly painstaking topographer, an acute winnower of men's evidence, a shrewd observer of their customs and beliefs. To be charming is not final proof of shallowness.

"I suppose that all men have equal knowledge about them" (ii, 3) is a curious sentence, which might be taken as a quip in another writer who made quips about such things. It does not, however, necessarily imply the cynical judgment that all men are equally well-informed and equally ill-informed about the gods,[5] as it might in Tacitus; for that is not what Herodotus says, and it is quite evident from the preceding sentences that it is not what he means.

[4a] See Chap. II, p. 50.

[5] Stein's interpretation, see How and Wells, *ad loc*. Professor Sayce, always eager to impute a base motive to Herodotus, characteristically says on this passage; "this affectation of religious scrupulosity on the part of Herodotus was probably a cover for ignorance."

He tells us that the Heliopolitans are reputed most learned among the Egyptians as to the gods, and he prefixes the statement that he wished to know the certainty; both of which clauses imply that the meaning of the cryptic sentence is not Tacitean in any way. Several suggestions have been made; Rawlinson supposes him to refer to the divine *names* when he says *them*; Sourdille urges that he refers to the mysteries which he supposes to be virtually the same among all peoples. But, whatever a stray sentence like this may mean or suggest, if it be what he actually wrote—and there is little in the style or construction to suggest interpolation or corruption, though there is always the possibility of a lost line—in any case a large part of Herodotus' interest and attention is given to inquiry that may bring him to fuller knowledge.

II

When we turn to closer study of what he does say, and try to relate it to what we know of his day, his home, and his inheritance, we find an environment of singular interest and complexity. Homer was obviously a large part of his education, and he says, in a passage to which we shall return at a later point, that he thinks Homer and Hesiod gave the Greeks their theogony (ii, 53). In other words, Homer and Hesiod were the great minds that brought order into things divine, which were confused enough, as Euripides says. The two old poets made the connexions between god and god clear, and gave to the gods those characteristics by which Greeks knew them. Homer, it is now generally recognized by scholars, was in a sense responsible for the order and clear presentment of things divine, in the Greek world; he was, more truly than archaeologists of an anthropological turn allow, the founder of Greek religion. Not that he knew it, or aspired to any such rôle; but, as I have tried to show elsewhere,[6] no other presentation of a divine scheme of things was embodied in poetry so compelling and so deathless. The lowly stuff of Hesiod influenced the Greeks; but the incomparable genius of Homer, even if he borrowed all he said about the gods, gave it an appeal that made all other traditions look parochial and old-fashioned; it made it necessary to relate them somehow to the splendid Olympus of the poet. However tenacious of life local cults and local mysteries remained—and today we do not under-estimate their power and vitality—the religion that Homer taught, or appeared to teach, was Panhellenic. In this Panhellenic religion Herodotus grew up. An uncle who "revived epic poetry" would secure that a nephew, who loved books and stories and inquiry, could not be ignorant of Homer's religion; that is an easy hypothesis, confirmed by constant references and implications in the History.

In the case of such a man it is impossible to suppose that interest in legend came only with manhood. The boy Herodotus must have known "divine tales" and legends of omens and oracles and theophanies, Greek and Carian. The uncle was, as well as a poet, a seer of signs; the nephew to the last could rarely resist them. Even with nineteen centuries of Christianity behind us, and two or three of natural

[6] *Progress in Religion*, Chap. III.

science, childhood still has far-travelled and native
tales of strange things and beings,—"the breath of
the bogey in my hair" as the little R. L. Stevenson
goes upstairs to bed, and many a tale of "little people" and magic to wonder at and turn over in mind.
Wonder—the word is a favourite with Herodotus;
and we shall not be far astray in guessing that he
used it early in life. Melissa was not the only spirit
to return from the dead in story (v, 92); and morality
rested from the nursery on many a tale of divine
justice. Strange oracles came true, everybody knew
that. We lose sight of childhood altogether sometimes in the great works of the adult minds of Greece;
let us think of our own fairy tales and recall the picture that Prudentius draws about 400 A.D. of the
religion of the little pagan child of the Roman Empire:—the sacred stone, growing black with holy oil,
the horn of fortune, the baby prayers, and the great
day when they lifted him up at his wish to kiss the
sacred image.[7]

As he grew older, Herodotus was led on to further
views of religion. He learnt the strange influences
that a hero's bones could lend to the land where they
lay, to the people who guarded them, to the troops
who carried them. Orestes helped the Spartans to
conquer Tegea (i, 67, 68). A Spartan law of about
508 B.C. laid down that only one of the Tyndarids
(the Dioscuri) should accompany a Spartan army,
and the other should stay at home (v, 75). In a
similar way on the island of Aegina the Aeacids and
their images are confused in thought (v, 80). At the
battle of Salamis an Aeginetan ship was despatched
to bring "the sons of Aeacus" to help the Greeks, and

[7] Prudentius, *Contra Symmachum*, i, 197-214.

she first (men said) began the fight (viii, 83, 84). Adrastos had his shrine at Sicyon and was honoured with dances (v, 67, 68); and on Aegina, choruses, with scurrilous jests at the women of the island, honoured Damia and Auxesia, or their olive-wood images (v, 82, 83). The hero counted in Greek religion to Herodotus' dying day and after, for the *Oedipus at Colonus* of Sophocles was produced a score of years after his death. This worship of the local hero, ancient or modern—for we remember Brasidas at Amphipolis—what did it mean? What reality lay behind it?

There were mysteries, too, with "holy legends" (ii, 48), and it would seem revelations, as the Homeric *Hymn to Demeter* reminds us, but Herodotus is careful to reveal nothing. Like his contemporary Pindar he will use words "with a voice for such as understand"—"whoever has been initiated into the rites of the Cabiri, which the Samothracians learnt from the Pelasgians and now practise, that man knows what I mean" (ii, 51). Many of his modern readers lack that initiation, but it is plain that Herodotus had had it, that he sought and obtained initiation elsewhere into other mysteries, and that altogether he attached to the mysteries a significance which he does not explain. In them, it would seem, he found confirmation for his belief in the existence of gods, and those gods generally the same in every part of the world, in spite of differences of name.

He believed further that communication was possible between gods and men.[8] The divine will was made plain to Xerxes in dreams, as Herodotus re-

[8] Cf. the account of Socrates' views upon this, given by Xenophon, *Memorabilia*, i, 1, especially § 19.

cords, and it is noteworthy that in the discussion about those dreams, a modern and rationalistic explanation is put forward by Artabanus, who sooner or later says a number of things that seem to fit the mind of Herodotus or his moods. "The roving dreams that visit men are such as I shall teach thee, being many years older than thou. For visions seen in dreams are most wont to come from what a man thinketh of by day; and we in these days past had most assuredly this expedition in hand" (vii, 16, β, 2). Others of the ancients had the same view. Thus the Hebrew *Ecclesiastes*[9] says, "A multitude of dreams results in many foolish words, for a dream comes through too much business, and a fool's voice is heard in many words." Cicero quotes the Latin poet Attius to much the same effect.[10] It is suggested that, in the case of the dreams of Xerxes, Herodotus borrows a motif from Homer. But, even if in the other cases he is "telling what he is told, which is his only business," it is tolerably clear that he was not quite prepared to accept the naturalistic view of Artabanus. Plutarch long after him, and John Evelyn later still, believed that a physical explanation of an occurrence does not invalidate its being a sign. The single horn of Pericles' ram may be due, as Anaxagoras showed, to some odd development within the skull; and yet, as Lampon the soothsayer foretold and events proved, a prophecy of Pericles' sole predominance in Athens.[11] Evelyn believes that comets "appear from natural causes and of themselves operate not,

[9] *Ecclesiastes*, v. 3; see Morris Jastrow, Jr., *A Gentle Cynic*, p. 217.
[10] Cicero, *de divinatione*, i, 22, 45.
[11] Plutarch, *Pericles*, 6.

yet I cannot despise them. They may be warnings from God, as they commonly are forerunners of his animadversions."[12] Later on we shall see a case where Herodotus finds it possible to combine a natural and a supernatural explanation of a geological phaenomenon.

Oracles offer better ground for certitude, for there in favourable instances verification is so far possible that a comparison of the forecast with the event may be made. So shrewd a traveller and inquirer as Herodotus did not miss the fact that not all oracles are genuine. He speaks now and again of a χρησμὸς κίβδηλος (i, 66, 75), which Mr. Godley translates as a "quibbling," Professor Rawlinson as an "evasive" response. When the Spartans, after expelling Hippias on the orders of Delphi, find out that the Athenian Alcmaeonidai had "persuaded the Pythian prophetess by gifts of money, that, whenever men of the Spartans should come to inquire of the Oracle, either privately or publicly sent, she should propose to them to set Athens free" (v, 63), the same adjective is used of the responses (v, 91), which were not quibbling or evasive but downright frauds and shams. Herodotus also tells how Hipparchus, the son of Pisistratus, caught Onomacritus tampering with the prophecies of Musaeus and interpolating a line (vii, 6). Herodotus was well aware that oracles and prophecies may be fraudulent, but he believed that not all are. He was interested, as men are still, in the coincidences (as we call them) of forecast and outcome. We put them down to accident or to shrewd observation, and on both scores justify our interest. He grew up in a *milieu*

---

[12] Evelyn, *Diary*, 12 December, 1680.

where it was believed that a god inspired the forecast; and the inquiry and investigation into cases of prophecy fulfilled bore upon his more general quest of certainty as to the gods and their existence. He did not exclude the possibility of a divine element in the forecasts of Delphi, though he clearly tells us that a human element might confuse the answer.

But that his disposition was in the main to believe, is the common conclusion of his readers. "Thus far I know the truth, for the Delphians told me," is Mr. Godley's rendering of a typical sentence, which Mr. Macaulay gave less forcibly but more literally: "Thus much I know by report of the people of Delphi" (i, 20). The sentence tells us a good deal that we otherwise surmise. He made a good many "inquiries" at Delphi, and he learnt a great deal there, most of it of one colour and uniformly favourable to the claims of the god. He learnt other stories elsewhere of the bribed priestess and the Medizing shrine, of "terrible oracles" sent to scare the Athenians. But, allowing for a certain amount of blunder and corruption, and a good many instances of studied ambiguity and sheer juggling with the unintelligible, though not allowing enough for the possibility of invention after the event, he came to the conclusion that, if there is any truth in human testimony, in face of so many instances of prophecy fulfilled, there remains a residue of cases of genuine foreknowledge, which must be due to divine inspiration; for how else could they have arisen? "With regard to oracles," he says at last (viii, 77), "I am not able to make objections against them that they are not true, for I do not desire to attempt to overthrow the credit of them when they speak clearly, looking at such matters as those which here follow;" and he quotes eight lines that refer quite distinctly to a sack of Athens, a sea-battle, and the day of freedom for Hellas, and he concludes: "Looking to such things as these and when Bakis speaks so clearly, I do not venture myself to make any objections about oracles, nor can I admit them from others."

At this point one may pause to note that, while we allow for sources of information which the priests of Delphi again and again could use without disclosure, while we allow for corruption, for ambiguity, for political shrewdness and knowledge of human nature, and for fabrication after the event, there remain cases of forecast in History for which ordinary shrewdness without amazing luck does not always sufficiently account. A recent Roman Catholic writer pleads, as he would, for what has always been the view of his church, that Delphi was conceivably in touch with the devil, whose agents conveyed the needed information. Few modern readers will have recourse to such a hypothesis. But the stories of Delphi may be taken with others; and, when all are sifted, what remains needs careful investigation. "A man's soul," wrote a rather sober old Hebrew, "is sometime wont to bring him tidings more than seven watchmen that sit on high on a watch-tower."[13] Modern psychologists are not at the end of their investigations of what is popularly discussed as telepathy and thought-transference.

[13] Ecclesiasticus, xxxviii, 14.

III

In any case, the reaction in the mind of Herodotus is not unlike what it would be in a modern researcher. He has not the apparatus of the modern man; he is less expert probably in the tricks of the conjurer; he has fewer things in the way of method or result or even question in his psychological armoury. That of course was to be expected. But, in a way very like our modern way, he enlarges his field of observation and anticipates the Stoic doctrine of the consensus of mankind. He does not so name his principle; he does not name it at all; but he devotes himself to learning the experience, the guesses and the beliefs and the theories, of other peoples. He observes well, as we have seen, and he is not to be blamed for sharing with the eighteenth century its ignorance of the discoveries of the nineteenth. He accepts oracles with discrimination; he does not exclude as automatically as eighteenth century scepticism would have tales of theophany[14] and of phantasms. These the nineteenth century joined with him in reconsidering, though it gave in general a different interpretation. He was initiated into mysteries in a number of places, and he carefully respects the pledges of secrecy. But he does not surrender his intelligence. He examines, he observes widely, and he compares; reason throughout is in the ascendant. Mr. Grundy, in an *obiter dictum*, calls him an "ultramontane," whose "critical capacity is laid aside

[14] E.g., of Phylacos and Autonoos when Delphi was attacked, viii, 39.

where he sees the hand of God."[15] That is not strictly fair; he brought his critical capacity to bear on everything submitted to him, and, where he sees the hand of God, it is a result of the exercise of this faculty and not of its dereliction. If he infers the hand of God, where Mr. Grundy or another would not, it does not in the case of such a man mean abandonment of intellectual integrity. It is equally possible, and a good deal fairer, to say, where we reject his conclusions, if we do, that a wider range of evidence, a closer examination of sources, lead us to another conclusion. We do not accept Apollo, but we may not be ready to exclude God from history without further consideration. In any case, it is easier to accuse Herodotus of credulity than to convict him of inattention to reason.

Before we convict him, or anybody else, it is reasonable to take a full view of the case, and part of the case here is his survey of the growth of Greek religious ideas. My phrase is not his; he is dealing not with those spiritual and moral conceptions that my phrase implies to an English reader, but with matters of divine nomenclature and development of ritual. Like many of the ancients, both Greek and Roman, he assumes that gods worshipped by one race may be identified in gods worshipped by another; Zeus will be Zeus the world over, "Jehovah, Jove, or Lord," as Pope put it with a novelty less triumphant than he perhaps supposed. Certain races worship only certain gods; but sometimes, at quite ascertainable dates, other gods are introduced or new names for old gods. It was Egypt that gave Herodotus his starting point; and modern Egyptologists offer

[15] G. B. Grundy, *Great Persian War*, p. 565.

us certain cautions.[16] He missed the importance of some gods, e.g., Râ (the Sun), Hâpi (the Nile), Thoth (ii, 67). He hellenized his data, as Greeks were apt to do, and did it too much; and partly so, and partly from defective information, he generalized too much. He ignored the large place that magic held in Egyptian religion. All these are essentially criticisms of his knowledge rather than of his judgment; and one may fairly infer from his treatment of what he has learnt and does know, that he would have been as apt and quick to use the fuller knowledge, which the modern Egyptologist draws from hieroglyph on monument or papyrus, as he was to seize such stories and traditions as "interpreters" or Greek residents could give him. Refusal of knowledge is the supreme intellectual crime, and none but the tribe of Sayce insinuates any such thing against Herodotus.

IV

With the information at his service, and with his canon of the identity of gods—an obvious canon then, however doubtful now, he maps out his scheme of things divine. He believed, and Egyptology confirms his belief, that Egyptian religion had received its existing form long centuries before Homer and Hesiod gave the Greeks a theogony (ii, 53). The

[16] See summary in How and Wells on book ii, chapter 35, following Sourdille; also severe criticism by Llewelyn Griffith in *Authority and Archaeology*, and criticism more genial in Erman, *Egyptian Religion*. T. E. Peet, in the *Cambridge Ancient History*, I, p. 326, says that Plato "was the one Greek who seems to have been unimpressed by that 'wisdom of Egypt' which was almost a by-word in the mouths of his fellow-countrymen."

Egyptians, he was told, "first used the appellations of twelve gods, and the Greeks afterwards borrowed them from them; and they were the first also to assign altars and images and temples to gods, and to carve figures of living things on stone. They showed me most of this by plain proof" (ii, 4). There stood that temple with three hundred and forty-one statues representing as many priests in as many generations (ii, 142, 143); and Greece had no such records—Homer and Hesiod lived only four hundred years ago (ii, 53). The Greeks talk of Heracles, he says in an important chapter (ii, 43), but the name came from Egypt to Greece—Amphitryon and Alcmene, his parents, were both of Egyptian descent; and Heracles is a very ancient god in Egypt. For, as the Egyptians themselves say, the change of the eight gods to the twelve, of whom they deem Heracles one, was made seventeen thousand years before the reign of Amasis; and even the Phoenician worship of Heracles, and their temple to him built on Thasos, are five generations earlier than the birth of the son of Amphitryon. The investigation of this was the cause of special journeys made to Tyre and to Thasos (ii, 44); and he thinks a line of distinction should be drawn between the Egyptian god and the Greek hero, one immortal and the other dead, even though both have the same name. He returns to this later on (ii, 145); among the Greeks, Heracles, Dionysus, and Pan are held to be the youngest of the gods; Pan is in Egypt the most ancient; the Egyptian Dionysus is 15,000 years before the time of King Amasis; but Dionysus the son of Semele only about 1,500 years, and Heracles 900 years, before Herodotus. The Greeks date the birth of these two gods by the time when they first heard of them. Further "the Egyptian ceremonies are manifestly very ancient, and the Greek are of late origin" (ii, 58), and it is the Egyptian way to "keep the ordinances of their fathers and add none others to them" (ii, 79).

On the other hand the religion of Greece was comparatively very modern; it was, some of it, clearly derivative, and even the names of some of the innovators and organizers were well known; and with Egyptian religion before him Herodotus could see quite clearly where some of the changes came from.

It was Melampus who taught the Greeks the name of Dionysus and his sacrifice and the pomp of the phallus. I would not in strictness say that he showed them completely the whole matter, for the teachers (*sophistai*) that followed set it forth more fully; but it was from him that the Greeks learnt to carry the phallus in honour of Dionysus, and they got their present practice from his teaching. I say then that Melampus showed himself a cunning man, in that he set himself up for a prophet, and, learning from Egypt much else but particularly the worship of Dionysus, he introduced it with but few changes to the Greeks. For I will not say it is a chance agreement between the Egyptian ritual of Dionysus and the Greek; for in that case the Greek ritual would resemble other Greek rituals and not be lately introduced. Nor will I say either that the Egyptians took it from the Greeks—either this, or any other custom. I think too that Melampus learnt about Dionysus chiefly from Cadmus the Tyrian and the men who came with Cadmus from Phoenicia to the land now called Boeotia (ii, 49).

From this statement about Dionysus Herodotus proceeds to a more general one.

Indeed, well nigh all the names of the gods came to Hellas from Egypt. For that they come from the barbarians, I find on inquiry to be true, and I think that they came chiefly from Egypt. Except the names of Poseidon and the Dioscuri, as I have already said, and Here and Hestia and Themis and the Graces and the Nereids, the names of all the other gods the Egyptians have always had in their land. I say here what the Egyptians themselves say. The gods, whose names they say they do not know, were, I think, named by the Pelasgians, save only Poseidon; and this god they learnt of from the Libyans. For no race of men have had the name of Poseidon from the beginning except the Libyans, and they have always honoured this god. The Egyptians did not so; nor do they honour heroes (ii, 50).

Other religious ideas and practices (with "sacred tales") the Greeks had from the Pelasgians, into whose connexion or identity with the Greeks we need not again look. Here the modern anthropologist is with the ancient historian in believing that Greek religion was a compound to which the old Mediterranean race contributed.[17] The Pelasgians, as we saw, called upon the gods (he learnt this at Dodona, a shrine in western Greece); but they called on them without names, for they knew no names for them, as is still the case in southern India and among other animistic peoples. Long after, they learnt the names of the gods, many of them from Egypt, and much later again the name of Dionysus. They were not sure about using the names of the gods that came from the barbarians, so they inquired at Dodona; for this oracle is considered to be the most ancient among the Greeks, and at that time was the only one. From that day onward, with the oracle's approval, they used the divine names, and the Greeks learnt them still later from the Pelasgians (ii, 52).

He digresses to tell the tale of Dodona's founding, and in two forms. The Egyptians in a matter-of-fact way say that two priestesses were kidnapped by

[17] E. E. Sikes, *Anthropology of the Greeks*, p. 76. See Chap. III, p. 88.

Phoenicians from Egyptian Thebes; one was sold in
Libya and the other in Greece, and they had taught
divination to those peoples. How did they know
all this? asked Herodotus; how could they be so
certain? And the priests replied that their people
had sought but never found the lost priestesses, but
afterwards had learnt the tale they told him. At
Dodona the story was more like a fairy tale. A black
dove settled one day on a beech tree and spoke with
a human voice. It said there must be a place of
prophecy of Zeus there, and the people understood
the message to be divine and founded the shrine.
He gives the names of the three senior priestesses
who told him this in Dodona; and his statement that
the rest of the temple staff confirmed it, hints that
he asked questions, for he did not believe that a dove
would really use human speech; a woman would have
to learn Greek and no doubt she did. "I suppose that
these women were called *doves* by the people of
Dodona because they were barbarians, and seemed
to speak like birds; after a while they say the doves
spoke with a human voice, because the woman spoke
what they could understand" (ii, 54-57). Bird talk,
the twittering of the swallow, was a Greek proverb
for the foreigner's speech.

> Well, if she be not, like a cheeping swallow,
> Possessed of some unknown outlandish tongue,
> My words must penetrate and speak persuasion.

So says Clytemnestra of Cassandra, and an elder
answers that the stranger seems to need some clear
interpreter; her ways are like a wild creature's made
captive.[18] Aristophanes, less sympathetically, says
of Cleophon:

[18] Aeschylus, *Agamemnon*, 1034 ff.

On the lips of that foreigner base,
Of Athens the bane and disgrace,
There is shrieking, his kinsman by race,
The garrulous swallow of Thrace.[19]

So perhaps that is why the priestess was called a dove; and Herodotus adds: "and when they say the dove was black, they signify that the woman was Egyptian."

Other Greeks spoiled the Egyptians beside Melampus, and taught their own people how to hold festivals (*panêgyris*) and pomps and services. All these, says Herodotus, are of very ancient date in Egypt and modern in Greece (ii, 58). Taboos as to actions, natural in themselves but unlawful in temples, were invented by the Egyptians and are observed by the Greeks, though not by other races. These other peoples hold man to be like the other animals, and what one tribe of animals may do in a precinct without displeasing the god, another may also do. But Herodotus likes neither their argument nor what they defend, and he commends the Egyptians (ii, 64). Herodotus alludes, and no more, to a lake at Sais, where at night they enact the story of the sufferings of a god, whom he "does not think it holy to name," a rite which the Egyptians call the mysteries.

I could speak more exactly of these matters, for I know the truth, but I will hold my peace (εὔστομα κείσθω), nor will I say aught concerning that rite of Demeter which the Greeks call Thesmophoria [a festival held by Athenian women in autumn], saving such part of it as I am not forbidden to mention. It was the daughters of Danaus who brought this rite out of Egypt and taught it to the Pelasgian women; afterwards, when the whole Peloponnese was cleared by the Dorians, it was lost, but the Arcadians, who

[19] Aristophanes, *Frogs*, 678 (B. B. Rogers).

alone of the Peloponnesians were left by the Dorians and not driven out, preserved it (ii, 171).

The Orphics and the followers of Bacchus derived from Egypt their prohibition of the use of wool in temples (ii, 81).

More interesting than any of these things is one of his few references to Immortality. "The Egyptians say that Demeter and Dionysus rule the world below"—the modern commentators point out that he means Isis and Osiris, whom Plutarch had less scruple in mentioning. "Moreover," he continues,

the Egyptians were the first to teach this word that the soul of man is immortal, and that, on the death of the body, it enters some other living thing then coming to birth, and when it has gone round all creatures of land and sea and air, it again enters a man's body then approaching birth; and the cycle takes it, they say, three thousand years. This word some of the Greeks used, some earlier and some later, as if it were their own; I know their names, but I do not write them (ii, 123).

Modern authorities have disputed whether the Egyptians taught the transmigration as well as the immortality of the soul, a question I would leave to Egyptologists; and they suggest that the unnamed Greeks, who borrowed the doctrine without acknowledgment, are respectively Pythagoras the earlier and probably the Orphics and Empedocles the later. It is suggested that Herodotus has a tender feeling for Pythagoras as a Samian, and so does not censure him by name here; but elsewhere he says that Salmoxis,—according to one story once the slave in Samos of Pythagoras, "one of the greatest of Greek sophists" [literally, "not the weakest"],—set up for himself in Thrace as a teacher of the doctrine of immortality. Herodotus himself believes he lived long before Pythagoras, "and whether there was a man called Salmoxis, or this be a name among the Getae for a god of their country, for me let him farewell" (iv, 95, 96). There the matter rests; Herodotus believed this doctrine was Egyptian.

Then there are the Greek poets to consider. Homer and Hesiod, not indeed after Pythagoras, but four hundred years before Herodotus, organized the Greek theogony, which is after all only "yesterday or the day before, as people say" (ii, 53). Egyptian divination, which is in Egypt an exact science, "has given material to those of the Greeks who deal in poetry" or "have busied themselves with poetry" (ii, 82), a phrase which does not suggest high regard in the historian, and may refer to Orpheus and Musaeus. And finally the Athenian tragic poet, Aeschylus the son of Euphorion, joined the great company of borrowers from Egypt, and from a story which Herodotus quotes, "and from none other, he plundered the idea which is found in none of the earlier poets, of making Artemis the daughter of Demeter" (ii, 156).

Modern students of Comparative Religion will make their own comments on this wholesale charge of derivation from Egypt, and they may be right. But for the student of the mind of Herodotus, the most interesting thing is not whether he is right or wrong as to Greek borrowing, nor whether his identifications are his undoing, as they probably are. A stranger in a strange land without the strange language, and a researcher into religion at any time in that millennium, would be equally at a loss. It is more important for us to notice the acute interest of the man in the legends and rituals and doctrines which he meets, and his instinctive application of new knowledge to old. Nothing, one might say, is with him mere antiquarian lumber. He uses everything he gets, now to make what he writes alive as few authors ever have, now for the more serious purpose of attaining truth on the most serious things a man can study,—his own nature, the past of his race, and the truth about the gods.

But poets were not the only teachers of Greece, and we have to ask how far Herodotus knew or was influenced by the great philosophers of the previous century or by the contemporary sophistic movement. He refers directly to Pythagoras, as we have just seen, and to Thales and his prediction of the eclipse. To the rest he does not refer, and there was perhaps no very obvious reason why he should. We may recall his remark about those captains of Xerxes, "whom I do not mention, for I am not compelled to do so by the necessity of my story" (vii, 96). He was undoubtedly influenced by the speculations of some of the philosophers; his wide range of inquiry proves that. Geology, as we say, and Anthropology, this comparative study of Religion, and much else, speak of the influence of the whole movement of illumination, even if he does not allude to individuals. But a historian has his own way of managing his reflections; and Herodotus, as already said, was more concerned with the acquirement of knowledge than with anticipations. When he expresses an opinion, it is not guess work but deduction from evidence before him. The great movement has had its effect on him. He does not speculate as to the original substance or production of the universe. But, in his proper field, of man and his habitat, his manners and his history, Herodotus shows by his handling of most questions that come before him that he has been trained in the great age of Greece. He has the stimulated and disciplined faculties which association, even indirect, with such intellects gives. He has the gift of asking the right questions.

The sophistic movement, it has been suggested, he did not entirely understand. He certainly stands with Socrates and Plato in not liking it altogether. The cool avowal of Protagoras that he did not know whether gods exist or not,[20] and his willingness to leave the matter there, would have jarred on Herodotus, who was at once simpler and more serious— was Protagoras taking any real trouble to find out? The suggestion in the well-known verses of Critias, probably written after the death of Herodotus, that the gods are the invention of a witty fellow who hocussed the simple with the fiction of invisible police and so saved order with a useful and ingenious lie[21]—perhaps such suggestions appeal more to clever people who have not seen or understood very much of the world.

Yet the great idea of the sophistic age, the contrast between Nature and Custom (φύσις and νόμος), does not escape Herodotus. We have seen how he quotes Pindar's saying that "Custom is King" (iii, 38). He is not unconscious, either, that many things which men have dragged in divine agency to explain, hardly need it, though sometimes he can reconcile Geology with Theology.

[20] Diogenes Laertius, ix, 50 ff. Diels, *Fragmente der Vorsokratiker*, II, no. 74, A, 1.

[21] Quoted by Sextus Empiricus, ix, 54; Diels, *Fragmente der Vorsokratiker*, Vol. II, no. 81, fr. 25.

The Thessalians themselves say that Poseidon made the gorge through which the Peneios runs; and what they say is likely enough. For whoever considers that Poseidon shakes the earth and that gaps rent by earthquake are the works of this god, would, on seeing the gorge, say that Poseidon made it; for it is the work of an earthquake, as is clear to me, this parting of the mountains (vii, 129).

The Athenians had a story of an oracle that bade them call on "their brother by marriage;" and they told him that in obedience they did sacrifice to Boreas and Orithyia, and prayed to them for help. They did this "when they perceived the wind rising or even before that"—and the storm rose and did great damage to Xerxes' fleet. "Whether it was for this reason that the wind Boreas fell upon the barbarians as they lay at anchor, I cannot say; but the Athenians at all events say Boreas helped them aforetime and did that deed then" (vii, 189). The storm raged for three days, "but at last the Magians, making sacrifice of victims and singing incantations to the wind, and in addition sacrificing to Thetis and the Nereids, stopped the storm, or else it just dropped of itself" (vii, 191)—an alternative that has often since then been suggested about prayer. Later on, when he described the second storm that broke upon the barbarian fleet, he says that "all this was being brought about by God in order that the Persian force might be made more equal to that of the Hellenes and might not be by very much the larger" (viii, 13).

V

The hand of God, or natural causes, or the one using the other? How often men have speculated so! Too often to let us ascribe the question to flippancy, Milesian or sophistic. This man, once more, is acutely interested, and "wishes to know." And he finds the hand of God not infrequently taking a part in man's life. There are divine warnings to men, "for he is wont somehow to give signs beforehand" (vi, 27), though the verb may be merely neuter; omens are given, though a man, like Xerxes, may misread an omen "easy of interpretation" (vii, 57); there are dreams, as we saw; Kolaios and his men reach Samos after their great discovery "thanks to divine escort" (iv, 152),—a passage where no irony can be supposed.

Many readers group Herodotus with those Greeks who count the divine envious; and so great a scholar as Eduard Meyer holds that this idea lies at the very centre of Herodotus' view of the world (*Weltanschauung*). But I notice that the outstanding passages where this occurs are in the speeches of his characters. That he is sympathetic with these characters, we can grant; he is so with all; but he has wrought a certain wisdom and feeling into their words and we can believe that he knew well what they meant. It was a popular view, and he understood such views. Still it is well to note that such thoughts are given in quotation. "Croesus," says the wise old Solon, "thou askest me of man's lot, me, a man who know that all the divine is envious and works trouble for us;" and Solon goes on to advise the king to "see the end" (i, 32). Amasis writes to Polycrates: "I like not these great successes of yours; for I know how jealous are the gods" (iii, 40). Artabanos moralizes to Xerxes on the same theme that God lets none have high thoughts save himself, "he loves to abridge the excessive;" on a great army "God in envy" casts fear or thunderbolt, and they perish (vii, 10, ϵ); in the period of life, he says, no man is so happy but he will often, and not once only, wish to die rather than to live, and "God giving man to taste of the sweetness of life is found therein to be envious" (vii, 46). Later on, Themistocles tells Xerxes that the gods grudge that one man should rule both Asia and Europe (viii, 109).

In his own voice Herodotus more explicitly shows his belief in divine judgments rather than divine envy. "Great *nemesis* from God" came upon Croesus (i, 34). The Spartans misused the heralds of Xerxes, and wrath came upon them for it, "the wrath of Talthybios the herald of Agamemnon" (vii, 134); "this I perceive to have been most evidently the act of God" (or literally, "one of the most divine things"); that the wrath of Talthybios fell on heralds and did not cease till it was satisfied, was plain justice; but that it fell on the particular men on whom it did fall "proves to me that the affair was of the gods" (vii, 137). It was remarked after the battle of Plataea that not a single Persian body was found in the precinct itself of Demeter's grove, though many fell in the unconsecrated ground beside it. "I suppose," says Herodotus, "if it be right to suppose about divine matters, the goddess would not suffer them to enter, seeing they had burnt her palace in Eleusis" (ix, 65). Evil comes back on the head of the man who does it, Herodotus clearly believes, and its coming is not unconnected with the gods or the divine; singular, plural, concrete, abstract, the words vary as ever in Greek speech. Δράσαντι παθεῖν was the teaching of Aeschylus, and Herodotus stands nearer him in belief than men sometimes allow; it is justice, retribution rather than envy, that he reads in the divine dealings, though he writes with a loving hand the words of Solon or Artabanus.

Probably few of us realize at all the difficulties of a polytheist, trained from infancy to believe in many gods, taught by life to see a certain justice slowly working in human affairs, and forbidden by all the philosophy available to lay much stress on any personal god known to his people, and yet pious, loyal to his training, "wishful to know" and fundamentally sincere. Herodotus represents the many minds of his day; perhaps more in him than in any of his contemporaries we can watch their interaction. He is neither orthodox with Aristophanes and Anytos, nor indifferent to the gods like Thucydides, nor angry with them like Euripides. He "wishes to know" about them and he studies every phase of religious thought presented to him, so far as he can get at it. We do not know of any Greek books about the religious beliefs of the barbarians; he was a pioneer, and his own book was the first.

Once he caught sight of a religion of another kind, a faith taught by one of the world's great prophets, exalted in its conception of God and consequently in its ethics, a faith still living in our world today. Persian religion, as he was able to see it, dimly but not wrongly, was not quite what Zoroaster had taught. Darius, it would seem, was a convinced Zoroastrian and a monotheist.[22] His people were confusing their faith with the superstitions of the races they conquered; and it had already that unhappy association with the Magians which has persisted to this day.

"As to the usages of the Persians," Herodotus says

I know them to be these. It is not their custom to make and set up statues and temples and altars, but those who make such they deem foolish, as I suppose, because they never believed the gods, as do the Greeks, to be in the likeness of men. But they call the whole circle of heaven Zeus, and to him they offer sacrifice on the highest peaks of the mountains; they sacrifice also to the sun and moon and earth and fire and water and winds. These are the only gods to whom they have ever sacrificed from the beginning; they have learnt later to sacrifice to the heavenly Aphrodite, from the Assyrians and Arabs. The Assyrians call Aphrodite Mylitta, the Arabs Alilat, and the Persians Mitra.

And this is their fashion of sacrifice to the aforesaid gods. When about to sacrifice they neither build altars nor kindle fire, they use no libations, nor music, nor fillets, nor barley meal. But to whomsoever of the gods a man will sacrifice, he leads the beast to an open space, and then calls on the god, himself wearing a garland on his tiara, commonly of myrtle. To pray for blessings for himself alone is not lawful for the sacrificer; rather he prays that it may be well with the king and all the Persians; for he reckons himself among them. He then cuts the victim limb from limb into portions, and having roasted the flesh spreads the softest grass, trefoil for choice, and places all of it on this. When he has so disposed it, a Magian comes near and chants over it the song of the birth of the gods [literally, a theogony], as the Persian tradition relates it; for no sacrifice can be offered without a Magian. Then after a little while the sacrificer carries away the flesh and uses it as he pleases (i, 131, 132).

[22] J. H. Moulton, *Early Zoroastrianism*, pp. 44, 52, 129, 131.

The value of this picture is attested by Dr. James Hope Moulton, who expresses definitely his opinion, based on profound scholarship, that here at least a generation of research has antiquated not Herodotus but Professor Sayce.[23] He translates in an appendix of his *Early Zoroastrianism* the passage given above and other chapters, with a commentary to which I would refer my readers. Even the historian's slip in making Mithras into a goddess he finds a "helpful mistake." Mistakes Herodotus might well make, in trying to clarify to himself the features of a religion which were presented to him in a foreign cult, confused by alien practices and explained by a translator. But it is surely impossible to read his words and not find sympathy in them. The antiquary is fascinated by Egyptian religion, the thinker is moved by the Persian faith; and Herodotus was antiquary and thinker at once.

Literature has been defined by Matthew Arnold as a criticism of life. Other definitions have been given of it, and will probably hereafter be given, but Arnold's will remain. What is the criticism of life that Herodotus offers us? Solon bids us see the end, and Artabanos from time to time sighs for death; and Herodotus understands both. He has seen the cities of many men and learnt their minds; he has made friends with men of all the world, men of every race, and they have told him the old stories of their peoples, have let him see their faith and manner of life; and he brings it all to us, and makes us the friends of Greeks and Persians, of Scythians, Egyptians, and Libyans. He teaches us a new humanity, a new sympathy, though he never uses such words. He

[23] J. H. Moulton, *Early Zoroastrianism*, p. 36.

makes us lovers of men, lovers of animals, lovers of the world and its wonders; and a lover always wants to know more of what he loves, and so do we as we read. He rambles and digresses, men say, and we say he does not do it too much, no! not enough. Who tires of the tale of Herodotus? Does it not make us love life more? Then what is his criticism of life? Is it not just this, that he loves it and makes it more divine and more wonderful for every one who reads his book?

ENVOY

A Hint from MARTIAL to the Reader of any Book

———

Some of the facts I never knew;
Some errors quite escaped my sight;
Some things I worked at got askew;
Some pages are obscure, if right;
—I own the truth of all you say,
But books are made no other way.

INDEX